ANCIENT ISRAEL, JUDAH, AND GREECE

Hebrew Bible Monographs, 111
Sheffield Centre for Interdisciplinary Biblical Studies, 9

ANCIENT ISRAEL, JUDAH, AND GREECE

LAYING THE FOUNDATION OF A COMPARATIVE APPROACH

Andrew Tobolowsky

SHEFFIELD PHOENIX PRESS
2024

Copyright © 2024. Sheffield Phoenix Press

Published by Sheffield Phoenix Press
Sheffield Institute for Interdisciplinary Biblical Studies (SIIBS)
University of Sheffield, Sheffield S3 7RA

www.sheffieldphoenix.com

A CIP catalogue record for this book
is available from the British Library

Typeset by the HK Scriptorium

ISBN 978-1-914490-47-7

CONTENTS

ABBREVIATIONS

AJA	*American Journal of Archaeology*
BA	*Biblical Archaeologist*
BibInt	*Biblical Interpretation*
CRB	*Currents in Biblical Research*
FAT	Forschungen zum Alten Testament
HKAT	Handkommentar zum Alten Testament
HTR	*Harvard Theological Review*
JAOS	*Journal of the American Oriental Society*
JBL	*Journal of Biblical Literature*
JEA	*Journal of Egyptian Archaeology*
JHS	*Journal of Hellenic Studies*
JNES	*Journal of Near Eastern Studies*
JSOT	*Journal for the Study of the Old Testament*
JSOTSup	Journal for the Study of the Old Testament, Supplement Series
KAI	*Kanaanäische und Aramäische Inschriften*
LHB/OTS	Library of Hebrew Bible/Old Testament Studies
OTS	Oudtestamentische Studiën
RHR	*Revue de l'histoire des religions*
TAPA	*Transactions and Proceedings of the American Philological Association*
VT	*Vetus Testamentum*
ZAW	*Zeitschrift für die alttestamentliche Wissenschaft*

Acknowledgments

This book, whatever its faults, is an attempt to distill the results of quite a lot of work over—well—a *reasonably* long period of time. In fact, I first became interested in what comparing scholarly approaches to these two sets of traditions could do all the way back in graduate school, call it a decade ago. I am far from the only person to have this interest, now or once upon a time, but it is still rarely enough pursued. This book is the fruit of my efforts to *pursue*—and to build such tools for pursuit as might make the mountain passes a little less steep the next time through.

Therefore, the first of many acknowledgments goes to my graduate school advisers, Saul Olyan, Stanley Stowers, and Pura Nieto Hernandez, who helped me begin pursuing an unusual quarry before I had any reason to know there was anything unusual about it. The second varietal of this species of thanks I present to Sheffield Phoenix Press. The truth is, I wanted to publish with Sheffield from the start because of its long history of publishing biblical scholarship that breaks with convention. I had an inkling, before I began, that a comparative perspective might lead me to some uncomfortably stark and uncompromising conclusions about past scholarly preoccupations—and indeed, from time to time, to the conclusion *that* compromising, which is to say, successively moderating certain older approaches, might look like wisdom but actually preserve what ought to have been left behind. I needed a press that let me lean toward, rather than away from, these conclusions when they presented themselves. And I found one. This book is therefore dedicated, too, to Meredith Warren, a personal friend and someone I deeply admire, who warmly embraced it from the beginning, and to Jeremy and Louise Clines for their generosity, enthusiasm, flexibility, and expert handling.

The third dedication goes to, well, lots of people. Much of the first two chapters, certainly, wandered in the fields of intellectual history, where I have been known, in the past, to get a bit lost. Among those who did their best to provide a map, I offer my thanks and appreciation to Ian Douglas Wilson, Daniel Pioske, Paul Michael Kurtz, Eva Mroczek, Jacqueline Vayntrub, Robyn Faith Walsh, and indeed many others. And the fourth dedication, of course, goes to my friends and family, who sustain me. I am grateful for text messaging services that have learned the deep magic of crossing international boundaries for allowing myself, Kerry Sonia, Daniel

Picus, and Zack Wainer to bring Willis Monroe back into the fold, at last, despite living 250 miles northeast of Bangor to share our excitements and frustrations, often about television shows. I am grateful, of course, to my parents, Paul and Judy Tobolowsky, and especially to my mother, whose personal interest in my work is all the more remarkable as I head toward my forties. I dedicate this, as well, to Mark Tobolowsky, my closest friend and still certainly top two among my most frequent conversation partners, as he has been ever since our shared birthdate sometime in the 1980s. I dedicate this to my wife, Robyn Schroeder, and to our so beloved son, Judah, light of my life, who have brought so much joy, fun, adventure, and love into my world. Strange as it may seem, I would consider myself a very lucky man, even if I never got to write a book comparing scholarly approaches to the study of the traditions of ancient Israel, Judah, and Greece. But I got to do that, too!

INTRODUCTION

One could be forgiven for thinking that ancient Israel and ancient Greece, like certain other famous couples, have grown a little more distant with time. Today, at any rate, they lead rather separate lives—on a modern university campus, in modern society, perhaps even in the modern mind. One is neatly packaged in something called "the classical world," kept safe in departments with similar names, while the other tends to hang its shingle in the realm known as "Religious Studies." One is placed in a context called "Mediterranean" or "Aegean," the other, "Near Eastern" or "Levantine." Those who study them have separate conferences and journals, separate training regimens for their intrepid, if desk-prone, explorers, and likely enough, separate sections of the library, the bookstore, and the museum to visit. For Israel, turn right at the mummy, or left at the Assyrian hunting frieze. For Greece, if you hit Augustus, you've probably gone too far.

The question of whether they were really so separate at the time, or if this is, instead, a reflection of *modern* intellectual history, is a good one to start with. If you take a step back—look at the right map, or, if possible, reserve a few hours on the time machine the Physics department has—I *think* that what you will see is a profoundly *connected* ancient world. This is especially true when we think of ancient Greece as it really was, not penned in by the confining coastline of the modern nation but a branching network of cities and colonies stretching from the Black Sea in the east to Iberia in the west. There were Greeks in Anatolia and Greeks in Egypt, where the famous *emporion* of Naukratis had been founded by the middle of the sixth century BCE. Already by the eighth, Greek trade flowed through al-Mina in Syria, at the mouth of the great Orontes River. And in the other direction sailed the Phoenicians, Israel's northern neighbors—a Semitic-speaking people whose gods and goddesses could play more than bit parts in certain biblical stories. They glided west as far as Spain, and even to Britain, on great wooden ships that inspired some of the prophet Ezekiel's most evocative poetry (Ezek. 27). And even today, believe it or not, Cyprus, home of Homer's Aphrodite, where both Greeks and Phoenicians lived, sits at anchor no more than 150 miles off the Levantine coast, closer than New York is to Boston.

We may not know quite what role the Israelites and Judahites played in all this, but they certainly lived among these tangling webs. And at least some of the authors in the Hebrew Bible knew of the Greeks. Rather, it is not the *Graikoi* who appear in the Hebrew Bible but the Ionian Greeks who lived on and off the west coast of Asia Minor and troubled the Assyrians with their raiding. In fact, the biblical genealogist who made Iawan a grandson of Noah, son of Japheth (Gen. 10.2) in the great "Table of Nations," knew enough, too, to record that this Iawan was the father of "Kittim," probably Cyprus, and very likely Rhodes as well.[1] Neither were these empty connections; the brother of the poet Alcaeus would fight in the armies of Nebuchadnezzar of Babylon, while Sappho's brother is supposed to have settled in Naukratis.[2] A bilingual tombstone (*KAI* 53) in Piraeus, the port of Athens, commemorates the life of the Sidonian Abdtanit son of Abdshamash—or, in the Greek, Artemidoros son of Heliodoros.[3] And Homer, if he lived, was a contemporary of Isaiah, Solon of King Josiah, Herodotus of Ezra. *This* is the world that we, like intellectual *Diadochi,* have divided.

I do not precisely propose here to put it back together again. In other words, this is not a book about cross-cultural influence or interactions themselves, and I want to be clear about that from the start. It does, however, begin with the fact that between ancient Greece and ancient Israel— really ancient Greece, ancient Israel and ancient *Judah,* whose distinctness from Israel will be emphasized throughout this book—we do have a great many similar traditions. These traditions were indeed written around the same time, not very far away from one another, and even, sometimes, under the shadow of the same geopolitical upheavals, especially the western march of the Persian Empire.[4] Even more importantly, they come from similarly fragmentary contexts, meaning that we can usually only guess how many other stories once existed or how representative what survives is of the intellectual diversity of the times and places in which they were

1. The text reads "Dodanim" (Gen. 10.4), which is a plural, but in Hebrew, the dalet ("d") and the resh ("r") are similar looking letters; so Rodanim—Rhodians—is very plausible, especially since a version of the same genealogy in 1 Chron. 1.7 actually does spell it "Rodanim."

2. Kurt A. Raaflaub, "The Newest Sappho and Archaic Greek-Near East Interaction," in *The Newest Sappho (P. Sapph. Obbink and P. GC Inv. 105, Frs. 1-4)* (ed. Anton Bierl and A.P.M.H. Lardinois; Studies in Archaic and Classical Greek Song, 2; Leiden: E.J. Brill, 2016), pp. 134-38.

3. Robert Parker, *Greek Gods Abroad: Names, Natures, and Transformations* (Berkeley, CA: University of California Press, 2017), p. 39. As Parker notes, the Phoenician name means "servant of Tanit" son of "servant of Shamash" while the Greek offers attempted equivalences—Artemis and Helios.

4. Arnaldo Momigliano, "Biblical Studies and Classical Studies: Simple Reflections about Historical Method," *BA* 45.4 (1982), p. 227.

produced. And they come from contexts where it is more or less equally true that we face difficult-to-answer questions about how well the testimony of archaeology and epigraphy does or does not corroborate the basic historicity of many important and influential accounts or reveal the context in which they emerged.

To be sure, in the case of the traditions themselves we must be clear that similar does not mean identical. I think there are very few cases, of which segmented genealogical traditions are the clearest examples, in which there is any reason to think compositions in one of these cultural contexts actually share a genre with the other, or are composed, or function, in much the same way.[5] Indeed, I will be especially cautious on this point because, in my opinion, the few past instances in which comparisons between biblical and classical compositions became popular were profoundly shaped by a parallelomania that repeatedly produced the opposite conclusion.[6] In other words, rather superficial similarities have very often been perceived as the hallmarks of identical phenomena instead.

At the same time, the similarities I am referring to are significant, and more than we often find between the Hebrew Bible's and Near Eastern traditions which are more often the focus of comparative investigations. There are lengthy, third-person narrative accounts of the national past and the deeds of founding figures.[7] There are traditions about the founding of cities and holy sites and the establishment of religious rites. There are the aforementioned genealogical traditions—accounts of ancestors and their descendants along multiple lines of descent that function as schematic representations of familial and ethnic relations and justifications for activities of all sorts.[8] There are stories of long journeys, and the eventful stops along

5. As Jacqueline Vayntrub observes, we are almost always better off building our sense of the genres that exist in different contexts from *within* those contexts (Jacqueline Vayntrub, *Beyond Orality: Biblical Poetry on its Own Terms* [The Ancient Word; London: Routledge, 2019], p. 24).

6. I discuss this issue in Andrew Tobolowsky, "On Comparison with Ancient Greek Traditions: Lessons from the Mid-Century," *Journal of Hebrew Scriptures* 23 (2023), pp. 1-30.

7. This is, if not precisely what Gerhard von Rad had in mind when he said that "there are only two peoples in antiquity who really wrote history—the Greeks and, long before them, the Israelites," the phenomenon that made him say it (Gerhard von Rad, *The Problem of the Hexateuch and Other Essays* [trans. E.W. Trueman Dicken; London: SCM Press, 1984], p. 167). Today, we can indeed recognize that, in fact, the biblical accounts are not "long before" but largely contemporaneous; von Rad was referring to his belief that the pentateuchal tradition really went back to the Yahwist and the court of Solomon, not his sense of when the Pentateuch *qua* Pentateuch was written down.

8. The fact that segmented genealogical traditions in particular—think the account of Jacob and his twelve sons—are common in the Hebrew Bible and ancient Greece

the way and much else besides. And they often stand in about the same chronological relationship to the events they purport to describe, which is to say that in both cases, many of our best known texts are from the mid-first millennium BCE and refer back to episodes that, if they occurred, would have occurred in the mid- to late-second millennium, raising similar questions about how well authentic memories of founding experiences might have been preserved over such a span of time.

Thus, these traditions are indeed not, for the most part, *identical* in character, in genre, in intent and function. But when we combine these similarities with the shared *evidentiary* challenges just mentioned, we find something that *is* genuinely identical: many of the questions they raise, and the problems they present, to contemporary researchers. That does not mean that the answers and solutions will be the same in both contexts. But it is nevertheless the case that two accounts of the deeds of legendary ancestors, or of the founding of cities, or of the genealogical relationship between subgroups within the embracing ethnic nation will require the scholar to address a great many identical concerns. We would like to know the relationship between these accounts and historical realities; we would like to know their relationship to earlier traditions about the same events. We would like to establish whether the archaeological and epigraphic record can be used to shed light on these stories, or even vice versa. We would like to know whether the details of these stories tend to preserve, even encode, the impression of more distant pasts, or mainly, the ideological projects of the authors composing the actual texts that survive. Both Genesis and the *Iliad*, Exodus and the Theban Cycle, as stories of founding ancestors doing founding things, raise these concerns and beg these questions, and whatever turns out to be true about one will help us investigate what might be true of the other without it being the case that what is true will be the same in both.

Arnaldo Momigliano, one of the few scholars in anything like a recent period to think systematically about what these comparisons can do, made a number of pertinent observations in this direction, especially in his essay "Biblical Studies and Classical Studies: Simple Reflections about Historical Method." In particular, he notes that there are far fewer practical dif-

---

and *not* in the Near East or Levant has been observed since at least the work of Robert Wilson on the subject of biblical genealogies in the 1970s, and subsequently noted by John Van Seters and Gary Knoppers well before more recent work on this topic (Robert R. Wilson, *Genealogy and History in the Biblical World* [New Haven, CT: Yale University Press, 1977], pp. 114-24, 132; Robert R. Wilson, "Between 'Azel' and 'Azel': Interpreting the Biblical Genealogies," *BA* 42.1 [1979], p. 13; John Van Seters, *Prologue to History: The Yahwist as Historian in Genesis* [Louisville, KY: Westminster John Knox, 1992], pp. 197-98; Gary N. Knoppers, "Greek Historiography and the Chronicler's History: A Reexamination," *JBL* 122 [2003], pp. 627-50).

ferences between biblical history, even if read as "sacred history," and the "profane history" of the classical world than we sometimes think: "I have never found the task of interpreting the Bible any more or less complex than that of interpreting Livy or Herodotus." And he adds the very apt point that

> the problems about understanding the texts, guessing their sources, and determining the truth of their information are basically the same in Roman as in Hebrew history. The similarity extends to the means and methods of supplementing and checking our literary sources by archeology, epigraphy, numismatics, and what not.[9]

We can certainly look to see whether our respective opinions on how much proof is needed to "supplement," what constitutes a source—and what not—are similar enough between the disciplines, and if not, why not. Might there be some reason for caution—or even for its lack—found by somebody in the other discipline that might be useful in our own?[10]

More broadly, we face many of the same general, even paradigmatic issues. How does tradition inheritance itself work? Should we think, with little enough evidence either way, that it tends to be conservative, in the sense that the heirs of early stories were rarely willing to change them very much, so that we can justly regard what survives as a *version* of a very early story? Or was it dynamic, the past constantly in flux, constantly being "improved" in one way or another, so that most narratives are best understood, first and foremost, as a product of the era in which they were actually written down? When addressing, say, an account of ethnic origins, how should we incorporate the last decades of arguments on the subject of the fluidity of ethnic articulations over time, or for that matter, of historical memory? What should we believe about the relationship between surviving texts and early traditions, or the stability of traditions over time in a mostly oral age? And how should we use extraliterary evidence to study them? What tasks are more important: historical reconstructions and the recovery of early traditions or the study of how later generations spoke through and reimagined the stories they inherited—or even, perhaps created? What, above all, should we think the compositions that survive *primarily* preserve, reflect, and reveal?

In all of these cases, we do not have nearly so much to *use* to answer these questions, or develop appropriate responses, as scholars working on more recent periods can generally take for granted. But we *do* have one signifi-

---

9. Momigliano, "Biblical Studies and Classical Studies," p. 224.

10. "I may well ask myself where a classical scholar can help biblical scholars most usefully. My answer would be that in the field of political, social, and religious history differences are more important than similarities—and therefore knowledge of Greco-Roman history can be useful only for differential comparison" (Momigliano, "Biblical Studies and Classical Studies," p. 227). I think this is often, but not always, true.

cant untapped resource: quite a lot of scholars *attempting* to answer them, from a wide range of different perspectives, utilizing different approaches, and incorporating new recognitions in new ways, between two disciplines that are unfortunately rarely in conversation with each other. Each could, therefore, benefit a great deal from a more extensive awareness of the state of the other, as much awareness as possible. But they have not been able to because they sit on opposite sides of the fence *we* built through a connected ancient world.

This is the engine that makes the book go: the conviction that there is much to be gained, not by comparing tradition to tradition between ancient Greece and ancient Israel and Judah, but approach to approach, and understanding to understanding between members of each *scholarly* community. And this is its central purpose: to help lay the groundwork for putting these communities in conversation with each other. We do this, first, simply by discussing how scholars in each discipline are currently investigating the same questions and problems where certain kinds of similar traditions are concerned, and, second, by suggesting what I think are the most promising approaches and why. And here I do not mean only which conclusions seem to me to be the most justified, but—if anything even more so—which approaches seem to me to best reflect what scholars in other fields have often more readily understood to be the full implications of the great shifts in how we think about ethnicity, memory, and tradition that have taken place over the last decades.

Of course, I do not mean to say that no work has yet been done in this direction, that I invented the idea of cross-disciplinary approaches, or that the following is a comprehensive treatment of the related issues. But I speak from experience here. I consider this book the culmination of roughly a decade's work on precisely these comparisons.[11] There have certainly been moments in the history of both disciplines where it was common to see a scholar of the Hebrew Bible refer to phenomena in ancient Greek traditions or vice versa. But these efforts had uneven results even then, and they have been extremely *un*common for quite some time now in any case, though, of course, not unheard of.[12] They are certainly rare enough that tak-

11. In, for example, Andrew Tobolowsky, "Reading Genesis through Chronicles: The Creation of the Sons of Jacob," *Journal of Ancient Judaism* 7.2 (2016), pp. 138-68; Andrew Tobolowsky, *The Sons of Jacob and the Sons of Herakles: The History of the Tribal System and the Organization of Biblical Identity* (FAT, 2; Tübingen: Mohr Siebeck, 2017); Andrew Tobolowsky, "The Problem of Reubenite Primacy," *JBL* 139 (2020), pp. 27-45.

12. In particular, a number of recent studies have advocated, and successfully performed, simply adding ancient Greece to the data set of comparative materials that might prove useful alongside more typical Near Eastern, for example, Anselm C. Hagedorn, *Between Moses and Plato: Individual and Society in Deuteronomy and Ancient*

ing a systematic view of how to approach shared problems might well do a great deal of good, and I mean to draw on my extensive experience to offer it. In addition, I mean to do so without suggesting that producing numerous scholars who are equally expert in both disciplines is an achievable goal. Which is to say that—especially because my focus is on scholarly approaches and not the intricacies of individual texts—I hope this book will show how these comparisons can be engaged in productively on quite a large scale without reinventing the wheel, so to speak.

This study has a second purpose too, however, and one that explains why I think a willingness to adopt a comparative approach is not just useful but actually vital. There is, in the study of ancient traditions, what I often think of as a kind of "sixth sense" problem. I refer, of course, to the well-known M. Night Shyamalan movie *The Sixth Sense*, and what I mean is simply this: there are any number of ideas and approaches still walking around that *do not know they are dead*. Or, to put it less colorfully, the study of ancient traditions exhibits a distressing tendency to preserve certain approaches to how they are produced and passed down, and what they preserve and reflect, that have elsewhere been quite discredited. Often, this is accomplished by vague and uninterrogated references to the supposed differences between ancient societies and our own, or to particularly advantageous interpretations of topics like "cultural memory"—advantageous, that is, precisely to the enterprise of reasserting the validity of older conclusions on supposedly new grounds. But other times, scholarship can simply be so path-dependent that having established a certain set of goals and norms for so long, it becomes very hard to really move on, and especially *to* assumptions that make achieving old ambitions harder, where the reconstruction of early traditions and early realities is concerned. Either way, these ghosts have proven quite stubborn, and I have come to feel that only an outside perspective can show how to exorcise them, and even how completely this needs to be done.

Indeed, I would go further; this sixth-sense problem is an issue in both fields, but it is, in general, much more of an issue in the study of the Hebrew Bible. There are some less-than-practical reasons for this difference, including, to put it bluntly, religion itself. Historically, Hebrew Bible as a field was often dominated by Protestant scholars working out of seminaries whose approaches to biblical traditions were shaped by their religious commitments—in some ways that they acknowledged, in some they may

Greek Law (Göttingen: Vandenhoeck & Ruprecht, 2004); Martti Nissinen, *Ancient Prophecy: Near Eastern, Biblical, and Greek Perspectives* (Oxford: University Press, 2017); Laura Quick, *Dress, Adornment, and the Body in the Hebrew Bible* (Oxford: Oxford University Press, 2021); Raleigh Heth and T.E. Kelley, "Isaac and Iphigenia: Portrayals of Child Sacrifice in Israelite and Greek Literature," *Bib* 102.4 (2021), pp. 481-502. I discuss this in "On Comparisons with Ancient Greek Traditions," 24-25.

not have realized, and certainly in some that they explicitly denied. It continues to be studied by a great many people who have more of a personal stake in demonstrating the basic reliability of many biblical narratives than we usually find elsewhere. This is not of course to say that it is impossible, or even unlikely, for someone who is deeply religiously committed to be a wonderful Hebrew Bible scholar, and there are many of this sort. But that doesn't change what has been true in the history of the discipline that is not true in the history of classics.

In addition, I would point to another issue that I think is very important but, as far as I know, has never gotten an airing. Simply put, the realities behind the production of the Hebrew Bible are far more in tension with traditional understandings than anything we could say about ancient Greek traditions even beyond questions of faith. Basically, we come to these, in our culture and often academia, as *the* traditions of ancient Israel. In reality, they are a collection of *some* ancient Israelite *and* Judahite traditions that were produced *in Judah,* and after quite a sequence of tumultuous, epoch-making events had already occurred.[13] What this means is startling for a discipline trained on ancient Israel—the religion of ancient Israel, the history of ancient Israel, the culture of ancient Israel, etc. In order to maintain even the basic premise that this *is* Israel's book, or Israel's traditions—as opposed to a Judahite book or a Judahite collection—we have to be able to explain why it doesn't really matter that Judah was separate from Israel for so long. This, typically, means embracing visions of the stability of identity, memory, and tradition over time that are often out of sync with how these topics are now understood elsewhere. Thus, many scholars, whether they realize it or not, are indeed incentivized to preserve outdated approaches in a way that has no counterpoint in the study of ancient Greece. We are not going to find out that Greek traditions are really Roman traditions, say—so there is less need to be concerned about what the fluidity of ethnic articulations over time means for the fundamentals of studying Greek narratives.

There are also quite a few eminently practical reasons why scholars of ancient Greek traditions have had an easier time moving on from what I will characterize in the first chapter as an essentially Romantic view of when and how a people's most important traditions developed, how they are passed down over time and what they represent. And this, of course, is why their work can be so useful where reconsidering assumptions and approaches are concerned in the other, biblical context. For one thing, there are a great many *more* ancient Greek compositions, and certainly of separate compositions, often by named authors from known and different contexts. By contrast, however many hands may have contributed to the pro-

---

13. It is, as Daniel Fleming calls it, "Judah's Bible" (Daniel Fleming, *The Legacy of Israel in Judah's Bible* [New York: Cambridge University Press, 2012]).

duction of the Hebrew Bible, and it is surely many, it is still a remarkable fact that virtually all the texts that survive from ancient Israel and Judah, from the main eras of biblical composition, survive *only* in this book. This they usually do anonymously, and sometimes interwoven with each other in such a way that disentangling one work from another and early notions from late is a formidable intellectual problem in its own right.

Thus, what is theoretical in one context—how one author might have influenced another, what one author might feel comfortable doing to the work of another—is often perfectly visible in the second. There is, to be sure, a great deal of multivocality in the Hebrew Bible, but the intellectually honest scholar of ancient Greece can hardly help but be aware of even more—a rather extreme diversity in Greek accounts of the legendary past, their contradictions, their disjunctions. Clear evidence of later authors taking ideas from earlier authors and running with them, greatly altering them, or ignoring them means these scholars must, perforce, be exposed to how dynamic tradition inheritance can be. They have clear examples of important early traditions told very differently across a host of compositions, sharply declining and increasing in importance, or even falling from grace altogether, to be replaced by totally new visions that arose in later circumstances. And no one who acknowledges that the very idea of Panhellenism was largely invented, likely enough accelerating in the early fifth century BCE, will have as easy a time treating later accounts of Greek identity as little more than versions of an original and eternal Greek ethnic vision in the way that it is common to treat biblical accounts of Israelite identity. All this is indeed in addition to the fact that the study of ancient Greek traditions often represents a less *fraught* context in which to work out intellectual ideas, because no one now regards these texts as scripture.

This is by no means to say that all scholars of ancient Greek traditions *do* acknowledge all of these things. "Zombie" approaches are alive and well in this discipline, too. Indeed, as we will see, many scholars in that discipline have the same romantic attachment to the Homeric poems as the fossilized remnant of Bronze Age memory and the same devotion to the somewhat outdated practice of sifting out kernels of truth from traditions of origin. Increasingly, in recent years, an idealization of the classical world has also played a part in contemporary white supremacist rhetoric and is popular, as well, among misogynists.[14] And as we will see in the first two chapters especially, the histories of inquiry into these traditions are deeply linked, and their modern history, similarly long. In the nineteenth century, similar ideas about traditions appeared at similar times, sometimes through direct

---

14. See especially the discussion in Donna Zuckerberg, *Not All Dead White Men: Classics and Misogyny in the Digital Age* (Cambridge, MA: Harvard University Press, 2018).

influence and sometimes, we might say, ambiently from a larger intellectual context. In the early twentieth century, similar challenges to familiar ways of doing scholarly business appeared at similar times and evoked similar responses. If the fields have parted ways to some extent since then—both in terms of approaches, and literally, as it is no longer common for scholars in one to be conversant with debates in the other—they are still both grappling with the same legacy of nineteenth-century approaches, and how precisely to move on from them. Certainly, both still struggle with the scope of what it would require of us if we really rejected inherited preoccupations with the original tradition, a romanticization of Homer, or early Israel, and a "pious historicism" that makes scholars in each react very strongly to any challenge to the basic historicity of certain traditions. Still, one field has certain advantages over the other where "exorcisms" are concerned.

Broadly speaking, then, I do think that comparing—not traditions but—scholarly approaches to traditions can prove extraordinarily useful in both directions. The greatest cause of the lack of certain kinds of progress, at least definitive progress, on some issues is, in my opinion, the simple circularity of disciplinary work: the rhythm of training and application, argument and response, that too often traps scholars in a linear pattern that acquires a gravity of its own. In this study, my purpose is to show how the circle might be opened through comparing approaches between fields—how an awareness of approaches and theories being deployed on shared issues, by a wider community of scholars *who have not been in much conversation with each other,* can make shifts possible that would otherwise be arrested in flight. We can, through what we might call "etic" comparison, help create this community, as well as increase the size of the data sets we have to work with, increase awareness of possible approaches, and much else besides. Perhaps most of all, we can help make the survival of flawed assumptions visible and provide new ways of thinking our way past them because, in the wider world of scholarship that a combined approach can bring us into contact with, someone already has provided it. At the very least, it will often be the case in what follows that someone has taken the challenge represented by a shifting foundational assumption about how peoples identify, remember, and tell stories *seriously* in a way that is not common in the other discipline and so provide a roadmap for what taking it seriously might look like somewhere else.

Even so, it will be the case that one discipline will more often show what is possible than the other, and more clearly how the other might break more thoroughly from outdated past assumptions, and I will not begin by denying it. I will simply state again that my *main* intention is to provide a foundation for future discussions between scholars in both fields. Regardless of who leads whom, exposure to a much wider spectrum of approaches to new challenges to older models than exists in either field alone is certainly useful. And this diversity will indeed make it easier to see—shall I say *incomplete exorcisms*—and to ask what really needs to be done to move forward.

This, then, is the broader shape and intention of the following study. In its particulars, it is broken up into four case studies, four attempts to come to grips with how scholars in two different fields *have* investigated a particular kind of tradition, how they *are* investigating them today, and what a combined approach can tell us about how they might do it in the future. Chapter 1, which will also offer a brief sketch of the history of disciplinary approaches through the nineteenth century and lay the groundwork for many discussions to come, will nevertheless focus on the study of ethnicity. In other words, it is concerned primarily with how scholars in both disciplines have, and should, incorporate the dramatic shifts in thinking about ethnic identity that have occurred over the last half-century into the study of traditions of ethnic origin. In Chapter 2, I will complete the historical sketch begun in Chapter 1, but in the broader context of a discussion of how to use extraliterary evidence in the study of surviving texts—the evidence of archaeology and epigraphy in particular. Chapter 3 will explore the study of genealogical traditions common to both corpora and Chapter 4 of foundation traditions and how to think about what kind of information they preserve and reflect. In all of these cases, I will particularly attempt to assess what newly fluid and reinventive models of how the past, and past ways of identifying, live on in later periods means for the study of ancient traditions. And I will explore which conclusions hold the most promise for finally exorcising the ghosts that haunt our fields, that truly belong in the pasts that made them possible.

Two last points before beginning the study. First, I have opted to use the term "ancient Greek tradition"—or in Chapter 4 "foundation traditions"—largely as a response to the commonplace use of "Greek mythology" *in opposition to* "biblical traditions." I have discussed the term "myth" at length in other studies, and my personal opinion is that an expansive view of the term would really cover both biblical and Greek traditions perfectly well.[15] At the same time, the kind of parsing required to pluck out myth from other kinds of ancient tradition feels to me like a distraction in a book that has so much other business to conduct, especially when it is clear that all of the stories discussed in this book *are* traditions, even if some—or all!—of them are also myth.

---

15. See Andrew Tobolowsky, "History, Myth, and the Shrinking of Genre Borders," *Eidolon*, May 16, 2016, https://eidolon.pub/history-myth-and-the-shrinking-of-genre-borders-e7ad46ca745, for an informal discussion of this issue. See also Andrew Tobolowsky, "The Hebrew Bible as Mythic 'Vocabulary': Towards a New Comparative Mythology," *Religions* 11.9 (2020), p. 459.

Second, I offer a genuinely heartfelt apology for any bibliographic failings in what follows. I can only say what will be obvious from the outset. Most chapters oblige me to sketch something of the history of two different disciplines and give an overview of contemporary approaches. There are, as a result, both prominent early scholars and wonderful contemporary studies that I could not discuss at length or, in many cases, even mention. In addition, and despite nearly a decade of work, I am under no illusions that I am as conversant with scholarship on ancient Greek traditions as I am with Hebrew Bible scholarship. If, while reading this book, you find yourself asking why I did not cite this or that study or discuss the work of this or that scholar, know that I would very likely agree with your complaint and regret the omission.

At the same time, a conviction that is crucial to this book's purpose is that if comparing scholarly approaches in these two disciplines is to be useful, it cannot belong only to the rare, if even extant, scholar who can claim genuine mastery over both disciplines. Still less should it belong to those who have only a vague sense of the approaches in the other field but are confident enough to proceed anyway, or the unfortunately common scholar who applies the lessons of one to the other but only on the basis of the big ideas of half a century earlier. In other words, you still often see, for example, biblical scholars doing comparative work by citing the ideas of Parry, Lord, or Nilsson without any apparent awareness of the ways their ideas have been challenged over time, or how they have been qualified even by those who still accept them in principle. One cannot simply read Parry, Lord, and Nilsson and get the sense of what twenty-first-century classical scholars believe, any more than one can read Albright, Alt, and Noth and understand how twenty-first-century Hebrew Bible scholars approach their task. So, someone who wants to apply approaches from one discipline to the other has to be as willing to investigate how they have changed over time as they would be where early twentieth-century arguments in their own discipline are concerned—and where they would certainly be aware that no major early twentieth-century idea remains unchallenged. This is no easy task.

Still, it is my view that the enterprise of comparing scholarly approaches to two such similar corpora, from similarly fragmentary contexts, similarly long ago and not too far apart in space, is valuable enough that it should be far more widely adopted, which requires, in this case, accepting limitations. And I hope that a thing done moderately well, under obvious constraints, is better than a thing done poorly or not at all. If I have achieved something that feels more toward the former than the latter, I will feel satisfied. However I have fallen short, I hope my effort will still prove useful to those interested in what a combined approach to the study of ancient traditions can reveal.

1

Ethnicity

Everyone knows the riddle of the two guards: one always tells the truth; the other always lies. This is a book in which every chapter is built around two *questions*. One always changes, while the other stays the same. The result is not a terribly high-stakes game—I cannot recommend it as entertainment at parties—but it is useful; and useful is something a book can hang its hat on. The stable question is, of course, "how can a combined approach help us see where the study of this topic ought to go next?" The changing one, bespoke for this chapter, is, "What do contemporary understandings of ethnic identity in particular mean for the study of ancient traditions?"

What I am referring to here, specifically, is the end of what is usually called the "primordialist" paradigm of ethnic identity. This is the idea that a given ethnic identity was defined once, long ago, in some distant—primordial—era and ever after remained functionally the same, carried on by biological descent. So, we are French, say, not only because we are descended from the ancient Franks in their era of primordial origins but because the ethnic identity we have today was formed in its particulars at that time. Then it was simply passed down by blood, generation to generation. Today, of course, we still acknowledge the important role of descent—not blood, in the sense of DNA or other biological or quasi-biological quantities, but descent in any case—in passing *conceptions* of ethnic identity on; but primordialism itself has been replaced with an increasing awareness of the inherent fluidity of ethnic constructions over time. This is called the "constructivist" paradigm because ethnicity is not just a construction, in the sense that it is something built rather than something we are born with, but something that is always being *re*-constructed in the face of new realities and challenges. And what it means for the study of the ancient traditions of Greece, Israel, and Judah is what I am to explore.

More precisely, the actual fact that primordialism is an outdated paradigm is not, for the most part, a new recognition that needs to be grappled with. What I will argue, however, is that its full ramifications have yet to be reckoned with in any meaningful way, and are much deeper than generally supposed. This is in part because primordialism itself survives in ancient studies better than it often does elsewhere. It is still, as Carly Crouch observes, "probably the form of ethnic identity which has most frequently found its way into discussions of biblical texts," even though it "is not adopted by the majority of ethnographers."[1] This is a polite way of saying that many Hebrew Bible scholars are still using a model that has long since been disavowed by those who study ethnic identity itself. And the situation is not so different where ancient Greek traditions are concerned.

Yet the greater problem, as far as I am concerned, is that lingering primordialist assumptions, acknowledged or not, provide the main justification for many still common approaches to the question of traditions and what they preserve and reveal. In other words, a number of typical ways of analyzing texts, as a practical matter, actually do require us to assume a people will have the same basic understanding of itself and its past throughout its history. But these methods and assumptions have become so second nature by now that their theoretical underpinnings have long since ceased being visible. Therefore, the need to change them *when* we change those underpinnings has not been visible either, and that is precisely what I hope to make clear.

I will argue that these include any variant of what has sometimes been called the "linear model" of tradition inheritance—the idea that surviving texts should be understood, first and foremost, as versions of much earlier traditions that enjoyed the same prestige and importance all along—so that scholars, working their way back to the earliest form, are inevitably recovering a centrally important early tradition.[2] And, it includes any version of

---

1. Carly L. Crouch, *The Making of Israel: Cultural Diversity in the Southern Levant and the Formation of Ethnic Identity in Deuteronomy* (Leiden: E.J. Brill, 2014), p. 99. The full quote is, "The primordialist framework, while not adopted by the majority of ethnographers, has profoundly affected archaeological interpretation of material culture and, in the form of its emphasis on genetic or biological connections among group members, is probably the form of ethnic identity which has most frequently found its way into discussions of biblical texts."

2. John H. Choi has provided an excellent critique of the "linear model" in the study of the Pentateuch, which he characterizes as the assumption that whenever references to stories that appear in the Pentateuch are found in the rest of the Hebrew Bible, they are *based* on the pentateuchal version, improperly retrojecting the authority the Pentateuch would come to have backwards into periods in which it would be anachronistic. See especially John H. Choi, *Traditions at Odds: The Reception of the Pentateuch and Second Temple Period Literature* (London: T. & T. Clark, 2010), pp. 15-16. Eva Mroczek has discussed, at length, the tendency to assume that earlier versions of traditions had the same role and status in their original context as they have in what survives with regard to the assumption of the perpetual canonical "hegemony" of biblical traditions prior to their actual canonization—for which, see Eva Mroczek,

the idea that tracing the historical development of a tradition can, by itself, explain the text we have, as if all someone who inherits a tradition can do is tweak it a little and send it on its way.[3] Both require the idea that an ethnic group keeps the same basic set of charter traditions throughout their history, which is also the idea that this group will have the same basic idea of who it is and where it comes from for that entire period—which is primordialism. But because the relationship between the method, the assumption, and the ethnic paradigm no longer has to be articulated to justify it, or even noticed, the downfall of the latter has not taken enough down with it.

Thus, the scale of the change that is needed to really move on from an outdated paradigm is much greater than it would be if all we had to worry about is how to talk about Israelite or Greek ethnicity itself. It requires a fundamental reassessment of how we think about what surviving traditions preserve, reflect, and reveal, and even of what it is *most important* to learn about—and from—them. After all, if we do not think the relationship between early ethnic constructions and later, or early charter traditions and later, is simply that between the original and the adaptation, and if we do not think the original is the "real" form and the later the corruption or invention, we will not think that studying early forms, by reconstructing them, is inherently more valuable than studying later ones *even when we feel confident that we can.* We will not view changes that are made over time as corruptions that need to be reverse engineered, and we will not think the development of either individual texts or whole complexes of tradition are necessarily linear. In other words, we simply will not be most interested in what surviving texts preserve about the earliest periods and earliest traditions it may reflect, and we will not find reflection itself an uncomplicated business. All of these common intellectual moves are fundamentally based on a primordialist vision of the stability of charter traditions over time, and, as a result, all of them need to be rethought.

"The Hegemony of the Biblical in the Study of Second Temple Literature," *Journal of Ancient Judaism* 6.1 (2015), pp. 2-35; Eva Mroczek, *The Literary Imagination in Jewish Antiquity* (Oxford: Oxford University Press, 2016). In addition, we have to consider all the traditions that once existed that simply did not survive and were not chosen for inclusion in surviving collections.

3. "It is a pervasive fallacy ... that the meaning of a text lies in its origins ... in biblical studies, there remains a persistent impulse to locate meaning in a text's origins and to approach that original moment through tracing a linear history of the text's formation. ... But what is remarkable is that although the goals of historicizing the biblical texts and tracing their development *appear* to take the opposite approach of a final form reading of the text, the search for an original moment of a text's formation can paradoxically echo a canonical and implicitly divine status of Scripture. Early stages of a text's history can prove informative. ... [but e]arlier iterations do not fix a text's meaning once and for all" (Vayntrub, *Beyond Orality*, p. 4).

Therefore, in what follows, I will begin by making the essential point: that primordialism is indeed gone beyond recovery, and we really do need to leave it behind. And I will end by attempting to answer the question: what contemporary approaches to the study of ethnic charter traditions, between the two disciplines at the center of this study, hold the most promise where successfully integrating fluid models of ethnic identifying into our analyses is concerned? But in order to make the scope of the problem visible, I also need to explain what made the role of primordialist assumptions in normal ways of proceeding *invisible in the first place.* And here, I will offer an essentially historical explanation that will occupy much of the middle of this chapter.

Specifically, I will argue that when the modern norms of textual and tradition inquiry were first developing, between the late eighteenth century and the end of the nineteenth, they were profoundly influenced not only by primordialist assumptions but a host of related ideas about the history of traditions and their relationship to ethnic nations. Indeed, in my view, this is where we find the fundamental significance of the fact that primordialism originated as the *Romantic* vision of the ethnic nation, especially as articulated in the work of Johann Gottfried Herder. As a result, it came packaged with other generally Romantic ideas about the nature of early traditions, what has sometimes been called the "developmental framework" or the "Great Divide" model of tradition production, which constructed early traditions as the pure, representative, and typically oral distillations of the beliefs and understandings of the entire group. [4] Indeed, in the period in question, they were often regarded as something very like the *collective memory* of the ethnic group concerning its own formative experiences.

The result, I will suggest, was a powerful "qualitative framework," a term that is not more descriptive than "developmental," but more useful for the argument I am making. This framework had less impact on the emergence of scholarly *methods* of investigation than on the importance and utility attributed to their ultimate task, the recovery of the original tradition. Specifically, I will show that the development of historical-critical approaches—and later, tradition-critical—aggressively cross-pollinated with these Romantic ideas about what early traditions were like. And, completely apart from the question of what historical critical methods *can* do, when used responsibly, I will show that many scholars embraced them precisely because of what they believed about the original tradition and how it compared to the surviving text.

---

4. See especially the discussion in Vayntrub, *Beyond Orality*, pp. 1-35. See also Robyn Faith Walsh, *The Origins of Early Christian Literature: Contextualizing the New Testament within Greco-Roman Literary Culture* (Cambridge, UK: Cambridge University Press, 2021), p. 49.

This discussion, once completed, will not only make the concluding consideration of contemporary approaches more straightforward, it will greatly simplify the task of later chapters. This will especially be the case after the second chapter's sketch of the second half of this history, how the Romantic roots of familiar approaches went underground and re-emerged as the animating force of the apparently empirical approaches of the early to mid-twentieth century. At the same time, it will also serve the specific goal of this chapter by revealing how the relationship between constructions of ethnic identity and the scholarly study of how traditions developed has historically worked. This, in turn, will lay the foundation of a consideration of why new assumptions should lead to new approaches, which will lead very naturally into my discussion of how scholars in both fields have attempted to reshape the study of charter traditions around the recognition of their constant fluidity over time.

In other words, we now know, as Jean-François Bayart put it, that "everyone is given to tinkering with his or her identity, depending on the alchemy of the circumstances."[5] Surviving texts are the medium through which that tinkering occurs; and tinkering, as a result, is not just what we can study through them, but in the case of charter traditions, the most important thing. The ballast we need to jettison to get there includes the idea of the early tradition as the real tradition, of the early ethnic group as the real ethnic group, *and* of a certain kind of tradition as a collective memory of a time long past. Stowed deep in the hold, where they cannot be seen, they have nevertheless kept a good deal of scholarship on a course plotted too long ago to a land that does not exist. It is time to toss them over the side and sail on.

Primordialism Problems

I would like to begin by stating as unequivocally as possible that primordialism is indeed an outdated model and that there is no path to recovering it, or even something vaguely like it.[6] Why I need to be so insistent will become

5. Jean-François Bayart, *The Illusion of Cultural Identity* (trans. Steven Rendall; Chicago: University of Chicago Press, 2005), p. 95. It is worth noting that Irad Malkin's claim that "genealogy can be an uncertain device for articulating ethnicity, because it is open to free manipulation and conflicting claims … capable … of differentiating and relating nations at the same time" bumps up against the fact that authors may *wish* to be able to differentiate and relate at *different* times, which means that genealogy might be a perfectly adequate device for articulating how ethnicity tends to work over time (Irad Malkin, *The Returns of Odysseus* [Berkeley, CA: University of California Press, 1998], p. 61).

6. There have been those who suggested that ancient ethnicity did not play by the rules of modern ethnic constructions. In addition, Kostas Vlassopoulos discusses the

apparent in later chapters, where the tenacity of the scholarly urge to find some justification for reviving older models on new grounds will be revealed again and again. And this, once more, is also the major inspiration for my desire to repeatedly emphasize the role a Romantic vision of *what* early traditions are like plays in preserving primordialist assumptions into the present. In other words, there is something more going on here than fidelity to an older way of thinking about identity itself; many scholars do not want to lose access to the kind of information an older way of thinking about *traditions* prioritized. And this is as much the explanation for why approaches that rely on linear models and assume a qualitative framework survive as it is for why, say, the skeptical arguments of Julius Wellhausen about what pentateuchal texts preserve and reflect were so roundly resisted for so long.

Yet, however we would have it, primordialism is a dead letter, and in fact, has been for quite a long time. We can trace its rejection as far back as the work of Max Weber, whose sociological analysis revealed, for example, that the marked differences between "the social and economic behavior" of Polish and German farmers was actually due to "historical and social causes" rather than an inherent Polish or German national *character*.[7] Others have credited the horrors of World War II for awakening the scholarly community to the dangers of perpetuating an ethnic model based solely on biological descent.[8] And, it is ultimately Frederik Barth who is most often credited with breaking from what Andreas Wimmer calls "the Herderian canon in anthropology, according to which each ethnic group represented a historically grown, uniquely shaped flower in the garden of human cultures."[9] This he did particularly influentially in the introduction to the

---

more or less dormant character of the discussion of ancient Greek ethnicity between the 1950s and the late 1990s because of certain doubts about the day-to-day importance of identities like "Dorian" or "Ionian" and the declining interest in older debates about "national" identities after the horrors of World War II (Kostas Vlassopoulos, "Ethnicity and Greek History: Re-Examining our Assumptions," *Bulletin of the Institute of Classical Studies* 58.2 [2015], pp. 1-2). Other studies have drawn attention to the way ancient constructions of identity may have blended what, at least in American contexts, is often treated separately—ethnicity and race, e.g. Erich S. Gruen, *Ethnicity in the Ancient World—Did It Matter?* (Berlin: de Gruyter, 2020), p. 4. Scholarship seems broadly to have moved on from any serious skepticism about the existence of ancient ethnic concepts that are similar to modern ethnic concepts in their construction.

7. Vivian Ibrahim, "Ethnicity," in *The Routledge Companion to Race and Ethnicity* (ed. Stephen M. Caliendo and Charlton McIlwain; London: Routledge, 2nd edn, 2020), p. 19. Ibrahim also offers an excellent discussion of the history of the term "ethnicity" and related ones like *ethnos* and *ethnie* [sic] (Ibrahim, "Ethnicity," pp. 18-19).

8. Jonathan M. Hall, *Ethnic Identity in Greek Antiquity* (Cambridge, UK: Cambridge University Press, 1997), p. 1.

9. Andreas Wimmer, "The Making and Unmaking of Ethnic Boundaries: A Multilevel Process Theory," *American Journal of Sociology* 113.4 (2008), p. 970.

1969 essay collection *Ethnic Groups and Boundaries*. And of course, the Herder of the Herderian canon is the Johann Gottfried discussed above and below.

Barth's argument is easy enough to follow and, in any case, is no longer controversial. He begins by acknowledging that since "anthropological reasoning" is generally based on the presumption that cultural groups *exist*— "that there are aggregates of people who essentially share a common culture, and interconnected differences that distinguish each such discrete culture from all others"—it is natural to assume that "there are discrete groups of people, i.e., ethnic units, to correspond to each culture."[10] In other words, since it is natural to talk about "the Spanish" or "Spanish people," it is natural, too, to think that "the Spanish" are a real group who can *operate* as a group, an ethnic collective.[11] In reality, however, we can observe that Spanish identity, or any other, is neither stable over time nor internally consistent. Instead, ethnic group identity is constantly being reshaped by new experiences and challenges, and especially by the challenge of maintaining ethnic boundaries in new situations.[12] Ethnic boundaries can grow and shrink; scholars generally suppose, as James C. Miller recently put it, that "the ongoing process of boundary definition and maintenance *is* ethnicity."[13] And this reveals the impossibility of imagining ethnicity as a transhistorical essence carried within each member of the group throughout its history.

Just as importantly, we now know that ethnic articulations have a strong relationship to political and social formations and, therefore, a strong tendency to shift when they shift.[14] Patrick Geary observes some of the

10. Fredrik Barth, "Introduction," in *Ethnic Groups and Boundaries* (ed. Fredrik Barth; Prospect Heights, IL: Waveland, 2nd edn, 1998), pp. 9-10.

11. This particular line of critique has been extended in recent years especially by the work of Rogers Brubaker, who has drawn attention to the fallibility of the idea of "group identity" in and of itself. See, for example, Rogers Brubaker, *Ethnicity without Groups* (Cambridge, MA: Harvard University Press, 2004); Rogers Brubaker, *Nationalist Politics and Everyday Ethnicity in a Transylvanian Town* (Princeton, NJ: Princeton University Press, 2006).

12. "When defined as an ascriptive and exclusive group, the nature of continuity of ethnic units is clear: it depends on the maintenance of a boundary. The cultural features that signal the boundary may change, and the cultural characteristics of the members may likewise be transformed, indeed, even the organizational form of the group may change—yet the fact of continuing dichotomization between members and outsiders allows us to specify the nature of continuity, and investigate the changing cultural form and content" (Barth, "Introduction," p. 14).

13. James C. Miller, "Ethnicity and the Hebrew Bible: Problems and Prospects," *CBR* 6.2 (2008), p. 173.

14. Ibrahim, "Ethnicity," pp. 19-20. As Carly Crouch observes, "There are perhaps as many specific kinds of social change which might impel the explicit articulation of identity discourse as there are ethnic groups" (Crouch, *The Making of Israel*, p. 97).

acknowledgments this fact requires of us. It is common, for example, for contemporary European ethnonationalists to assert their rights on the basis of the various population movements and conquests that occurred during the first millennium CE.[15] In reality, however, the *way* they articulate the national identity they retroject into this distant past only became imaginable after the development of *nationalism itself* in the late eighteenth and nineteenth centuries. Thus, "The real history of the nations that populated Europe in the early Middle Ages begins not in the sixth century but in the eighteenth."[16] Similarly, where ancient ethnicity is concerned, we have to realize that the disruptions that accompanied the passage of ancient time from the Archaic to the Classical Age in Greece, and over the course of the Iron Age in Israel and Judah, raise serious questions about how relevant early constructions of Greek or Israelite identity even are for understanding later.

For now, however, it is enough to say that we understand ethnic identity as fundamentally fluid, not just from period to period but in different contexts, and that this is called the "constructivist" view of ethnicity. This is because, in it, ethnicity is understood not just as "dynamic, negotiable, and situationally constructed," as Jonathan M. Hall put it, but perpetually *re*constructed era to era and context to context.[17] There are still, to be sure, disagreements about just how "constructed" ethnicity is, since it is hard to determine how consciously it is being remodeled in various cases, and since we do often inherit our sense of ethnicity, to some extent, from prior generations. There are, therefore, those today who see ethnic articulations as essentially strategic, the province of "ethnopolitical entrepreneurs" manipulating their followers for diverse reasons.[18] There are those who

15. Patrick J. Geary, *The Myth of Nations: The Medieval Origins of Europe* (Princeton, NJ: Princeton University Press, 2002), pp. 15-16. He further notes that "the very tools of analysis" we use to discuss ethnic groups were also "invented and perfected within a wider climate of nationalism and nationalist preoccupation at that time." An excellent book by Stefani Engelstein explores the way that Europeans, in the late eighteenth century—the time of Herder—"embarked on a new way of classifying the cultural and natural human world," which included thinking in terms of the interrelationship between ethnic nations and language families—"languages, religions, races, nations, species, or individuals" (Stefani Engelstein, *Sibling Action: The Genealogical Structure of Modernity* [New York: Columbia University Press, 2017], p. 2).

16. Geary, *The Myth of Nations*, pp. 6-8.

17. Hall, *Ethnic Identity in Greek Antiquity*, 2. Referring to Hall's study, Vlassopoulos notes that Hall's presentation of ethnicity, even in the ancient Greek world, as "a social construction and not an objective reality ... has been universally accepted by subsequent scholars," and was essentially an act of "bringing classicists in contact with the development of anthropological, sociological, and historical studies of ethnicity in the last few decades" (Vlassopoulos, "Ethnicity and Greek History," p. 4).

18. Brubaker, *Ethnicity without Groups*, p. 10.

imagine this manipulation as conscious, even cynical, while others see it as essentially unconscious.[19] There are those who lean toward an ethnic "essentialism" that "privileges the transcontextual stability provided by ethnic cultures," while others stress "situationalism ... how individuals identify with different ethnic categories depending on the logic of the situation."[20] Even so, we are "all constructivists now."[21] So much for primordialism.

It is at this point, however, that I need to remind readers that this chapter is not really about how contemporary scholars in both disciplines should talk about ethnic identity itself. It, is instead, about what constructivist understandings of ethnicity, in whatever form, demand of us where the study of traditions is concerned. Above all, I am arguing that the familiar image of an original set of charter traditions precipitating through the ages is far more dependent on primordialist constructions of ethnic identity itself than has been acknowledged virtually anywhere. Basically, as I have already suggested, it stands to reason that if ethnic actors are always changing their sense of who they are, even in small ways, they will also change the stories that provide the charter for who they are in the ancient world as much as in later periods. This acknowledgment must surely change how we imagine the relationship between surviving traditions and the earlier narratives they draw from, or are based on, but not only that. They will change what kind of information we expect to find preserved within them. Indeed, they should even change how we feel about the fact that we cannot reliably recover early "kernels of truth" about the original ethnic group from them, but largely the record of later ideological interventions.

In other words, the ongoing fluidity of ethnicity should change how we understand the *significance* of new ways of expressing ethnic belonging. These are not corruptions; they are not inventions; they are ethnicity taking its natural course. They are not simply the next step in a predetermined evolutionary process because an ethnic articulation that exists can neither explain nor predict the next formulation to arise. Broadly, I suggest that someone who imagines that the most vitally important thing to do with an ancient text is discover what kernels of truth it contains can hardly interpret the ongoing fluidity of visions of the past as anything but a threat to this enterprise, whether they would put it that way or not. But

---

19. Werner Sollors refers, critically, to the instrumentalist assumption of ethnicity as "a conspiratorial interpretation of a manipulative inventor who single-handedly made ethnics out of unsuspecting subjects" (Werner Sollors, *The Invention of Ethnicity* [Oxford: Oxford University Press, 1989], p. xi).

20. Wimmer, "The Making and Unmaking of Ethnic Boundaries: A Multilevel Process Theory," p. 971.

21. Miller, "Ethnicity and the Hebrew Bible: Problems and Prospects," p. 28.

as Jonathan M. Hall put it, in his pathbreaking 1997 study, *Ethnic Identity in Greek Antiquity*:

> If ... we accept the view that ethnicity is not a primordial given, but is instead repeatedly and actively structured through discursive strategies, then clearly myths of ethnic origins are among the very media through which such strategies operate.[22]

In other words, recognizing that traditions of ethnic origin were the means through which ethnic groups redescribed themselves repeatedly over time does not make them corrupt—or fake, or less than—it makes them interesting as a record of the history of ethnic redescription.

Indeed, I would go further. Among the most important consequences of the end of primordialism we must include a considerable lessening of the importance of certain kinds of distinctions that have previously seemed almost intuitive. These include, of course, the distinction between the early and the late tradition: the earlier is *only* earlier, not more authentic. They should also include even the seemingly commonsense distinction between what are sometimes called "genuine" and "invented" charter traditions, which is to say, traditions that have some basis in real, historical events, and those that do not.[23] This is, above all, an outsider's view of the situation. The evidence suggests that the heirs of ancient traditions neither knew nor marked which was which, and that both of what we might regard as genuine and invented accounts operated in much the same way.[24] So, the distinction may matter to the ethnic group and their competitors a great deal, but it does little to add to scholarly analysis. In other words, since a tradition that is "genuine"—based on real events—and "invented"—not based on real events—is treated the same way, and has the same kind of things happen to it, over the course of its history, it does not add to our analysis of the tradition as tradition to make that distinction, even though it seem as if it must.

In addition, we simply have to regard those who inherit traditions as having more creative agency with respect to what they do with them—

---

22. Hall, *Ethnic Identity in Greek Antiquity*, p. 41.

23. The term was pioneered in Eric Hobsbawm and Terence Ranger, eds., *The Invention of Tradition* (Cambridge, UK: Cambridge University Press, 1983).

24. "To the biblical authors there is no difference between the 'historicity' of, for instance, the Primeval story and that of other stories in the Hebrew Bible" (Hans M. Barstad, *History and the Hebrew Bible: Studies in Ancient Israelite and Ancient Near Eastern Historiography* [Tübingen: Mohr Siebeck, 2008], p. 8). See also Daniel Pioske's recent discussion of how much the contemporary epistemological framework for thinking through what people who are describing the past *must* be doing has shaped inquiries into what biblical traditions *are* doing in ways that might not be appropriate (Daniel Pioske, "An Archaeology of Ancient Thought: On the Hebrew Bible and the History of Ancient Israel," *HTR* 115.2 [2022], pp. 171-96).

intentional agency or quite unintentional. And we can think about what this might mean through the lens of an analogy I have employed before, between the inheritance of traditions and the work of the museum curator.[25] In the museum, of course, a great deal of energy goes into identifying where and when the artifacts came from, and it would make a great difference—to the curators, to the museum-going public—whether they are real or fake. Even so, imagining a museum exhibit as nothing more than a neutral presentation of artifacts is a poor way of understanding it *even when* the artifacts are real. Instead, the curators still have a great many choices to make, which to include and exclude among them. They have to decide what story to use them to tell, and we have to realize that two different curators can tell very different stories even through the same artifacts.[26] We have, indeed, to realize that curation does not change only how we encounter the artifacts, and what we learn from them, but even, in some cases, what they fundamentally seem to be. This means that, where studying surviving ethnic articulations is concerned, identifying what they were built from or developed further tells us far less than we used to think because inherited elements can be presented in so many different ways. Or, more plainly: the fact that a surviving text may be built around an early tradition, or multiple early traditions, does not really change how new it might be as a vision of identity and the past, the same way that the presence of real artifacts in a museum exhibit does not keep curators from being able to present them in very different ways without physically altering them.

At the same time, a good deal of contemporary scholarship remains primarily interested in the question of what texts preserve about earlier periods, ideologies and ethnic articulations. Many of these scholars, indeed, use the existence of real artifacts as the centerpiece of arguments as to

25. Andrew Tobolowsky, "The Primary History as Museum Exhibit: Rethinking the Recovery of the Hebrew Bible's Artifacts," *Method and Theory in the Study of Religion* 32.3 (2020), pp. 233-58.

26. The "act of display is always simultaneously one of definition and attribution of value" (Rhiannon Mason, "Cultural Theory and Museum Studies," in *A Companion to Museum Studies* [ed. Sharon Macdonald; Chichester: Wiley-Blackwell, 2011], p. 18). In other words, as Shelly Shenhav-Keller observes, exhibits that present the past through objects function "as a master-narrative, a story that weaves the facts into a fabric of a plot" but—and here she cites Amos Funkenstein—it "does not represent the facts ... but takes part in their creation," including by determining "the facts that will be selected," and "emplotting" them in a way that is unique to that particular exhibit (Shelly Shenhav-Keller, "Invented Exhibits: Visual Politics of the Past at the Museum," in *Memory and Ethnicity: Ethnic Museums in Israel and the Diaspora* [ed. Emanuela Trevisan Semi, Dario Miccoli, and Tudor Parfitt; Newcastle upon Tyne: Cambridge Scholars Publishing, 2013], pp. 25-26; Amos Funkenstein, "History, Counter History and Narrative," *Alpayim* 4 [1991], p. 208). Shenhav-Keller is referring to the Museum of the Jewish Diaspora, and the Funkenstein quote is translated from Hebrew.

why invention and reinvention—description and redescription—are not powerful forces in shaping what survives. If the artifacts are real, how can the exhibit be an invention? Likewise, they tend to treat those elements of surviving texts that reflect early ethnic visions as, inevitably, the first step on the journey toward later ones. We can think of early tradition elements and the remnants of early identity constructions instead as artifacts, *from a much wider range of available artifacts,* which were chosen for specific reasons and presented in specific ways, even when they are perfectly real and perfectly ancient.

Of course, I stress that even in the museum the curator is not an entirely free agent but is influenced on many different levels by social, cultural and presumably occupational forces. Even so, curation is a creative act, and so is retelling the story of the past. And so is rehashing inherited ethnic identities. And unlike in the museum, where ethnic articulations are concerned, there is absolutely no reason to be less interested in what the curators are doing than in what the artifacts are that they are doing it with—if not more so because, in this case, exhibiting the artifacts is expressing or creating identity, not corrupting identity. And this, in my view, is indeed the basic significance of the shift from a primordialist to a constructivist view of identity for the study of traditions, that traditions about identity always reflect how identity is understood in that era, and the identity constructions of one era are no less interesting than that of another. Even so—as I intimated in the introduction to this chapter—there are historical reasons why the move to a more dynamic vision of tradition inheritance, and a move away from these linear and qualitative imaginings, has been difficult to effect. I turn my attention to them now.

Romantic Roots

There is something usefully instructive for the main topic of this book, the study of traditions, about the fact that tracing the exact nature of the influence of philosophical ideas, movements and treatises on individual arguments and formulations is so challenging. Everyone knows—so to speak—that someone is not necessarily a capital "R" Romantic just because they have some Romantic ideas, or present arguments that show the influence of Romanticism. Everyone knows that "the Romantics" themselves did not speak with one voice, not even the German Romantics, not even the "Jena Romantics."[27] And this is because the influence of ideas is not linear. Their

27. The early epicenter of Romanticism *qua* Romanticism was the city of Jena where a group of German intellectuals gathered in the late 1790s, including the Schlegel brothers, Novalis, Friedrich Schleiermacher, Ludwig Tieck and others (Judith Norman and

reception is shaped by the idiosyncrasies, individual apprehensions, beliefs and agendas of those doing the receiving in ways that are hard to trace or reconstruct. All of which, of course, cuts against familiar linear models of tradition inheritance, too.

Then, of course, influences can happen below the level of the historian's sight. Almost every scholar discussed in this chapter is a German man, usually a Protestant, born between 1744 (Herder) and 1862 (Hermann Gunkel), who went to the same schools, sometimes had the same teachers, and were frequently connected through family and marital ties.[28] We know much of what was written down by one scholar or another; but what was said at the dinner table, in the classroom, at coffee, that, of course is another matter. If someone we think of mainly as a figure of the Enlightenment, or unaffiliated, has one opinion that we generally associate with the Romantics, they might have been convinced of it at a wedding reception or a birthday party as easily as by an essay from a major figure of intellectual history.

Time and time again, however, those who inherit *traditions* or *ethnic constructions* are not supposed to have idiosyncrasies, individual opinions about which stories are important and why, or individual understandings of which figures and events are the most central in shaping the nation. We do not imagine that someone who was not very interested in the Trojan War, say, might nevertheless have some stories about Odysseus they particularly like, and a different sense of what the important episodes in that story were than most other people. We do not think an ethnic actor can be our imagined curator, building something not only new but idiosyncratic out of the same inherited artifacts. In short, we can certainly ask why anyone should think the history of ethnic concepts is linear when the history of ideas is not.

At any rate, our interest here is in the "Herderian canon" of ethnicity mentioned above. Its influence is indeed diffuse and can certainly be difficult to

---

Alistair Welchman, "The Question of Romanticism," in *The Edinburgh Critical History of Nineteenth-Century Philosophy* [ed. Alison Stone; Edinburgh: Edinburgh University Press, 2011], pp. 49-50; Richard Littlejohns, "Early Romanticism," in *The Literature of German Romanticism* [ed. Dennis F. Mahoney; Martlesham, Suffolk: Boydell & Brewer, 2004], p. 65; Andrew Webber, "The Afterlife of Romanticism," in *German Literature of the Nineteenth Century, 1832–1899* [ed. Clayton Koelb and Eric Downing; Woodbridge, Suffolk: Boydell & Brewer, 2005], p. 23; Louis Dupré, "What Was and What Is Romanticism?," in *The Quest of the Absolute: Birth and Decline of European Romanticism* [Notre Dame, IN: University of Notre Dame Press, 2013], pp. 8-10).

28. Paul Michael Kurtz relates the surprising fact that "Throughout the nineteenth century, somewhere between half and a third of scholars in the human sciences were related to another academic either by affinity or consanguinity" (Paul Michael Kurtz, *Kaiser, Christ, and Canaan* [Tübingen: Mohr Siebeck, 2018], p. 26).

trace. But we can begin with the fact that Johann Gottfried Herder—along with Johann Gottlieb Fichte and a few others—was, in many ways, the father of primordialism.[29] The term did not exist yet and would not until the mid-twentieth century. But Herder was still the most influential shaper of this vision of ethnic groups, which he understood to be bound together primarily by shared language, as ancient in origin, transhistorically stable, and possessed of a shared set of innate attributes that constituted their national *character*.[30] The Basque, for example, might be "alert, active, valiant, and lovers of freedom"; the French might have a "gay and enlightened genius."[31] If so, the Basque would always be alert, active, etc., and the French always, etc., and so on. This would be, on some level, what it *meant* to be Basque or French.

What we have to understand, however, is that from the start, Herder's was not merely a vision of ethnic nations. It was a vision of traditions as well, and of the relationship between the two. Herder himself famously analogized the historical development of nations to the course of a human life, progressing from infancy to the heights of civilization—in some cases anyway—through a series of stages. But where infancy, so to speak, was concerned, he had something of Jean-Jacques Rousseau's idealization of childhood in mind.[32] So, the early nation was not just primitive but innocent and pure; not just untutored but natural and unfiltered. In that period, the character of the ethnic nation was believed to exist in its least adulterated form, the moment

---

29. Fichte's contributions are usually traced to a series of lectures he gave on the subject of the German nation between 1807 and 1808—on the heels of Napoleon's defeat of the Prussian army at Jena in 1806—in which he articulated a vision of ethnic nations in general as primordialist entities defined by a shared language and the German nation in particular as superior in various respects. Among many useful discussions, see Nakul Kundra, "Understanding Nation and Nationalism," *Interdisciplinary Literary Studies* 21.2 (2019), pp. 135-36; Adeed Dawisha, "Nation and Nationalism: Historical Antecedents to Contemporary Debates," *International Studies Review* 4.1 (2002), pp. 10, 17.

30. As Jennifer Fox put it, "At the heart of Herder's schema is the concept of *Das Volk,* meaning 'folk' or 'nation.' In Herder's thought this nation is the most fundamental social collective, and the existence of multiple, diverse national groups represents the natural order. The quintessential nation constitutes a culturally homogenous, organic whole. ... The hallmark of each nation is a shared language, history, and environment, all of which contribute to the collective consciousness ... of a people" (Jennifer Fox, "The Creator Gods: Romantic Nationalism and the En-Genderment of Women in Folklore," *Journal of American Folklore* 100.398 [1987], pp. 565-66). See also William A. Wilson, "Herder, Folklore, and Romantic Nationalism," in *The Marrow of Human Experience: Essays on Folklore by William A. Wilson* (ed. Jill Terry Rudy and Diane Call; Boulder: University Press of Colorado, 2006), p. 110.

31. Johann Gottfried Herder, *Outlines of a Philosophy of the History of Man* (trans. T. Churchill; London: Luke Hansard, 1800), p. 470.

32. Engelstein, *Sibling Action,* p. 134.

when it was *most* itself.[33] The same is true of its traditions, which were imagined to be usually oral, simple, short, unfiltered and so on.[34]

In addition, Herder's arguments gave a boost to the idea of "folk genius": that in early periods, ethnic nations thought and acted much more collectively than they do now, that they had a *collective* genius. As Jacqueline Vayntrub established in her recent study, this is an idea that had already appeared in the work of Giambattista Vico and Francis Bacon.[35] Indeed, Vico had already described Homer as little more than a conduit for the *spirit* of ancient Greece, "or, in the idiom of Herder ... the summation of the national soul expressed in the poems of the folk."[36] But in Herder, certainly, "folk poets ... were national poets, the agents through whom the true character of a nation made itself manifest."[37] Finally, early authors—national authors—were often imagined as too unsophisticated for true invention, even if they were also too unsophisticated for historiography.[38]

We need to consider what the combination of all of these ideas did together—producing a quite familiar vision of early traditions, even if we do not always recognize how instinctively we reach for it. The early tradition, in contrast to the later text, was not just a story but a kind of memory of real experiences, even if distorted by the vagaries of poetic recollection. It was not just a narrative but an expression of "the collective memory of the people," even when it was, of course, "collected ... or written down

33. "What were these inclinations? ... The most natural, strongest, simple ones!" (Johann Gottfried Herder, *Another Philosophy of History and Selected Political Writings* [trans. Ioannis D. Evrigenis and Daniel Pellerin; Indianapolis, IN: Hackett Publishing Company, 2004], p. 5).

34. See the discussion in Vayntrub, *Beyond Orality*, pp. 2-3, 9, 11.

35. "Auerbach notes that it is easy to show that Vico, long before Herder and the Romanticists, discovered their most fertile aesthetic concept, the concept of folk genius. He was the first who tried to prove that primitive poetry is not the work of individual artists but was created by the whole society of the primitive peoples which were poets by their very nature" (Vayntrub, *Beyond Orality*, p. 47). See also Fabian Lampart, "The Turn to History and the Volk: Brentano, Arnim, and the Grimm Brothers," in *The Literature of German Romanticism* (ed. Dennis F. Mahoney; Martlesham, Suffolk: Boydell & Brewer, 2004), pp. 174-75; Wilson, "Herder, Folklore, and Romantic Nationalism," p. 110.

36. Wilson, "Herder, Folklore, and Romantic Nationalism," p. 115.

37. Wilson, "Herder, Folklore, and Romantic Nationalism," p. 16.

38. As Hermann Gunkel would later articulate the view, "Uncivilised races do not write history; they are incapable of reproducing their experiences objectively ... only in poetical form, in song and saga, are unlettered tribes able to report historical occurrences. ... Thus we find among the civilized peoples of antiquity two distinct kinds of historical records side by side: history proper and popular tradition, the latter treating in naïve poetical fashion partly the same subjects as the former, and partly the events of older, prehistoric times" (Hermann Gunkel, *The Legends of Genesis* [trans. W.H. Carruth; HKAT, 1; Chicago: Open Court Publishing, 1901], p. 7).

in a specific historical version by one single author."[39] And unlike in later periods, national consciousness in the formative era was understood to be at such a peak that it stamped itself on everything, the "literature, religion, customs, and laws" that were produced at that time.[40] As a result, it was widely believed that the pure form of national character could be *reconstructed* through the study of any of these in their original form. And indeed, there were even those who believed that a nation *could* only compose its great traditions during its long-ago "heroic age" since only its pure character could give rise to charter accounts of sufficient power to last the ages. The famous Brothers Grimm certainly thought as much.[41] Later, and despite the skeptical views that are usually associated with him, Wellhausen himself would refer to the time of Moses as the only "properly creative period" in Israel's history, "giving the pattern and norm for the ages which followed."[42]

In short, the way arguments like Herder's entangled views about the early ethnic group with a specific, linear model of tradition development produced a vision in which early traditions were the most important to study—and recover if necessary—not simply because they were early traditions, but because they were by far the most revealing, the most important, the most genuine. Perhaps the most famous result of all of this theorizing was a positive obsession with the recovery of folk *lore*. The Grimms themselves were the best-known collectors, and it is indeed worth noting that they were not just collectors but intellectuals—both worked as professors at one point or another—and committed Romantics. They were, by their own admission, after what they called *Naturpoesie*, "natural poetry," which is to say, the unaffected natural poetry of the uncorrupted *folk,* which they contrasted with *Kunstpoesie* ("cultivated literature"), which had none of the former's charm.[43]

39. Lampart, "The Turn to History and the Volk," 171.

40. George S. Williamson, *The Longing for Myth in Germany* (Chicago: University of Chicago Press, 2004), pp. 1-2. Indeed, the Brothers Grimm, who were primarily motivated, in their more famous efforts, by their interest in recovering "the spirit of the German people" *through* the recovery of its folk traditions, had actually set out to study *law* at Marburg under Friedrich Carl von Savigny before changing their approach (Walsh, *The Origins of Early Christian Literature*, p. 76; Jack Zipes, *The Original Folk and Fairy Tales of the Brothers Grimm: The Complete First Edition* [Princeton, NJ: Princeton University Press, 2014], p. xxii).

41. The Grimms were sure that "there is no way to create something like Volkspoesie"—or Naturpoesie—"under the conditions of modern life" but only in the era of "the foundations of a nation" (Lampart, "The Turn to History and the Volk," 178).

42. Julius Wellhausen, *Prolegomena to the History of Ancient Israel with a Reprint of the Article "Israel" from the Encyclopedia Britannica* (Gloucester, MA: Peter Smith, 1973), p. 432.

43. Over time, they believed, German civilization had progressed, and *Naturpoesie* had been forced to "recede ... and take refuge among the folk in oral traditions" (Zipes,

And they employed what would come to be known as the "generic method," the effort to study traditions by first identifying the genre in which it had been composed. This served as their guide to the history of traditions; they believed, for one thing, that "legends," or "*Sagen*," had "almost the authority of history" by their very nature.[44]

There were a number of others like them in the mid-nineteenth century, and in many other places, collecting folklore in similar pursuit of the genuine national spirit: Lady Charlotte Guest in Wales and Elias Lönnrot in Finland among them.[45] Indeed, Herder himself collected folklore, as in his *Volkslieder* (1778–1779). Others would go after ancient monuments, or manuscripts.[46] In each of these cases there operated the belief, as Elliott Oring put it, that "the unlettered peasants, uncorrupted by civilization, were the remnants and spiritual heirs of a native heathen nation," which meant that their "folklore" preserved "the fragments of the philosophy and way of life of an ancient people." This could "be reconstructed through the judicious analysis and comparison of contemporary peasant tales and customs."[47] In other words, there was the model just described—

The Original Folk and Fairy Tales of the Brothers Grimm, p. xxv). See also Walsh, *The Origins of Early Christian Literature*, p. 76.

44. Patricia G. Kirkpatrick, *The Old Testament and Folklore Study* (JSOTSup, 62; Sheffield: JSOT Press, 1988), p. 77. It is worth noting that the generic method was by no means defunct in other disciplines in later periods either; one landmark study, by G.L. Gomme, would appear in 1908 (George Laurence Gomme, *Folklore as an Historical Science* (London: Methuen, 1908).

45. Lady Charlotte created the *Mabinogion,* a collection of Welsh legends in the 1830s and '40s, and did not believe herself to be merely translating traditions, but to be in pursuit, in a sense, of a "Cymric nation" that is "not only … an early offshoot of the Indo-European family, and a people of unmixed descent, but … it has strong claims to be considered the cradle of European Romance" (Lady Charlotte Guest, *The Mabinogion: From the Welsh of the Llyfr Coch o Hergest [The Red Book of Hergest] in the Library of Jesus College, Oxford* [London: Quaritch, 2nd edn, 1877], p. 22). Lönnrot published the *Kalevala Epic* in 1835, "… a huge collection of folk poems," intended in part to "restore to the Finnish people … the national characteristics and cultural values" it depicted (Wilson, "Herder, Folklore, and Romantic Nationalism," p. 132).

46. As Abrahams puts it, each aspirationally "national" entity "has its own body of tradition that records and represents the history and accrued wisdom of 'the people.' Evidences of the past are inscribed in the present, in monuments and piles in the landscape, and in the scarce remains of ancient beliefs, practices, and performances, as they were recorded from the old people—or even better, as they were discovered from manuscript sources" (Roger D. Abrahams, "Phantoms of Romantic Nationalism in Folkloristics," *Journal of American Folklore* 106.419 [1993], p. 9).

47. Elliott Oring, "On the Concepts of Folklore," in *Folk Groups and Folklore Genres: An Introduction* (ed. Elliott Oring; Logan, UT: Utah State University Press, 1986), pp. 5-6.

the pursuit of the "original" tradition because of the belief that it revealed the ethnic nation as it "really" was. And in addition, for the true Romantic nationalists, these acts of recovery were also the key to national *revival,* since they could tell the ethnic nation who it "really" was, and therefore, could be again.[48]

For us, however, the focus remains on the impact ideas like these had on the study of ancient traditions. And here I reiterate that we need not imagine their influence as either consistently direct or total in character. But the era of Herder was also the era when both modern disciplines were beginning to take shape. And when we realize how common the idea not only was, but is, that early traditions are essentially national memories, this is the context in which we can realize that this idea is not natural, inevitable or obvious. It appeared in a specific historical era—the era in which the Romantic nationalist imagination of the nation, its history, *its* traditions and *their* history flourished—for specific reasons.

Correspondingly, my point in what follows will not be that traditions have no histories; it will not be that we cannot, sometimes, reconstruct those histories; and it will not be that this is a useless thing to do. It will be that when we do not think the early ethnic group can act collectively, we should not think it can produce traditions collectively. When we do not think the history of ethnic constructions is linear, we should not think that later generations simply rehearse and adapt what is handed down rather than making more dramatic changes within a larger and more diverse complex of ideas. And when we do not think it is better to study early ethnic articulations than later, we will not be more interested in the question of where an ethnic concept came from than how it is redeployed in the particular context that interests us. Thus, once again, even when we can recover earlier elements or reverse engineer earlier versions of surviving stories, what we really reveal is *only* early elements and earlier narratives, nothing more. But in part because they began to take shape during the precise era I have been discussing, a preoccupation with the question of what a text preserves of earlier materials and realities moved quickly to the center of what it meant to study a text in the first place and has largely remained there since. The relationship between this preoccupation and an older set of ideas about ethnic groups themselves is what I aim to make clear.

The Original Tradition

On one level, the idea that the Hebrew Bible and ancient Greek traditions, especially the Pentateuch and Homer, might come in for the same kind of

---

48. Wilson, "Herder, Folklore, and Romantic Nationalism," p. 122; Abrahams, "Phantoms of Romantic Nationalism in Folkloristics," p. 9.

analysis that the Grimms brought to bear on folktales might seem a little surprising. The folklorists, after all, were interested in recovering traditions that they generally characterized as older, simpler, shorter, poetic and oral. The *Iliad* and the *Odyssey* might be poems, but they are lengthy, complex, written compositions that are already of a very great age. The Hebrew Bible is the same, and largely executed in prose. Yet Vico, as we have seen, was already willing to see Homer as an expression of Greek folk genius before even Herder picked up his pen. Herder, who wrote *Vom Geist der Ebräischen Poesie* (*The Spirit of Hebrew Poetry*) in 1782, was just as happy to add the Hebrew Bible to the mix.[49] In fact, so were the Grimms themselves.[50] *Naturpoesie,* it seems, is something you know when you see it.

Yet superficially, at least, it would be another one of Herder's observations that would echo how the scholars of his day would begin to evolve new approaches to ancient traditions. This was his insistence that the Hebrew Bible could be understood merely as the traditions of ancient Israel in the same way that the *Nibelungenlied* could be understood as German tradition, rather than something more universal like "scripture." Again, I do not mean to suggest a perfectly direct line from one to the other, but around the turn of the eighteenth century, ideas like these would fuel not only Romantic approaches to these texts but the fires of the willingness of thinkers more in the mode of the Enlightenment to perform "dispassionate" inquiries upon them.[51] In other words, the idea that biblical traditions were fundamentally like other traditions meant they could be studied like other traditions.

This brings us to a consideration of historical criticism which, as John Barton observes, was the "dominant" approach to the study of ancient traditions "from the mid-nineteenth century until a generation ago," if not an even wider span.[52] Barton lists four attributes characteristic of the interests

49. Vayntrub notes that "Herder went beyond Vico" who "exempted the ancient Hebrews" from his scheme because, in the words of Isaiah Berlin, he "'had not dared to touch' the Bible other than to create pietist theoretical exceptions, but Herder, by contrast, understood the Bible to be the literature of the ancient Hebrews. For Herder, the Bible was no more sacred than the literature of any other nation" (Vayntrub, *Beyond Orality*, p. 47).

50. Christa Kamenetsky, "The Brothers Grimm: Folktale Style and Romantic Theories," *Elementary English* 51.3 (1974), p. 383.

51. George S. Williamson describes how it also fueled Romantic inquiries into Germany's own traditions "because it was no longer possible for educated Germans to identify reflexively with the travails of the Hebrew people or to see themselves as part of the 'children of Israel' or the 'new Jerusalem'" (Williamson, *The Longing for Myth in Germany*, p. 10).

52. John Barton, "Historical-Critical Approaches," in *The Cambridge Companion to Biblical Interpretation* (ed. John Barton; Cambridge, UK: Cambridge University Press, 1998), pp. 9-10. Rather, Barton makes this claim for the Hebrew Bible, but it

of historical critics: "genetic questions," "original meaning," "historical reconstructions," and "disinterested scholarship."[53] They were also interested in history *qua* history—"concerned with history in the straightforward sense of the term"—and often saw the effort to work back to what the text "really" said as the first step toward recovering what had "really" happened.[54] But above all, historical critics study texts by attempting to reconstruct the history of the traditions they present from the finished product back to their original sources, and from there, the circumstances that gave them shape.

As with "folk genius," historical criticism has a history stretching back beyond the eighteenth century—to Spinoza, for one—but began to take on the appearance of the familiar method particularly in the work of scholars like Johann Gottfried Eichhorn and Friedrich August Wolf. Eichhorn, a Hebrew Bible scholar, produced his multivolume *Einleitung ins Alte Testament* (*Introduction to the Old Testament*) in the early 1780s, at just the same time that Herder was publishing his *Vom Geist der Ebräischen Poesie*. Wolf, a classicist, published his still-more-influential *Prolegomena ad Homerum* in 1795.[55] Wolf and Eichhorn had much in common with each other, as they did with a great many other scholars discussed below. They were both, for example, educated at Göttingen "under Heyne and Michaelis." And Wolf, it seems, was inspired by Eichhorn, just as Eichhorn "had drawn on" the studies of the classicist Heyne.[56] They both, also—interestingly for this study—were quite conscious of working along parallel lines. Eichhorn, for example, would suggest, perhaps ironically, given Wolf's conclusions, that since Homer's "genuineness" had been, in his view, successfully defended, "the same grounds ... support also the genuineness of each separate book of the Old Testament."[57]

Wolf, meanwhile, would ground the new history of the Homeric poems that he laid out—the birth of the modern "Homeric question"—in large part

applies to the study of Homer as well. See also Paul Michael Kurtz, "A Historical, Critical Retrospective on Historical Criticism," in *The New Cambridge Companion to Biblical Interpretation* (Cambridge, UK: Cambridge University Press, 2022), pp. 15-36.

53. Barton, "Historical-Critical Approaches."
54. Barton, "Historical-Critical Approaches," p. 11.
55. Kurtz, "A Historical, Critical Retrospective on Historical Criticism," pp. 21-22.
56. Grafton, Most, and Zetzel, "Introduction," p. 20. They point out that Wolf sketched, but never wrote, a further section of his study which would "compar[e] at length the textual histories of the Old Testament and Homer" (Grafton, Most, and Zetzel, "Introduction," pp. 20, 25). As Wolf put it, "by comparing both of these farragoes, the Greek and the Hebrew, we will finally be able to gain a more profound knowledge to the beginnings from which the emendation of manuscripts and the art of criticism developed" (Wolf, *Prolegomena to Homer*, p. 51).
57. Eichhorn, *Introduction to the Study of the Old Testament*, 47.

on a manuscript of the *Iliad* published by Jean-Baptiste-Gaspard d'Ansse de Villoison in 1788. This was Venetus Marcianus Graecus 454, which was complete with "scholia," essentially ancient text-critical notations, going back to Alexandrian scholarship of the third century BCE.[58] And he would refer to these scholia specifically, perhaps even tauntingly, as "a sort of Greek Masorah, one far superior to the other in both age and variety of leaning, and far better preserved."[59] In other words, Wolf asserted that classical scholars now had as much to work with, with respect to text-critical apparatuses, as biblical scholars, if not more.

At any rate, their conclusions, though quite different in certain respects, were nevertheless fundamentally historical-critical in nature. Eichhorn, who may have been the first to call historical criticism "higher criticism" as opposed to the "lower criticism" of purely textual inquiries, is best known for restarting biblical scholarship down the path to the famous Documentary Hypothesis[60]—even if his identification of two sources in the book of Genesis in some ways replicated the earlier argument of Jean Astruc, who had died two decades before,[61] and even if he personally believed originally that it had been Moses himself who had *used* these sources to write Genesis, which were therefore, of course, actually even older.[62]

58. Robert Fowler, "The Homeric Question," in *The Cambridge Companion to Homer* (ed. Robert Fowler; Cambridge Companions to Literature; Cambridge, UK: Cambridge University Press, 2004), p. 220. A good discussion of the relevant scholia to both the *Iliad* and the *Odyssey* can be found in Eleanor Dickey, *Ancient Greek Scholarship: A Guide to Finding, Reading, and Understanding Scholia, Commentaries, Lexica, and Grammatical Treatises, from their Beginnings to the Byzantine Period* (Oxford: Oxford University Press, 2007), pp. 18-23. Dickey suggests there is some ambiguity in the modern use of the term scholia, though it is usually used today to refer to marginal notations on the text of the poems. However, "Scholars working on philosophical and scientific texts ... have a tendency to use 'scholia'" to refer to standalone commentaries. Even more confusingly, many marginal notations are in fact copied from standalone commentaries (Dickey, *Ancient Greek Scholarship*, p. 11 n. 25).

59. The full quote is, "let the masters of Oriental literature, proud of their Masorah, cease at last to deplore the ill fortune that makes us rely for the authority of the Homeric text on such recent manuscripts. ... If we put together all our excerpts from all sources, we ... now have a sort of Greek Masorah, one far superior to the other in both age and variety of leaning, and far better preserved" (Wolf, *Prolegomena to Homer*, 51).

60. Kurtz, "A Historical, Critical Retrospective on Historical Criticism," pp. 21-22.

61. As Rogerson notes, Jean Astruc had already divided Genesis into two sources in 1753 but Eichhorn "undertook the work afresh" (Rogerson, 19).

62. John Rogerson, *Old Testament Criticism in the Nineteenth Century: England and Germany* (London: Fortress Press, 1985), pp. 20-21. "Supposing the Mosaical books in their present disposition not to be the work of Moses, still they are composed of Mosaical materials, merely put into form by a later hand" (Johann Gottfried Eichhorn, *Introduction to the Study of the Old Testament* [trans. George Tilly Gollop; London: Spottiswood, 1888], p. 49). However, Eichhorn eventually "abandoned the

As for Wolf, his conclusions were in some ways even more striking, and likely more influential. First, he denied that the surviving texts were meaningfully the work of Homer, whom he imagined as an illiterate poet, very much in the Romantic mode. Then, from the evidence of the scholia, he concluded (he was not the first to reach this conclusion) that it was the sixth-century BCE Athenian tyrant Pisistratus who "*was the first to set down the poems of Homer in writing and to have put them into the order in which they are now read.*"[63] Indeed, noting "passages which are cited from Homer by Plato and his contemporaries but do not appear in him today," Wolf actually believed that there was no "fixed text until the age of the Ptolemies."[64]

Before long, Wolf's approach would give rise to the "analyst" and "unitarian" approaches to the study of Homer, just as Eichhorn's would inspire others to explore the Documentary Sources of pentateuchal traditions. The former, the analysts, sought to identify pre-existing poems and traditions that had, over time, gotten swept up in the *Iliad* and combined together. By contrast, the unitarians attempted to identify a single core poem around which the familiar *Iliad* and *Odyssey* would eventually be built, especially the *Iliad*.[65] These scholars would come to a range of different conclusions as would those who followed after Eichhorn. But all agreed with these antecedents that, as Grafton, Most, and Zetzel put it, "the true history of the text was its ancient history, before the standardized manuscripts now extant had been prepared."[66] We might say that they were therefore uninterested in the text as it actually is, though it would often be fairer to say that they understood the text to *be* nothing more than the end product of its history.

The point that I am making here begins with the obvious: there is nothing wrong with the idea that texts like the Pentateuch and the Homeric

idea of Mosaic authorship altogether" in response to some of the work of Wilhelm de Wette, discussed below (Joseph Blenkinsopp, *The Pentateuch* [New York: Doubleday, 1992], p. 3).

63. Wolf, *Prolegomena to Homer*, 137. He "commanded above all that Homer be sung in a new order by the rhapsodes at the quinquennial Panathenaic festivals" (Wolf, *Prolegomena to Homer*, 144).

64. Wolf, *Prolegomena to Homer*, 137, 142.

65. Whether these early efforts were valid or not, it is "historical criticism to which we owe the suggestion that any books are composite, put together out of a number of originally separate source documents," which is surely correct (Barton, "Historical-Critical Approaches," 9). As Dickey observes, the *Iliad* was analyzed by scholars of this sort much more often than the *Odyssey*, as it was considered to be "the superior work" in many ancient contexts (Dickey, *Ancient Greek Scholarship*, p. 21).

66. Anthony Grafton, Glenn W. Most, and James E.G. Zetzel, "Introduction," in *Prolegomena to Homer*, by Frederick A. Wolf [Princeton, NJ: Princeton University Press, 1988], p. 21.

poems have sources and layers. [67] They clearly do, and the nineteenth century saw a great deal of progress toward identifying them. At the same
time, what we often see in nineteenth-century historical criticism is that
scholars were interested in the results of this method because they believed
it revealed not only the original tradition but, on some level, the "real"
tradition. And, whether it shaped how they approached their project or not,
we see that they were often influenced by Romantic ideas about what early
traditions were like, both in terms of what they were imagined to be and,
often explicitly, in terms of the scholar's understanding of why recovering
them was so valuable. They were also often interested in them as a reflection of true national spirit—which, again, requires a primordialist vision of
what ethnic identity is to even entertain.

A paradigmatic case in point, where both sets of ideas are concerned,
appears in the work of the famous analyst Karl Lachmann, who, fittingly,
came to the study of Homer from the study of the *Nibelungenlied,* the
beau ideal of German Romanticism.[68] Having supposedly found many
original songs in the *Nibelungenlied,* he turned to the task of finding
them in the *Iliad.*[69] But his approach was explicitly motivated by his belief
that "the authorship of the *Iliad,* like that of the *Nibelungenlied,* could
be seen as in some way originating in the collective genius of the Greek
people," if one could work back to the *real Iliad,* from what survives.[70]
Lachmann, as Martin Nilsson would observe already in the early twentieth century, certainly combined the mechanics of historical criticism
with "the romantic idea of popular collective poetry" and Nilsson was
already able to trace the thread of this "back to the great German poet

67. For recent treatments of this topic in Homer, see especially Margalit Finkelberg, "The Cypria, the Iliad and the Problem of Multiformity in Oral and Written
Tradition," *Classical Philology* 95.1 (2000), pp. 1-11; John M. Foley and Margalit Finkelberg, "Meta-Cyclic Epic and Homeric Poetry," in *The Greek Epic Cycle and its
Ancient Reception* (ed. Marco Fantuzzi and Christos Tsagalis; Cambridge, UK: Cambridge University Press, 2015), pp. 126-38.

68. As Lampart observes, to the Grimms and others like them "The exemplary
form of Volkspoesie or Naturpoesie is a medieval epic such as the Nibelungenlied; like
legends and myth it is created by the people" (Lampart, "The Turn to History and the
Volk," p. 178).

69. Frank Turner, "The Homeric Question," in *A New Companion to Homer* (ed.
Ian Morris and Barry B. Powell; Leiden: E.J. Brill, 1997), pp. 131-32. At the time,
others were doing much the same. Kurtz mentions Theodor Nöldeke, who "separated
sources in the Pentateuch, Qur'an, and Alexander Romance" (Kurtz, "A Historical,
Critical Retrospective on Historical Criticism," p. 29).

70. Turner, "The Homeric Question," pp. 132-33. As he put it, "In this regard, the
destruction of the unity of Homeric authorship opened the way for the erection of a
collective ancient genius."

and scholar, Herder."[71] It is worth asking whether Lachmann would have found his project worth pursuing if he felt differently about what early traditions *were*.

Then there was Ulrich von Wilamowitz-Moellendorf, who was an arch-analyst, and likely the most influential classicist of the second half of the nineteenth century.[72] Wilamowitz was in many ways a different sort of scholar than Lachmann and made and contributed to many genuine advances in the study of ancient Greek traditions, including his insistence on the importance of philological expertise and his willingness to combine the study of texts with emerging extraliterary evidence of various sorts.[73] But his internalization of the qualitative framework is certainly visible in his oft-cited view that the *Iliad* as it stands, one of the most beloved and widely read compositions in history, was really "a miserable piece of patchwork."[74] Further, his debt to Herder was self-acknowledged: "without Herder, where would all research be into the origin of language, and the organic evolution of individual nations and mankind as a whole, all comparative study of parallel phenomena throughout the world?"[75] These convictions were presumably among those that inspired his dictum, "anyone who is incapable of working his way back from the surviving manuscripts to the author's autograph ... had better leave textual criticism alone."[76] But then we can also ask: What assumptions make the recovery of the "auto-

71. Martin P. Nilsson, *Homer and Mycenae* (New York: Cooper Square Publishers, 1968), p. 12.

72. Foley calls Wilamowitz's *Homerische Untersuchungen* the "apogee" of analyst scholarship "with its minute and thoroughgoing dissection of the *Odyssey* that combines the flower of Analytic technique with a command of the possibilities for the history and transmission of the poem" (John Miles Foley, *The Theory of Oral Composition: History and Methodology* [Bloomington: Indiana University Press, 1988], p. 5). Kurtz refers to "the empire of classics, where 'Wilamops' long reigned supreme" (Kurtz, *Kaiser, Christ, and Canaan*, 200).

73. William M. Calder III describes Wilamowitz's approach as an effort to combine *Wortphilologie*—the study of individuals words through analogy, developed by Gottfried Hermann—and the *Totalititsideal,* developed by Friedrich Gottlieb Welker, "the conviction that the particular can only be understood from out of a knowledge of the whole," into an embracing science of the study of Greek texts in, supposedly, their own context (William M. Calder III, "How Did Ulrich Von Wilamowitz-Moellendorff Read a Text?," *Classical Journal* 86.4 [1991], p. 347).

74. Fowler, "The Homeric Question," 221; Turner, "The Homeric Question," 137; Cedric H. Whitman, *Homer and the Heroic Tradition* (Cambridge, MA: Harvard University Press, 1963), p. 2.

75. Ulrich Von Wilamowitz-Moellendorff, *History of Classical Scholarship* (ed. Hugh Lloyd-Jones; trans. Alan Harris; Baltimore, MD: Johns Hopkins University Press, 1982), p. 106.

76. Wilamowitz-Moellendorff, *History of Classical Scholarship*, 170.

graph" *more* valuable than the study of the text qua text, even if we believe that they both have value? What models of tradition development make one believe that an autograph, in the sense of an original, authentic tradition from longer ago, inevitably exists?

In short, Robyn Faith Walsh is of course correct that "the Analyst debate was itself couched in Romantic ideas about oral tradition's national ethos."[77] By "national," she means what I have meant throughout, that the early tradition was qualitatively different from the later because it was supposed to represent what the whole nation believed. The unitarian debate was too, in the sense that these scholars did not generally regard the *Iliad* and the *Odyssey* themselves as Homer's work but imagined them more as elaborations on a lengthy poem that was.[78] And the same patterns would appear in the study of the Pentateuch, which I will return to below.

It did not have to be this way, which is a crucial point. There is nothing about the exercise of identifying the sources that compose a surviving text, or earlier elements, or tracing the processes through which they came together, that is *necessarily* Romantic. Again, the Pentateuch and the Homeric poems certainly are texts in which the operation of multiple hands is clearly visible. It is good, and illuminating, to know more about them, and the sequence of their operation. At the same time, the apprehensions of what many nineteenth-century historical critics, and not a few twentieth, thought they would find were clearly shaped by the set of ideas that I described above about what early traditions were like. The assumption of their historiographical value lay in the corresponding assumption that early traditions are like memory. The assumption of their explanatory value lay in the corresponding assumption of linear processes of tradition development over time, and so does the idea that the surviving text is *simply* the outcome of a history of development. The belief that the original tradition was the real, or authentic tradition, the tendency to view alterations as corruptions of its original purity, has its roots in the Great Divide. And we can only guess just how much the desire to recover the original tradition, instead of studying the surviving text, inspired scholars to complete their investigations successfully, where failure, meaning, a willingness to con-

---

77. Walsh, *The Origins of Early Christian Literature*, 54.

78. Turner mentions G.W. Nitzsch, who thought of Homer as an aggregator of earlier poems; G. Hermann, who "in ... 1831 and 1832 argued that there had been an original Homer, and that he had composed original poems much shorter than the present *Iliad* and *Odyssey*," which were later expanded; and George Grote, who made a case for important early poems in various ways (Turner, "The Homeric Question," pp. 134-37). Fowler notes that these Unitarians "stressed the planful design and artistic quality of the poems, which argued for a great poet's involvement at a late stage in their evolution" (Fowler, "The Homeric Question," 221).

clude that the early tradition is beyond recovery, might have been the more responsible choice.

In addition, we can question the tendency among many of the practitioners of historical criticism to *ignore* the surviving text, or to treat the study of its sources as a totally sufficient inquiry.[79] As Barton puts it, in the biblical case,

> Historical-critical approaches generated the hypothesis that Genesis-Deuteronomy should be read, not as five discrete books, but as the interweaving of four separate, older sources. ... Once they had established the existence of these sources, Pentateuchal critics took little further interest in the Pentateuch as it now stands. To the question "What is the Pentateuch?" they answered "The amalgam of J, E, D and P": thus a question potentially about the *nature* of the work was given an exclusively genetic answer.[80]

Likewise, Homer was often regarded as an amalgam of sources rather than, even in this model, as a poet creatively welding sources into a new and interesting whole. It is one thing to say that a text is based on an early tradition and even that it should be regarded as an evolution of that tradition. It is another to suppose that those who actually produced our texts did nothing more than set down or combine what they received.

Thus, once again, the importance of the end of primordialism for historical criticism in particular lies less in its ability to call into question whether early sources, kernels and cores *can* be recovered than in the changed *significance* of what is uncovered, even when successful. If we find, say, an eighth-century BCE element in a fifth-century BCE text we have only found an earlier element of discourse, not the real, not the revealing, not the superior account. It may or may not be likely, but for all we know the fifth-century BCE author might have plucked the eighth-century BCE text from an obscurity it had enjoyed even in its original context and given it new life for reasons that are entirely rooted in the later period. It could even be that the curator has made the artifact look very different from what it would have seemed to be in its original context, even without physically altering it at all.

Then, beyond historical criticism itself, the same set of concerns applies generally to how we understand what the texts that survive fundamentally are, just as I have been arguing throughout. We should not think of surviving visions of the past as the neutral outcome of *longue durée* processes. We should not think of the artifacts they contain as the most, or the only,

---

79. "Often the finished product seems to be of less interest to such critics than the underlying sources" (Barton, "Historical-Critical Approaches," pp. 9-10).

80. Barton, "Historical-Critical Approaches," pp. 9-10.

interesting thing about them. We should not be overconfident about what these artifacts will reveal in any case. And if we do not prefer to study early periods and early materials, both because they are no more valuable and interesting than later and because they are not as explanatory as they used to seem, we should not be less interested in what authors do with what they inherit than what is inherited.

In short, ethnic actors, influenced by past discourses but not bound by them, and always in the process of reinventing who they are, do not take dictation from inherited traditions. They dynamically reimagine them, add to them, even replace them with others when it seems useful to do so. Text and tradition histories can tell us what they were working with but cannot predict or define what they will do next. This is why I have throughout called attention to the necessity of a shift from viewing texts as a repository of kernels and cores to one in which we ask, first, how the actual authors of the actual text are *using* the past. Before we can consider the ramifications of this view, however, we must fill in more of the story on the Hebrew Bible side of the ledger.

Taking Stock

Again what I am arguing in this chapter—and soon, from a comparative perspective—is that the ongoing preoccupation with early traditions relies far more heavily on outdated primordialist assumptions about ethnic nations than is usually realized. However, I note again that scholarship on ethnicity actually moved beyond primordialism some time ago, which brings us in range of one of the true leitmotifs of this study: scholarly *resistance*, because I consider it a mystery that needs solving before further steps can successfully be taken. Why have so many scholars of ancient traditions been so resistant, specifically, to acknowledging the full ramifications of more fluid models of inheritances of all sorts than scholars in other disciplines often are? Obviously, one answer is the theological commitments of many of those who have studied the Hebrew Bible in the past and, to some extent, today. But the fact that the same pattern appears in many studies of ancient Greek traditions reveals that something more is going on. I have presented an argument—part of an argument—for what that something is. In the nineteenth century, the recovery of the earliest version of a text was, fairly often, considered to be much more than merely interesting and useful. It could be, in a way, the only version of the tradition that mattered. It could be a collective memory of which the later text was only a distortion. Many of the norms of inquiring into these texts were deeply influenced by these premises as they developed, and so were many of the tools. Thus, any attempt to rethink either the efficacy of these tools *or* the value of what they can achieve, can seem to deny to the scholar the ability to do important work—sometimes, the only important work—and thus, resistance.

Another way to think about the current situation is to suggest that the history of resistance I will describe throughout this book is itself evidence for my argument; it proves how indelibly the idea that the early tradition, or the original tradition, is more than merely an earli*er* tradition, but something grander and more revealing that stamped itself on scholarly understandings early on, and gave fundamental shape to what it seemed to mean to study a text. The end result has not only been a preoccupation with recovery and reconstruction but a continued neglect of what the actual authors of our actual texts do, want or understand. But these are precisely the aspects of traditions that reveal how Israelite or Greek identities were constructed *in the period in which the texts themselves actually emerged.* And under the aegis of constructivist, rather than primordialist, models of ethnic identity, these are the identity projects that really produced the discourse, and no less interesting or valuable than any other. And it is this neglect, which no longer makes any sense, that continues to be justified often through baseless assertions about the difference between ancient traditions or oral traditions and other traditions that are always *merely* assertions.[81]

The diverse features of this history of resistance happen to be reflected unusually well in the history of Hebrew Bible scholarship from Wilhelm de Wette to Julius Wellhausen, which is why I have separated out that discussion from the prior one. To begin with, the difference in the impact of theological concerns is on full display. Intellectual historians will be well aware that the idea most associated with Wellhausen—that pentateuchal traditions really emerged only in the era in which they were actually composed—was present already in the very early nineteenth century in the work not only of De Wette but others like Johann Severin Vater and Johann Karl Wilhelm Vatke.[82] It is de Wette, however, whom John Rogerson describes, with justice, as the first to even attempt to present the history of Israel and its institutions in a way "that is radically at variance with the view implied

81. The idea that ancient traditions are often seen through the lens of a variant of the Great Divide that constructs an inaccurate distinction between ancient and modern composition has been explored by Paul S. Evans in Paul S. Evans, "Creating a New 'Great Divide': The Exoticization of Ancient Culture in Some Recent Applications of Orality Studies to the Bible," *JBL* 136 (2017), pp. 749-64.

82. See Thomas Römer, "'Higher Criticism': The Historical and Literary-Critical Approach—with Special Reference to the Pentateuch," in *From Modernism to Post-Modernism (The Nineteenth and Twentieth Centuries)* (ed. Magne Saebø, Peter Machinist, and Jean Louis Ska; Hebrew Bible/Old Testament: The History of its Interpretation; Göttingen: Vandenhoeck & Ruprecht, 2013), pp. 395-401; Rogerson, *Old Testament Criticism in the Nineteenth Century*, p. 35.

in the OT itself."[83] Among de Wette's various important observations, he pointed out that in much of the rest of what passes as historical narrative in the Hebrew Bible, almost no one seems aware that a Pentateuch, or Torah, even exists, or seems terribly concerned with following its laws.[84] It stands to reason, then, that it did *not* exist in early periods. Then, since in Chronicles, a Persian period text, the kings and others do tend to act in accordance with pentateuchal law, it seemed clear to de Wette that the latter had only developed some time after the end of the monarchy, [85] which is to say that the Pentateuch was essentially a postmonarchical production.

Yet this early progress toward more modern conclusions would almost immediately be stalled in the face of a conservative counter-reaction, especially as reflected in the work of Heinrich Ewald.[86] Rogerson tells a compelling version of this story, how, for example, the death of Friedrich Schleiermacher in 1834 resulted in the elevation of the conservative Ernst Wilhelm Hengstenberg to a position of influence at the University of Berlin. This was the year before the publication of at least three studies that should have moved biblical studies further down the road de Wette and others had begun to mark out: Vatke's *Biblical Theology,* Johann Friedrich Leopold's *The Older Jewish Festivals* and David Strauss's *The Life of Jesus.* Rogerson describes how the middle of the nineteenth century was instead dominated by the work of Ewald, who made some enduring contributions and was

83. This was part of a broader shift, what Kurtz describes as "this conceptual move, from Bible as history to history behind Bible" (Kurtz, "A Historical, Critical Retrospective on Historical Criticism," p. 23). The classic treatment of this shift can be found in Hans W. Frei, *The Eclipse of Biblical Narrative* (New Haven, CT: Yale University Press, 1974). De Wette, as Jean Louis Ska observes, "is famous for several reasons. He is the one that identified ... the book discovered in the temple under King Josiah ... [as] Deuteronomy. This discovery was the starting point of many other observations," which included the recognition that "the centralization of the cult required by Deuteronomy 12 cannot be older than Josiah" (Jean Louis Ska, "The 'History of Israel': Its Emergence as an Independent Discipline," in *From Modernism to Post-Modernism* [ed. Saebø, Machinist, and Ska], p. 327).

84. Rogerson, *Old Testament Criticism in the Nineteenth Century*, p. 34. Wellhausen would describe de Wette as the first "clearly to perceive and point out how disconnected are the alleged starting-point of Israel's history and that history itself" (Julius Wellhausen, *Prolegomena to the History of Israel. With a Reprint of the Article Israel from the "Encyclopedia Britannica"* [trans. J. Sutherland Black and Alan Menzies; Edinburgh: A. & C. Black, 1885], p. 5).

85. Blenkinsopp, *The Pentateuch*, p. 5.

86. Kurtz adds that "de Wette was dismissed from his professorship in Berlin and Strauss impeded from taking one in Zurich. ... Such conflict turned into trench warfare with de Wette's ultimate successor, Ernst Wilhem Hengstenberg, whose control extended beyond the Berlin theological faculty" (Kurtz, "A Historical, Critical Retrospective on Historical Criticism," p. 29).

best known for his massive *History of the People of Israel*, but was, from the perspective of the conservatives at least, "on the side of ... the angels."[87]

For us, however, the main point is that this pattern existed largely in one field and not the other. To be clear, there was resistance to what Wolf had opened up in the study of Homer too. Kurtz cites the amusing fact that Elizabeth Barrett Browning damned him by name, in verse, in her *Aurora Leigh*.[88] But even more telling is Kurtz's reference to a comment by "the Oxford bishop Samuel Wilberforce" in response to Barthold Georg Niebuhr's analysis of the traditions in Livy. Here Wilberforce expresses his concern with "whether the human mind, with which Niebuhr has tasted blood in the slaughter of Livy, can be prevailed upon to abstain from falling next upon the Bible."[89] In other words, the anxiety of Browning *et al.* already had something in it of an awareness that the Bible would be next, and not just the Hebrew Bible.[90]

As a kind of aside, one interesting aspect of Ewald's work, which would dominate much of the mid-nineteenth century, is how representative it is of conservative efforts to respond to the type of critiques that would really change approaches both then and now. Practically, his inquiries resonate, certainly, with how the writing of ancient history was performed already in the early part of the nineteenth century. In some ways, it was like Niebuhr's *History of Rome* (1811–12), which supposedly "demonstrated how classical legends and other literature could furnish a solid basis of history." And Ewald was a colleague, at Göttingen, of Karl-Otfried Müller, who is perhaps the best-known early nineteenth-century proponent of the idea that ancient traditions are the distilled and distorted memories of early nations in their formative era. His *Die Dorier* (*The Dorians*, 1841) is the archetypal account of the historical "Dorian invasion" behind the Greek tradition of the "Return of the Herakleidae."[91]

The benefit of these kinds of efforts, where a conservative establishment is concerned, is that they can code as radical; as Rogerson notes, Ewald's

87. Rogerson, *Old Testament Criticism in the Nineteenth Century*, pp. 90, 101-102.

88. Browning describes him as a "kissing Judas" and an "atheist"—correctly intuiting that his work dissecting Homer would soon lead to dissections of the Bible (Kurtz, "A Historical, Critical Retrospective on Historical Criticism," p. 15).

89. Kurtz, "A Historical, Critical Retrospective on Historical Criticism," p. 16.

90. There is no space to discuss it here, but scholars will be aware of similar controversies attending the publication of studies like David Strauss's *Das Leben Jesu* in 1835.

91. Rogerson, *Old Testament Criticism in the Nineteenth Century*, pp. 92-93. Ska mentions that Ewald noted the influence of Müller in the foreword to his history in the first two editions, but that this reference no longer appears in the third edition (Ska, "The 'History of Israel,'" p. 330).

certainly was in comparison to Eichhorn's views.[92] But they really preserve the basic premises of more conservative approaches intact. In other words, espousing the idea that these traditions are not literal history, but still memory, however distorted, can make it seem as if the scholar is granting the validity of more skeptical critiques while actually allowing them to go on being interested in these texts mainly for the historiographical information they preserve about early realities. In a similar vein, the introduction even to the 1981 edition of Martin Noth's *History of Pentateuchal Traditions* could still refer to his "radical historical scepticism about the Mosaic tradition." Noth believed that the Pentateuchal narrative had formed in all of its particulars by the end of the Bronze Age and still regarded Moses as a historical figure.[93]

Here, however, is a sort of irony that, as far as I can tell, has not yet been articulated. As I say, the scholarly establishment in the discipline of Hebrew Bible successfully resisted conclusions like Wellhausen's for decades. This comparative investigation puts us in a position to realize, however, that Wolf's *condemnatio* where the accessibility of the "real Homer" was concerned was far more like the start of modern efforts *to* recover him than the end. In other words, as soon as something like Wolf's skeptical conclusions were in the world, other scholars could begin to find their way around them. The same pattern would repeat itself here, with Wellhausen, but only once critiques like his were actually able to be made. Thus, the conservative reaction to the work of de Wette *et al.* only *delayed* the emergence of efforts to demonstrate that the Pentateuch preserved what was really a very early narrative *despite* the late composition of the familiar text. These would follow very shortly after Wellhausen and last well into the late twentieth century.

This is what is so interesting about the history of resistance I will be discussing throughout. No matter how arguments and assumptions develop, a large number of scholars have generally found a way to resume the traditional preoccupation with the recovery of the original tradition, and through it, the supposed image of real events. And here we come to the main component of Wellhausen's new argument, his synthesis of earlier recognitions into the traditional "Documentary Hypothesis." This Wellhausen did in *Geschichte Israels* (1878), originally intended to be part one of a two-volume history. The second volume would never appear, and it would instead receive its more familiar title, the *Prolegomena zur Geschichte Israels,* for the 1883 edition, perhaps as "a subtle claim to par-

---

92. Rogerson, *Old Testament Criticism in the Nineteenth Century*, p. 92.
93. Bernhard W. Anderson, "Introduction," in *A History of the Pentateuchal Traditions*, by Martin Noth (trans. Bernhard W. Anderson; Chico, CA: Scholars Press, 1981), p. xxii.

allel rank with Wolf's *Prolegomena*."[94] It set out a four-source hypothesis in which P, the Priestly source, was the last and most important.

As a practical matter, it is true that the basics of this hypothesis had already appeared in the work of Karl Heinrich Graf and, perhaps, in the thought of his teacher Édouard Reuss, with other roots in the arguments of Hermann Hupfeld.[95] But Wellhausen made his case so convincingly that his version of it would survive for almost a century virtually intact. Even today, though the traditional Documentary Hypothesis has fractured, most still regard the Priestly author, authors, or, most likely, authors and editors as the most important shaping force behind the Pentateuch as we have it, and especially of the books of Genesis through Numbers. And most suspect that this shaping action largely took place in the postexilic period, if not, in some cases, even later.[96]

In other words, since Wellhausen, there has been *very broad agreement* that the Pentateuch was essentially a postexilic production. And yet, if this aspect of his case has fared enormously well, the opposite is true of his additional argument: that, as a result, the Pentateuch did not preserve early traditions or early realities to any meaningful extent.[97] This is what Lawson G. Stone refers to as Wellhausen's "axiom" that "a text is evidence not for the era it narrates but rather for the era of its composition."[98] Kurtz echoes him: "More often than not, and not infrequently with force, Wellhausen argued that textual sources conveyed information first and foremost on the time of their production."[99] My argument is similar in some ways, different in others, but for now we return for the moment to the theme of resistance.

---

94. Frank Moore Cross, *From Epic to Canon: History and Literature in Ancient Israel* (Baltimore, MD: Johns Hopkins University Press, 1998), pp. 34-35. Although, unlike Wellhausen, Wolf did not have a particularly low opinion of the quality of what survived (Fowler, "The Homeric Question," p. 220).

95. See, generally, Römer, "'Higher Criticism,'" pp. 413-15.

96. To be clear, Wellhausen had quite a specific date in mind for the completion of the Priestly work—444 BCE, which he calculated as the year in which Ezra had read a book called "the book of the law of Moses" to an assembly of Judahites in Neh. 8.1 (Wellhausen, *Prolegomena*, 405). It has been far more common, since then, to speak in more general terms, but still within similar time horizons.

97. As Wellhausen himself put it, he believed that in Genesis "we attain to no historical knowledge of the patriarchs, but only of the time when the stories about them arose in the Israelite people ... this later age is here unconsciously projected, in its inner and its outward features, into hoar antiquity, and is reflected there like a glorified mirage" (Wellhausen, *Prolegomena*, pp. 318-19).

98. Lawson G. Stone, "Early Israel and its Appearance in Canaan," in *Ancient Israel's History: An Introduction to Issues and Sources* (ed. Bill T. Arnold and Richard S. Hess; Grand Rapids, MI: Baker Academic, 2014), p. 132.

99. Kurtz, *Kaiser, Christ, and Canaan*, p. 88.

To be sure, Wellhausen's arguments would enjoy a vogue of perhaps twenty years.[100] However, from at least the time of Hermann Gunkel's *Die Sagen der Genesis* (*The Legends of Genesis*, 1901), the study of the Pentateuch, on both sides of the Atlantic, was largely characterized by the conviction, as Martin Noth put it, that these later texts were essentially crystallizations of much earlier narratives which reflected essentially real events.[101] In other words, Wellhausen's chronology of when and how the sources had been put together was about right, but it hardly mattered. The basic narrative was still the early, (often) oral charter tradition it had long been imagined to be.

Indeed, Gunkel's work is a case in point, where these acts of resistance are concerned, given that he agreed with Wellhausen in almost every respect. This not only included the still common idea that P was the last and most important shaper of the collection, but even Wellhausen's understanding of this actor as suffering from, in Gunkel's words, a "grandiose want of respect for what had been the most sacred traditions of his people"; an author and editor who had "no conception of the fidelity of the older authors," and who "worked over" inherited "material … very vigorously indeed."[102] But Gunkel, quite implausibly—what should have seemed quite implausibly, in any case—essentially argued that P was completely an aberration. Every single other link in the chain of transmission was a "reverent hand." As a result, "the attempt of P to supplant the older tradition had proven a failure," and the hunt for that older tradition could go on as before.[103] Well might one offer the rejoinder that if we acknowledge the ability of even one heir of traditions to display substantial creative agency, we have to begin to account for the operation of creativity on inheritance more generally. But this is not what happened.

Instead, in Gunkel's specific case, this argument is what opened the door for what would be called "form criticism," a term he never much liked.[104]

100. Kurtz notes, "The decade following the publication of the *Prolegomena* saw the capitulation of almost every influential Old Testament scholar in Germany to the new teaching" (Kurtz, *Kaiser, Christ, and Canaan*, p. 71).

101. Martin Noth, *A History of Pentateuchal Traditions* (trans. B.W. Anderson; Englewood Cliffs, NJ: Prentice Hall, 1972), p. 1.

102. Gunkel, *The Legends of Genesis*, pp. 129-31. "It is Wellhausen's immortal merit … to have recognized the true character of this source, which had previously been considered the oldest, to have demonstrated thus the incorrectness of the entire general view of the Old Testament" (Gunkel, *The Legends of Genesis*, p. 123).

103. Gunkel, *The Legends of Genesis*, p. 132.

104. "Despite his dissatisfaction with the terms *Formgeschichte* and 'form criticism,' Hermann Gunkel became the methodology's progenitor" (Peter Benjamin Boeckel, "Exploring Narrative Forms and Trajectories: Form Criticism and the Noahic Covenant," in *Partners with God: Theological and Critical Readings of the Bible in Honor of Marvin A. Sweeney*, vol. 2 (ed. Shelley L. Birdsong and Serge Frolov; Clare-

Form criticism, not at all coincidentally, borrowed very heavily from the Grimms's "generic method" in order to make the case that identifying the form of the original tradition, and its genre, was the key to recovering its original shape, even as far back as its oral prehistory.[105] At any rate, this was tradition criticism, not historical criticism, in the sense that it added to the effort to reconstruct the original text and the sources that were combined within it a belief in the capacity of scholars to recover even the oral tradition upon which the earliest text had been based. And if this seems, with the benefit of hindsight, like wishful thinking, this brings us back to the question of what shaped the wish, what value this recovery had, what it was supposed to do.[106] Even more, it shows what I have argued all along: the ubiquity of the view that we should study texts primarily in their capacity as repositories of early traditions.

Yet one additional clue where the question of why Wellhausen's account of the significance of his arguments had the destiny it did comes from this surprising fact: he *himself* did not deny the fundamental superiority of early traditions to later. He himself embraced the qualitative framework in very familiar terms, literally. For him, too, the original traditions of Israel had been, in a familiarly Herderian metaphor, the "green tree which grows out of the soil as it will and can," and the "water which … rose from a spring," natural and pure.[107] What survived, by contrast, was the tree "cut and made to a pattern with compass and square," the water of the well "stored up in cisterns."[108]

More, it was "the residuum of a ruined state"—an "artificial product" that was "estranged from the heart."[109] The original composition, by contrast, was connected to a historical Moses and was supposed to be a product of "national being" and an expression of "national consciousness."[110] Mean-

mont, CA: Claremont Press, 2017), p. 27. Gunkel "preferred the term 'literary history' since he was not concerned with a text's form alone" (Boeckel, "Exploring Narrative Forms," p. 27 n. 2).

105. The Grimms had divided the traditions that interested them into three categories, *Mythus, Märchen* and *Sagen,* which is to say, myths, fairytales, and legends, each of which genre was supposed to reveal certain things about the history of the tradition in question (Kirkpatrick, *The Old Testament and Folklore Study,* pp. 17-18).

106. I discuss the operation of desire on early- to mid-twentieth-century pentateuchal scholarship in "On Comparison with Ancient Greek Traditions: Lessons from the Mid-Century," *Journal of Hebrew Scriptures* 23 (2024), pp. 1-30.

107. Wellhausen, *Prolegomena,* pp. 81, 361, 410.

108. Wellhausen, *Prolegomena,* pp. 361, 410.

109. Wellhausen, *Prolegomena,* pp. 422, 425.

110. Wellhausen, *Prolegomena,* p. 425. Wellhausen was to some extent in conversation with well-known Romantics. In fact, Bernard M. Levinson notes the very interesting fact that Wellhausen "several times emphasized that his 'discovery' that Exod. 34 preserved the original Decalogue had been anticipated a century earlier by Johann

while, the pious Gunkel echoed Wilamowitz in criticizing the surviving text, so beloved by so many for so long, in favor of the hypothetical original. P, "this order-loving man has ensnared the gay legends of the olden times in his gray outlines, and there they have lost all their poetic freshness."[111] In short, Wellhausen by no means denied the tremendous relative value of the reconstruction of the early tradition as opposed to the study of the surviving text; he simply denied the *possibility* of that reconstruction. It can hardly be surprising, then, that almost immediately a great many scholars indeed went to work on explaining why it was possible after all, just as they did with Wolf.

Here we find a remarkably clear illustration, not of the point we started with but of its most important counterpoint. In order to overcome this history of resistance to acknowledging that later compositions should not be understood simply as corruptions of early ones, oral or otherwise, it is not enough to argue that these early ones are beyond the reach of traditional assumptions and methods. The desire to recover them, because of the value historically imputed to the exercise, is too strong. Someone will find an apparent way. And in this case, where it *is* often possible to recover earlier elements, earlier discourses, and sometimes even earlier realities, it creates a situation where, in order to make the case that reconstructing early traditions still has the same value, it seems enough to point out merely that it is still *possible*. The reality, however, is, once again, that even achieving these aims has a far different significance in a context where we cannot imagine later generations simply passing on *the* original traditions of the ethnic nation, more or less in their entirety, than they had under primordialism. This is what needs to be explained, asserted, insisted upon; and this, above all, is why what I am arguing for here is indeed not an effort to go "back to Wellhausen," a common enough phrase in the contemporary study of the Hebrew Bible.

In short, then, the case of Wellhausen's skepticism, so to speak, demonstrates the operation of a pre-existing scholarly desire for a particular outcome on the course of intellectual history in a number of different ways. Indeed, among the most striking is the scope of the success of Gunkel's argument. In my opinion, Gunkel himself was, in many ways, a man out

Wolfgang von Goethe"—in an early story of his, which described a young pastor who came to a similar conclusion—and who also, in the words Goethe puts into his mouth regarded "the Jewish people ... as a wild, infertile stock that stood in a circle of wild and barren trees, upon which the eternal Gardener grafted the noble scion Jesus Christ, so that, by adhering to it, it ennobled the nature of the stock and from there slips were fetched to make all the remaining trees fertile" (Bernard M. Levinson, "Goethe's Analysis of Exodus 34 and its Influence on Wellhausen: The Pfropfung of the Documentary Hypothesis," *ZAW* 114.2 [2002], pp. 215-16).

111. Gunkel, *The Legends of Genesis*, p. 124.

of time, someone whose arguments are visibly based on little more than Romantic intuition in an era when others were already turning to philology, archaeology and epigraphy.[112] But even in America, Gunkel was largely viewed as a fellow traveler, which is precisely the opposite of what should have happened. The Albright school in particular was typically insistent on the use of archaeological, epigraphic and philological evidence that Gunkel lacked capacity for and was, anyway, generally quite acerbic about contemporaneous European contributions. Yet Albright himself was complimentary of Gunkel's conclusions, and so was Frank Moore Cross.[113] The explanation, in my view, lies in the promise Gunkel's work held out where preserving familiar preoccupations were concerned. They appreciated the service he had provided to the discipline.

Meanwhile, at least as telling, if not more so, is the fact that Wellhausen aside, scholars who did not think the "original" Homer, or the earliest traditions of Israel, could be recovered *were also the ones least troubled by this conclusion.* Wolf, for one, was perfectly content with the idea that the "real" Homer was lost: "If we demand the bard in simon-pure condition, and are not content with what contented Plutarch, Longinus, or Proclus, we will have to take refuge either in empty prayers or in unrestrained license in divination."[114] De Wette, too, was not disturbed by the historiographical skepticism his arguments introduced into the study of pentateuchal traditions that upset so many others; he thought that the ethical message of the text could survive its historical inaccuracy.[115] And Vatke, unusually,

112. Gunkel, *The Legends of Genesis*, p. 47.

113. Albright would argue, in the introduction to a 1964 edition of *Die Sagen*, that Gunkel was "right much of the time," as opposed to Wellhausen, who was "wrong almost throughout." And "where Gunkel was mistaken," he wrote in a quite atypical forgiving spirit, "the state of our knowledge in 1901 was far too sketchy for positive conclusions" (William F. Albright, "Introduction," in *The Legends of Genesis*, by Hermann Gunkel [New York: Schocken Books, 1964], p. x). Likewise Frank Moore Cross would credit Gunkel with having "forged" the "tools for the analysis of the preliterary history of the old traditions" (Frank Moore Cross, *Canaanite Myth and Hebrew Epic: Essays in the History of the Religion of Israel* [Cambridge, MA: Harvard University Press, 9th edn, 1997], p. 3).

114. Wolf elaborates: "This doubt may carry the implication that these sources cannot enable us to restore Homer's work to the genuine, pure form which first poured from his divine lips. If so, I shall say later how willingly I follow this school of thought and line of reasoning" (Wolf, *Prolegomena to Homer*, pp. 45-46). In addition, he had considerable respect for the Alexandrian scholiast—that "thanks to [them] ... we doubtless read a Homeric text more correct in many passages than they themselves could read" (p. 46). In other words, as Turner puts it, "The text could not be regarded as impure or incorrect simply because it did not mesh with modern taste" (Turner, "The Homeric Question," p. 126).

115. Ska, "The 'History of Israel,'" pp. 328-29. Blenkinsopp notes that de Wette

imagined religious progression, rather than decline, over time, and thought the Persian period that actually, most likely, saw the formation of the penta-teuchal text must therefore have been the "apotheosis" of Israelite religion.[116] Obviously then, the lack of a *desire* for the outcome described above played a considerable role in allowing scholars to fail to achieve it.

I do think that texts are, pretty much always, a product of the discourses that emerged in a given context, often acting on inherited materials, but also moderated through the individual apprehensions of their actual authors. I think that this is true for a number of reasons, many of which will appear in other chapters. My argument here, however, is that the end of primor-dialism makes the idea that—more or less as Wellhausen supposed!—tra-ditions about ethnic origins are always essentially the product of the era in which they were composed inescapable. People are always reimagining and redescribing their own ethnic pasts; traditions are the medium through which they do that; texts are individual representations of traditions that double as examples of these efforts. And again, I think this more fluid way of thinking about the relationships between traditions, their own histories, and the cultures they emerge from is not only among the fundamental sig-nificances of the necessary shifts in scholarship but a fairly straightforward and uncomplicated result thereof. The ethnic nation lacks the *coherence* in early periods to tell any one story about who it is. It lacks the *stability* over time to simply rehearse it. It—to the extent there is an "it"—lacks the desire to do so, because the past is alive when it is useful and relevant, and that requires making it useful and relevant anew.

If, however, what we have seen throughout this chapter up to now is why making this straightforward shift has proven difficult—because the central goals of nineteenth-century scholarship are only practical within the linear models primordialism allows, because the qualitative framework made linear models so desirable to maintain—what we see in Wellhausen's argument and the responses to it are what it would really take to move on. In other words, one more rejection of the feasibility of restoring the "autograph" to "simon-pure condition"—to blend Wilamowitz with Wolf—is not going to have any more impact than others, no matter how well-grounded, than the ones that came before. Not unless we change how desirable achieving the task seems.

What I am arguing here is that this is precisely what we can do when we start to think differently about the history of ethnic articulations, and so turn a kind of crisis into an opportunity. The end of primordialism allows

---

argued "that the early narrative traditions in the Pentateuch ... cannot be used as his-torical source material. They represent rather Israel's mythic view of its origins, its place in the world, and its destiny." But he also believed that they were "of great reli-gious value to the reader sensitive to their appeal" (Blenkinsopp, *The Pentateuch*, p. 5).

116. Römer, "'Higher Criticism,'" p. 410.

us to acknowledge that earlier layers of discourse are not more revealing; they are simply earlier. Later articulations of ethnic identity are not corruptions of an original purity, but authentic ethnic visions in their own right. And the more creativity we can imagine someone who creates a new representation of the ethnic self and the past is possessed of, the less we will think the developmental history of earlier visions can really explain what happens next. This frees us up to acknowledge that the early and the late text are equally valid constructions of self and the past, equally interesting, and equally important. And this is what allows us not just to acknowledge but to embrace the fact that one might be more accessible than the other and to believe that even when both are accessible, the older does not need to be privileged over the newer as an object of study. I suspect that these recognitions, if they could be more broadly adopted, would indeed by themselves limit the kind of efforts I will critique throughout because these are generally motivated by a misplaced faith in the importance of the task of recovering early traditions. But either way, they should change how we approach texts in a very general way.

Moving On

It might seem odd to leave this sketch of intellectual history here, just across the border of the twentieth century. I did it for three reasons, the first and second of which are purely practical. Maybe someone else could sketch two and a half centuries of intellectual history in a single chapter, while doing justice to both, *and* address contemporary trends in two different disciplines, but I could not. Second, the rest of this history will simply make more sense in the context of the second chapter's discussion of the use of extraliterary evidence in the study of ancient traditions: how it has been used and how it should be used. As we will see, a great many twentieth-century scholars were most interested in this emerging evidence, quite improperly, as a way of reasserting the validity of nineteenth-century preoccupations against late nineteenth-century skepticism. I consider this, as I will discuss in the next chapter, a great wrong turn akin to the seventy years between de Wette and Wellhausen when progress toward better conclusions was stalled by conservative counter-reaction.

The third reason, however—and really the main one—is this. Demonstrating the rootedness of common ways of thinking about what texts are and of how to study them in outdated assumptions was my first goal. Revealing the fundamental nature of the relationship between that paradigm, primordialist assumptions, and Romantic fictions about early traditions was the second. I believe both have been achieved. We will not imagine surviving texts *only* as the heirs, corrupted or not, of a much earlier set of central traditions unless we embrace a linear model through which the

latter gradually evolved into the former. We will not imagine the reconstructed tradition as the single goal of study, or the superior composition,
or collective memory, or a complete representation of the beliefs of the era
that formed it, without a qualitative framework. The former has no basis
without primordialism, the latter without some of the other assumptions
about the history and nature of traditions that emerged within the same circles that gave shape to primordialism. I think, therefore, that even this brief
sketch has indeed served the purpose of positioning us to ask the central
question: what can a combined approach tell us about what it would really
take to move on?

In my view, the contemporary landscape of discussions suggests three
distinct answers to this question. First, we can reconsider the comparative importance of studying early and late articulations of ethnic identity
relative to the history of the groups under consideration here. And this is
a reconsideration that I think is forced on us as soon as we consider something like Panhellenism, in many ways the archetypal expression of Greek
identity. After all, what we now know about Panhellenism is that it did
not exist in early periods; it, very likely, only took on familiar form in the
early fifth century BCE, in part as a response to the Persian wars.[117] But if
we chose to ignore it as an invented identity, or de-emphasized its study
in favor of the study of earlier articulations of Greek identity, as scholars
often do with Israelite identity, how little would we learn about the world of
Socrates, Plato, Pericles and so on? And this recognition ought to shape not
only what we are interested in, where the history of ancient Greek ethnicity
is concerned, but how we study the traditions that charter it.

After all, consider the tradition that describes Greek identity as,
largely, a consequence of descent from the Hellenic *Urvater*, Hellen himself. As I will discuss in the chapter focused on genealogical traditions,
the familiar way of investigating these traditions privileges efforts to
sieve the representation of the relationships between Hellenic subgroups
for kernels of truth about their actually early arrangement. Now, however,
we realize that it is precisely these relationships that were invented later
on. As Hall put it,

> In making the eponymous Aiolos, Doros, Ion, and Akhaios sons and
> grandsons of the Hellenic *Urvater,* Hellen, the "Hellenic Genealogy"
> sought to project the view that a single undifferentiated population of
> Hellenes had existed prior to a series of subdivisions. ... In reality ... the
> opposite was the case ... the Dorians, Ionians, Aiolians and Akhaians are

---

117. David Konstan, "To Hellēnikon Ethnos: Ethnicity and the Construction of
Ancient Greek Identity," in *Ancient Perceptions of Greek Ethnicity* (ed. Irad Malkin;
Washington, DC: Center for Hellenic Studies, 2001), p. 33; Irad Malkin, *The Returns
of Odysseus* (Berkeley: University of California Press, 1998), p. 18.

actually attested prior to any unitary subscription to a common Hellenic consciousness.[118]

Therefore, what was once regarded as a schematic representation of early Greece and population movements becomes instead a guide to the process through which a later ethnic concept was first *developed.* Should we lament this fact? Or should we be just as happy to learn about how Panhellenism developed as about what early Greek identity was like?

This brings us to the second answer to the question of what it would take to move on. We need to reconsider the importance, along with the explanatory power, of reconstructing the earliest articulations of a familiar ethnonymic identity in the first place. What could seem more natural than assuming that we learn best about an ethnic identity by uncovering its ultimate origins? And yet, when we imagine fluid rather than stable histories of ethnic articulation, the original form can have rather limited explanatory power. And unfortunately, it is particularly the case in the study of the Hebrew Bible that investigations into the origins of something we can call Israelite identity—and of markers like circumcision and dietary laws—are treated as if they *were* studies of what Israelite identity fundamentally is, even given that biblical representations are, for the most part, literary constructions from a much later period.

In other words, there have certainly been impressive monographs on Israelite ethnicity in recent years, including Ann Killebrew's *Biblical Peoples and Ethnicity* (2005), and Avraham Faust's *Israel's Ethnogenesis: Settlement, Interaction, Expansion and Resistance* (2006), and not these alone.[119] Generally, however, these treat the study of ethnogenesis and ethnic histories as the same thing. Kenton Sparks's *Ethnicity and Identity in Ancient Israel: Prolegomena to the Study of Ethnic Sentiments and their Expression in the Hebrew Bible* (1998)—prolegomenas again—is better in that it does spend some time tracing what he sees as the *development* of ethnic articulations in Israel.[120] But he, too, does so in something of a linear fashion, assuming that the familiar biblical construction is mainly a variation of a version of Israelite identity that had been handed down from the beginning. Indeed, only rarely do any of these studies, or others like them,

118. Jonathan M. Hall, *Hellenicity: Between Ethnicity and Culture* (Chicago: University of Chicago Press, 2002), p. 56.

119. See, e.g., Elizabeth Bloch-Smith, "Israelite Ethnicity in Iron I: Archaeology Preserves What Is Remembered and What Is Forgotten in Israel's History," *JBL* 122 (2003), pp. 401-25; Ann E. Killebrew, *Biblical Peoples and Ethnicity: An Archaeological Study of Egyptians, Canaanite, Philistines, and Early Israel, 1300–100 BCE* (Atlanta, GA: Society of Biblical Literature, 2005); Avraham Faust, *Israel's Ethnogenesis: Settlement, Interaction, Expansion and Resistance* (London: Equinox, 2006).

120. Largely in Chapters 4 through 7.

even address the question of what the origins of something called Israelite identity is *supposed* to explain about biblical constructions that emerged in Judah, so much later; it is assumed that it does.[121] And with this, there is the assumption that there was never any truly dramatic transformation like we see in the history of Greek ethnic constructions.

And here we reach the final and I think most important point, which is that the study of ethnic concepts and the study of the traditions that reflect them need to be separated by an awareness of the individuality of each presentation, no matter how we reconstruct these conceptual histories. Or more simply, we ought to understand a *general* ethnic concept as the *starting point* for the specific, individual, and idiosyncratic visions that actually exist in different texts. I have made this point before while discussing a new way of thinking about ethnic identity in ancient Israel which suggests that something rather similar to the development of Panhellenism occurred there.[122] Indeed, since the 1990s, certain scholars have been making this case: that the Judahites did not originally think of themselves as Israelite, but only came to do so sometime after the Assyrian conquest of Israel in 722 BCE.[123] This means that a "Panisraelitism" embracing Israel and Judah was invented in a relatively late period.

---

121. Carly Crouch's more recent investigation is, in my view, particularly sophisticated, and breaks from the mold of previous studies in acknowledging the ongoing fluidity and reinventive capacities of ethnic articulations over time; and James C. Miller's *CBR* article is absolutely exemplary, one of the few studies to really take direction less from how scholars of antiquity have thought about ethnicity and more from how scholars of ethnicity itself have (Crouch, *The Making of Israel*; Miller, "Ethnicity and the Hebrew Bible: Problems and Prospects"). Miller is right to observe how few studies of Israelite ethnicity are even interested in ethnicity in the monarchical period, which says a lot about what has and has not happened in this discipline, especially since this is less true of the exilic and postexilic period. In other words, scholars are mainly interested in the origins of anything like Israelite identity and biblical constructions of Israelite identity and not in what happened in between (Miller, "Ethnicity and the Hebrew Bible: Problems and Prospects," p. 189).

122. Andrew Tobolowsky, *The Myth of the Twelve Tribes of Israel: New Identities across Time and Space* (Cambridge, UK: Cambridge University Press, 2022), pp. 45-52.

123. This idea was first argued in an influential way by Philip Davies in the early 1990s and has since become relatively common, if still not the dominant position. See Philip R. Davies, *In Search of "Ancient Israel": A Study in Biblical Origins* (JSOTSup, 148; Sheffield: JSOT Press, 1992); Philip R. Davies, *In Search of "Ancient Israel": A Study in Biblical Origins* (Edinburgh: T. & T. Clark, 2nd edn, 2004); Fleming, *The Legacy of Israel in Judah's Bible*; Lauren A.S. Monroe and Daniel Fleming, "Earliest Israel in Highland Company," *Near Eastern Archaeology* 82.1 (2019), pp. 16-23; Nadav Na'aman, "The Jacob Story and the Formation of Biblical Israel," *Tel Aviv* 41.1

It might seem obvious— in my opinion it *has* seemed obvious—that this vision of Israelite identity in Judah as a cultural invention is a dynamic, modern vision of ethnic identifying. And of course, in some ways, it is. What I have argued, however, is that it is actually afflicted with many of the same issues as the premise that biblical constructions of Israelite identity are only versions of the earliest Israelite identity there was. In other words, this is still a history of the origins of an ethnic concept, and *not* a full accounting of the ethnic expressions that actually appear in biblical texts. We would still have to discuss how this concept was used by different authors in different contexts, whenever it emerged, and toward what ends. In ancient Greece, we face different Panhellenistic articulations. In the Hebrew Bible, we have different Panisraelitisms. As a result, the recognition that the biblical vision of Panisraelite identity might reflect a concept that was invented in later periods, rather than very early ones, is *not* by itself a sufficient response to the recognition of the fluidity of ethnic articulations over time. And it does not keep us from having to think of specific biblical texts as containing specific and discrete visions.

Here, above all, is where we see the value of a combined approach to the study of ancient ethnicity and its ramifications. Again, there is simply so much more evidence for how ancient Greek ethnic concepts could and did change over time and in response to circumstances than we have from ancient Israel, because we have the work of so many different authors, from different periods, in different compositions. This is not to say that we should expect the same kind of phenomena to appear in both contexts with any regularity. But it is to say that the ancient Greek world, with its larger and more diverse corpus, can give us a more *realistic* picture of the range of identity phenomena that we might face anywhere at all than the Hebrew Bible can. The fact that the latter is still a multivocalic corpus does not mean it is close to a match for the actual multivocality of the actual world of ancient Israel and Judah, and that is a problem Hebrew Bible scholars can use some help to solve. Thinking of ancient Greek phenomena as examples of what can or might have happened can provide it.

We can include in this category treatments of the overall picture of shifts in basic ethnic conceptions over time such as Jonathan M. Hall's famous study, *Ethnic Identity in Greek Antiquity* (1997), which identified an "aggregative phase" in the history of Panhellenism and an "oppositional," phase where the familiar "Greek" and "Barbarian" distinctions became central. Other studies have added new and interesting wrinkles since: Kostas Vlassopoulos's article "Ethnicity and Greek History," for example. Here, he brings out the variety of how ethnicities were constructed in different parts

---

(2014), pp. 95-125; Israel Finkelstein, *The Forgotten Kingdom* (Ancient Near East Monographs, 5; Atlanta, GA: Society of Biblical Literature, 2013).

of Greece, from *poleis*-based to trans-regional, embracing ethnic groups who shared territory and those who didn't, those with religious centers and those without. He also investigates the complicated relationship between what are sometimes called "sub" ethnicities and Panhellenic ethnicities in a subtle and sophisticated way.[124]

The greatest benefit of this particular comparison, however, emerges from the studies that show *how* Panhellenic ethnic formations can be adapted, what *circumstances* can call adaptations forth, and how constantly, as a result, adaptation happened. We can consider here studies like Lee E. Patterson's *Kinship Myth in Ancient Greece,* which shows how frequently ancient authors invented new stories about their ancestors as a way of participating in "kinship diplomacy."[125] Erich Gruen, in a recent exploration of foundation traditions, which I will discuss at greater length in a later chapter, has underscored the fact that the extent of ethnic refashioning in the context of interchange between groups in the ancient world could be extreme enough to be regarded as "identity theft"—the borrowing and repurposing of other people's stories of origin as a way of shifting a group's position on political and social maps.[126]

Irad Malkin has contributed a number of useful studies. In one, he shows how the place actual historical colony founders had in the memory of Greek colonizers was gradually usurped by traditions about heroic founders—like Herakles or Odysseus—who then served an important role in future efforts to build connections between regions through heroic genealogies.[127] In another, he describes how traditions about the heroes of the Trojan War, especially Odysseus, were repeatedly adapted to serve as charter traditions of a wide variety of places.[128] In addition, the Greek world can also show something that is very hard to see in the biblical context: how the stories we know may have operated outside of their texts. Elizabeth Irwin points to the social role played by traditions about heroic ancestors in ancient Greece, how it insured that the very nature of the heroic past was continually "contested within the fluid and fragile grouping within

124. Vlassopoulos, "Ethnicity and Greek History."

125. Lee E. Patterson, *Kinship Myth in Ancient Greece* (Austin: University of Texas Press, 2010).

126. As Gruen observes, this is because "group identities in antiquity did not possess a pure and unadulterated character. Nor were they meant to do so. Communities and peoples, rather than considering themselves hermetically sealed entities, regularly proclaimed ties to other societies, even inserting themselves into their history and traditions" (Gruen, *Ethnicity in the Ancient World,* p. 223).

127. See Irad Malkin, *Myth and Territory in the Spartan Mediterranean* (Cambridge, UK: Cambridge University Press, 1994); Irad Malkin, *A Small Greek World* (Oxford: Oxford University Press, 2011).

128. Malkin, *The Returns of Odysseus.*

the *polis* known as the *agathoi.*"[129] What would ongoing contestation look like in ancient Israel and Judah, and what would its effects be on surviving accounts of Israelite origins?

I do not intend here to say that Hebrew Bible scholars, or religious studies scholars generally, have nothing to contribute to this conversation, or that only classicists have made any of the arguments just described. The overall recognition I am describing here is reflected, for example, in Ian Douglas Wilson's recent argument that even though the Hebrew Bible's accounts of Israel's history drew on "older sources" and are on some level "composite," the result of drawing and combining was nevertheless "new discourse, and ... for the most part, received as such." More specifically, the surviving biblical account is not a compendium of all ages, it *uses* materials of different ages to represent "a particular discursive horizon, located across the fifth to early third centuries BCE."[130] Other useful studies of memory in particular repeatedly emphasize the crucial point that references to memory cannot be used to *avoid* having to acknowledge how visions of the past are repeatedly redescribed and reinvented over time, including those by Daniel Pioske, Ehud ben Zvi and others.[131] Jacqueline Vayntrub's study of orality as a concept in the study of biblical poetry contains many useful insights regarding the importance of avoiding justifying older Romantic models of tradition histories through references to the supposed difference between oral and more literate societies. This is another

---

129. Irwin adds that "the elite of a given polis were not a well-defined class, but a loose group of contenders asserting their entitlement to this label," and something like this is broadly true between poleis and ethnic groups as well (Elizabeth Irwin, "Gods among Men? The Social and Political Dynamics of the Hesiodic Catalogue of Women," in *The Hesiodic Catalogue of Women* [ed. Richard L. Hunter; Cambridge, UK: Cambridge University Press, 2005], p. 83).

130. Ian Douglas Wilson, *Kingship and Memory in Ancient Judah* (New York: Oxford University Press, 2017), p. 10.

131. Daniel Pioske, *David's Jerusalem: Between Memory and History* (New York: Routledge, 2015); Daniel Pioske, *Memory in a Time of Prose: Studies in Epistemology, Hebrew Scribalism, and the Biblical Past* (Oxford: Oxford University Press, 2018); Ehud Ben Zvi, "On Social Memory and Identity Formation in Late Persian Yehud: A Historian's Viewpoint with a Focus on Prophetic Literature, Chronicles, and the Deuteronomistic Historical Collection," in *Texts, Contexts and Readings in Postexilic Literature: Explorations into Historiography and Identity Negotiation in Hebrew Bible and Related Texts* (ed. Louis Jonker; Tübingen: Mohr Siebeck, 2011), pp. 95-148; Ehud Ben Zvi, "The Memory of Abraham in the Late Persian/Early Hellenistic Yehud/ Judah," in *The Reception and Remembrance of Abraham* (ed. P. Carstens and N.P. Lemche; Piscataway, NJ: Gorgias, 2011), pp. 13-60; Philippe Guillaume, "Exploring the Memory of Aaron in Late Persian/Early Hellenistic Period Yehud," in *Remembering Biblical Figures in the Late Persian and Early Hellenistic Periods* (ed. Diana Vikander Edelman and Ehud Ben Zvi; Oxford: Oxford University Press, 2013), pp. 95-105.

crucial set of recognitions where completely moving on from older models of ethnicity itself is concerned.[132]

Another idea that I think might have broad, practical utility from at least a religious studies context, if not per se a biblical one, is the concept of the "plural actor." This is the idea that we all, to some extent, are capable of identifying in multiple different ways in different contexts, so that we are all in a sense, multiple people at once. And it has seen some use in the study of early Christian constructions of identity.[133] I suspect that it might offer a helpful way of negotiating how Judahites and Israelites could both identify as participants in their separate regional cultures and eventually in their shared Israelite one.[134] But I also think it could help clarify discussions of how different Greeks navigated their own complex systems of identifying—by poleis, by region, by sub-ethnic group, within Panhellenism and so on. The question of *which* of these was more prominent might not be the right question; what *circumstances* brought which to prominence might be instead.

For us, however, what matters is the simple fact that the clearer context shows constant processes of adaptation, *not* transhistorical stability. James C. Miller is right: the fact "that ethnicity is a changing social phenomenon rather than a 'thing' possessed by a group" actually means that "no single configuration of Israel's ethnic identity existed"—or Greek.[135] It has no stable core either; it is a set of ideas that are inherited but can emerge in new configurations, and can be swapped out for others more readily and more often than we might think. Every articulation plays with a particular set; every articulation is its own. Because the ones that survive are neither simply the heirs of an original vision nor corruptions of it, there is no reason to be more interested in *what* it plays with than *how*. And if what we want to understand *is* a particular articulation, the relationship decisively reverses. We should be very much more interested in how what is inherited is used than in what those inheritances *are*.

This is even more the case if we really rid ourselves of the linear model, if we see a garden of forking paths, in Borges's phrase, stretching backwards into the mists of time. Still more if we do not think there is a qualitative distinction between an early and a late tradition. Still more when we acknowledge that when we have recovered an early tradition, we

132. Vayntrub, *Beyond Orality*.

133. Bernard Lahire, *The Plural Actor* (trans. David Fernbach; Cambridge, UK: Cambridge University Press, 2011). See Eric Rebillard, "Material Culture and Religious Identity in Late Antiquity," in *A Companion to the Archaeology of Religion in the Ancient World* (ed. Rubina Raja and Jörg Rüpke; Chichester, UK: Wiley Blackwell, 2015), pp. 427-32.

134. Tobolowsky, *The Myth of the Twelve Tribes of Israel*, pp. 103-105.

135. James C. Miller, "Ethnicity and the Hebrew Bible: Problems and Prospects," *CBR* 6.2 (2008), p. 173.

have with us *only* an early tradition, not a distorted memory of the events that gave the ethnic group its shape, ever central, down through the eventful ages. And so the ramifications of a more fluid model for the study of ethnicity itself become the ramifications for the study of *any kind of tradition* that gives shape to how the people of a nation, a family, or a place understand themselves and their past. In every case, we are in the presence of a past constantly reimagined to meet the needs of a changing present, and so we should want to understand what is being imagined and why, most of all.[136] And what is inherited very often has the role in these efforts of *ingredient* for a new act of becoming, not of "kernel of truth," preserving the old.

We are, however, still far from the sea change I mentioned at the beginning of this chapter, and further, generally, in Hebrew Bible than in the study of ancient Greek traditions. A greater commitment to asserting the accessibility of "the" early traditions of Israel, and to insisting what survives prominently reflects early Israelite concepts, institutions and beliefs, is a clear historical phenomenon. And even more so, as we will see in the next chapter, the commitment to asserting that traditions about the patriarchs, the exodus and the conquest *must* reflect genuine people movements, Bronze Age experiences, some half-remembered realities is still with us. Less willingness to entertain the creative agency and individual intentions of the actual authors of the actual texts, even when their work largely consisted of choosing and combining older materials is also a feature here. And so this discussion continues in chapters to come.

Conclusion

By a fortuitous coincidence, I happened to be reading David Graeber and David Wengrow's *The Dawn of Everything: A New History of Humanity* as I finished up the first draft of this book.[137] I do not mean to comment here on its overall argument, which is not terribly relevant for mine. However,

---

136. A number of examples of what I am talking about can be found in Michael D. Hattem's *Past and Prologue,* which includes an account of how colonial visions of who their antecedents were repeatedly shifted as part of the process of breaking away from Britain and creating a new identity. For example, the Glorious Revolution shifted in colonial historical memory from an event that had restored the "ancient constitution" between king and parliament; to one that achieved parliamentary supremacy over the king; to one which had unfortunately upset the balance between parliament and king, as American antipathy shifted between parliament and king depending on the circumstances (Michael D. Hattem, *Past and Prologue: Politics and Memory in the American Revolution* [New Haven, CT: Yale University Press, 2020], pp. 39, 118-20).

137. David Graeber and David Wengrow, *The Dawn of Everything: A New History of Humanity* (New York: Farrar, Straus and Giroux, 2021).

I was struck by a pattern they identified in the history of another tremendously influential eighteenth-century idea: Jean-Jacques Rousseau's vision of primitive man living in a state of equality until the rise of private property. Graeber and Wengrow note that a number of contemporary scholars—they mention Stephen Pinker and Francis Fukuyama among them—offer supposedly modern, sophisticated and nuanced versions of Rousseau's vision.[138] Rather, in another pattern presaging discussions to come, these scholars often establish the validity of their approach by *dismissing* Rousseau's original account. Pinker, for one, claims that Rousseau and Hobbes "were talking through their hats."[139] Then, however, they work their way back to very similar conclusions, now supposedly justified by new evidence.

The problem, however, is that Rousseau's vision was not a good idea, badly supported. It was not the instinctual discovery of a genuine reality waiting for a sophisticated contemporary scholar to flesh out with the proper kind of proof. It was *literally* based on nothing—no proof, and no possibility of having any.[140] It has not gained any in the interim. As a result, when modern scholars replicate this vision, however much more carefully and skeptically, they are *still* reproducing an argument that has no basis. And I would think that if Rousseau had not come up with it—if no one else with similar cachet had, and so etched it on our intellectual imagination—no one would now be rediscovering it, with however much greater sophistication. Thus, the best thing to do is, very likely, to forget we ever heard of Rousseau's idea—and then see what the actual evidence might actually say.

It is the same with primordialism, at least in many respects. The noble savage does not have what primordialism has, which is a world full of people who understand their own identities according to it.[141] As a result, its presence or absence is not challenging to navigate in the way that the absence of primordialism is, because the persistence of the vision of ethnic nations as real entities with ancient histories continues to play an important role in shaping what rights are deserved by whom.

138. Graeber and Wengrow, *The Dawn of Everything*, p. 13.

139. Graeber and Wengrow, *The Dawn of Everything*, p. 12.

140. Indeed, Graeber and Wengrow suggest Rousseau himself might not have viewed the vision he constructed as more than a hypothetical. They claim that "Rousseau himself never suggested that the innocent State of Nature really happened. On the contrary, he insisted he was engaging in a thought experiment" (Graeber and Wengrow, *The Dawn of Everything*, p. 11).

141. Another problem is that ethnic actors tend to imagine their own ethnicity in primordialist terms, so it remains the most intuitive way of thinking about what ethnicity is. As Rogers Brubaker put it, "It is participants, not the analysts, who are the real primordialists, treating ethnicity as naturally given and immutable" (Brubaker, *Ethnicity without Groups*, p. 83).

As an intellectual idea, however, it, too, is based on nothing. If we started over, innocent of inherited ideas and built only from observation, we would find only what scholars have been finding since the days of Max Weber. At no point in the history of a self-described ethnic group is there a single ruling construction of what "their" ethnic identity *is*. To the extent that the members of an ethnic group can be characterized, or caricatured, in any one way with even general efficacy, this is surely due to social and cultural influences, not biological ones. And instead of as a stable, transhistorical core, ethnicity exists as a flexible set of ideas that are repeatedly and dynamically remixed—even added to, subtracted from, or replaced—in response to new situations. These ideas can mean different things, and be organized in different ways, from person to person, let alone era to era.

The same is true of the linked Romantic assumptions about the history of traditions that created this enduring vision of an ethnic nation transforming its foundational experiences into charter narratives, then handing those down, generation to generation, from the beginning to the very end of ethnic time. Some stories are based on real events, and some are not. Some are very early and survive a long time; some are invented in living memory. But there is no proof, and there never will be any proof, that early ethnic actors reliably transmute history into story, or that surviving early stories that do reflect historical events look, seem, or are inherited differently from those that do not. There is no evidence that later compositions present anything other than the same confusing mélange of fact, fiction, collectivity and individuality as earlier. And in any case, as I have argued throughout, postulating linear tradition histories for traditions that reflect how a people imagines its own past absolutely requires us to assume linear ethnic histories, which are no longer plausible. And when we do not imagine one generation handing its core traditions on to the next in a stately procession, but instead a mass of stories from different circles surging onwards from diverse channels into a great ocean of traditions, through which succeeding generations may swim, we can square the circle between the fact that we certainly do inherit a great many of our imaginations from the past, and the reality that inheritance is dramatically fluid nonetheless.

And so, if we had to do it over again, I do not think we would arrive at primordialism either, or any close relative. This means that if it did not already exist, it, too, would not be reinvented, however superficially plausible the reinventions seem. Because it exists as an idea, because so many others were built on the foundation it provides, there is immense resistance to leaving it behind, however poorly formed we can acknowledge it was when it first burst onto the scene. Indeed, what we will see in the next chapter is that, just as with Pinker above, not a few efforts to reinvent this particular wheel in the early to mid-twentieth century begin precisely by denigrating the premises that gave it its original shape before working back to them by some supposedly new path. We should, instead, leave it behind.

I have tried in this chapter to gesture at what else that means leaving behind and discuss why that has not happened yet. I have argued that the history of resistance has, as its cause, an inherited set of ideas about how scholars are supposed to study ancient traditions, and what is supposed to be interesting about them. These ideas, as I have tried to show, are not, however, neutral nor obvious; they are the result of a particular, flawed conception of traditions and their histories that is the specific historical product of specific historical assumptions. And I have argued that a combined approach can offer what decades of internal debate has not been able to offer, a way to really work our way free of them. The fact, for example, that Panhellenism was a relatively late innovation forces us to reckon with the likelihood that Israelite and Judahite authors were also ethnic innovators, even if we do not think anything of that precise sort happened in the latter context. The fact that the larger corpus of ancient Greek traditions affords us many examples of Classical Greeks, and post-Classical Greeks, innovating new visions *of* Panhellenism forces us to reckon with the likelihood that various biblical Panisraelitisms are more than merely versions of the original concept, whether that emerged in earliest Israel or relatively late Judah. They *are* innovations which can tell us a lot about, well, themselves. They can tell us what developments called for innovation, and how someone answered the call. From this perspective we can even acknowledge that early realities might be preserved in texts and *still* insist that the important thing is not that they exist, which does not tell us very much, but what is being done with them, which does.

What we will see in the next chapter will strengthen both parts of the discussion started here. On the one hand, we will see that the desire to construct surviving texts as the heirs of early traditions, which were the reflection of real experiences, survived the end of the nineteenth century intact. It also survived the turn to a new paradigm of investigation, one founded less on the study of texts alone and more on extraliterary evidence—archaeology, epigraphy and anthropology—that authorized claims of empirical proof that were qualitatively different from what came before. As we will see, the early- to mid-twentieth-century efforts to deploy this proof were largely occupied with using it to reassert the validity of older preoccupations.

At the same time, we will also see more and more recent discussions of how to break away from older approaches and understandings, and more proofs that we need to do precisely this, as completely as possible. We will see more confirmation of what I mean when I say an embrace of the shift to a fluid, constructivist model of ethnic identifying is what opens the door to all kinds of changes in how we think about what traditions preserve and reflect. If we are always in the process of reinventing ourselves and our past, surviving texts will reveal how ancient peoples *did that,* through the medium of whatever they inherited, and not a little of what they developed themselves. This is the kind of information we should expect to find in what we have, and not the dim reflection of long ago, *even when the dim reflection seems, in fact, to be there.* This is the sea change we need, and it starts here. A comparative approach can help us see precisely what to do to bring it about.

2

PROOF

The title of this chapter is a little tongue in cheek. My topic is what a combined approach, as I have been calling it, can tell us about the role various kinds of extraliterary evidence—archaeological, epigraphic, anthropological, sociological, etc.—should play *not* in the reconstruction of past reality, but specifically in the study of ancient traditions. I needed a term that could serve as a catch-all and chose proof, as in evidence, for obvious reasons. But I also wanted to gesture at an increasingly well-known problem, the fallacy that the use of this evidence is what makes a study perfectly objective or defines it absolutely against those that rely on literary evidence— proof as in a mathematical proof. One of the recognitions we now have to grapple with is precisely how it changes things when we recognize that choosing which proofs to emphasize, and how to interpret them, is deeply subjective. Nobody *really* wants to read a history that merely relates what the finds are, and what little they can definitively prove by themselves. Almost nobody writes them.

Thus, this chapter, too, is built around two questions. Or perhaps I should say three, given that "how can a combined approach help us see where the study of this topic ought to go next" is the centerpiece of each of our discussions. One new question for this chapter, however, is "what *does* proof prove?" What should we think, after a century of skeptical reassessments, is actually true about the relationship between traditions such as the Pentateuch and Homer and historical realities? What seems to be the most justified position, not just about the reality of the events described in these texts according to the proofs we now possess, but the role of real events in giving shape to the stories?

The other question, at least as important, is "what *can* proof prove?" Or, rather, we might think of the proverbial woodchuck: what could proof prove, if proof could prove, etc.? Today, we are, of necessity, much more skeptical about the accuracy of most surviving ancient traditions and about how early they really emerged than scholars were at the beginning of the twentieth century. But *say that we weren't.* Would even the conclusion that a given example is very accurate, or very early, seem to mean the same thing as it meant in that era? Or would we see a greater difference between event and representation no matter what relationship we thought we espied? I think we would, and this, above all things, is what a combined approach can clarify.

In other words, I think that, broadly speaking, many twentieth-century scholars thought it was still possible to prove not only that a tradition was accurate and early but that it was, *as a result*, a different kind of tradition altogether; *in its essence* a memory of that event, as opposed to a story about it. And I think that even if a tradition gets quite a lot right, this idea is passe for a host of reasons. Thus, while there are still many scholars who take for granted that it matters a great deal whether the *Iliad*, the *Odyssey*, the Pentateuch, and other stories about Heroic Israel and Heroic Greece have a foot or two in historical reality, the question of precisely *why* is one that now needs to be asked in a serious way. And even if we think we can answer it, we still might find that it matters for different reasons than scholars once thought—for the historiographer, perhaps, but not so much the textual scholar, and so on.

In order to arrive at this point, however, this chapter will continue the discussions of the previous in two key regards, the first of which is quite literal. There, I offered a sketch of how late eighteenth- and nineteenth-century developments in the study of traditions entangled essentially Romantic assumptions in the norms of scholarly process, its goals and understandings. That is, I argued that the influence Romantic ideas about what early traditions and early nations were like exerted on developing tools of historical-critical and tradition-critical inquiry preserved the idea of a fundamental difference between early traditions and later texts long past the era when the presence of such a difference should have been able to be justified without challenge.

More specifically, I argued that many nineteenth-century scholars were preoccupied by the hunt for the, or an, "original tradition"—the earliest version of a text or story—*because,* whether they were avowed Romantics or not, they tended to understand original and early traditions much as Johann Gottfried Herder or the Brothers Grimm imagined them. They embraced, explicitly or implicitly, a linear model of tradition development, and of a divide of sorts, in which the earlier was not *just* earlier but the more accurate and superior.[1] They could believe, as Herder had believed, that the original tradition was an expression of the collective memory of the

---

1. For one thing, "the linear developmental model adopted in these early studies that advocated a stark division between an older, oral mindset and the sudden appearance of a literate one ... no longer holds. Instead, it is increasingly apparent that written and oral forms of discourse were continually intertwined throughout the centuries in which the Hebrew Bible was composed," leading, as well, to an ongoing dynamism in composition (Pioske, *Memory in a Time of Prose*, pp. 17-18).

nation, perhaps even authored, in some mysterious way, by the collective consciousness of that nation. They could think, in fact, that certain kinds of traditions could *only* be authored early on, in a heroic age, when the fires of national creativity burned with enough purity. They could think—à la the Great Divide—that early traditions, and especially oral traditions, were genuine, pure, and representative of national *character,* while later texts were artificial, corrupt, and individual representations of something much finer. As a result, nineteenth-century scholarly tool kits often developed to facilitate the pursuit of increasingly outdated preoccupations, and so continually re-instantiated them. These same preoccupations consistently incentivized resisting, and finding ways around, negative conclusions where the recoverability of these original traditions was concerned, as in the failure of the more skeptical aspects of the arguments of Wolf, de Wette, and Wellhausen to prove enduring.

In this chapter, I will describe how the same beliefs, preoccupations, and assumptions gave fundamental shape to the first serious encounters with the new accesses of "proof" that greeted twentieth-century scholars. In other words, the first influential attempts to use newly available archaeological and epigraphic materials and the results of anthropological and sociological inquiries were still profoundly shaped by the *desire* to prove that surviving texts were really based on much earlier traditions, and that these were essentially accurate. As a result, these inquiries not only preserved flawed assumptions about "what can proof prove"—that it *can* prove that a text is quite another kind of tradition after all—but reinvented them in the guise of empirical propositions. That is, I will argue, many early twentieth-century attempts to employ new proofs, even early to mid-twentieth century, gave the impression that *if* one could prove that a given text was really based on an early tradition, a real event, or both, one could also prove—or even *would* also prove without additional effort—that it was in fact something like the collective memory of the ethnic nation after all. Then, I will argue that because subsequent reassessments of these early arguments typically focused on their historicist claims and *not* the assumptions and beliefs that inspired them, they were far more successful, just as in the last chapter, at moderating the robustness of early conclusions than changing the paradigm of investigation.

In the process of this discussion, I will, therefore, complete the sketch I began and bring it into the present. The result, however sketchy, so to speak, will be a history of entanglement, which, in the parlance of this study's introduction, will double as an attempt to make the presence of inherited ghosts fully visible where they have long been hidden away. And this, of course, will prepare us for the exorcism that a combined approach to the question of how to respond to changed assumptions can provide. But I will also continue to grapple with this *legacy* of entanglement, and with what cutting our way free of it would really take. In the first chapter, this meant showing how new understandings of ethnic identity had greater implications for the older paradigm than we often realize. In other words, I argued that the recognition that we ourselves are more than merely the linear descendants of our biological ancestors in terms of our ethnic formation must also lead to the recognition that our traditions are not merely versions of our original, long-ago ones either. If we constantly reinvent our identities, then we also reinvent the visions of the past that charter them. If we cannot call one era's ethnic constructions the authentic ones, in contrast to another, we cannot treat one way of explaining the ethnic past through traditions as more authentic than another or superior on other grounds. And the less linear we imagine subsequent processes of tradition inheritance to be, the less the discovery of the early tradition or text will even seem to *explain* the version we actually have. This, in turn, will mean that we should most often study traditions in search of a different kind of information, imagining a different kind of process of development. In this chapter, however, grappling with inherited legacies will mean precisely what I implied in the second central question above: a reassessment of what it would seem to mean today, even if the presence of robust correspondences between text and extraliterary evidence could be demonstrated far more decisively than is likely at this late hour.

Thus, I will indeed discuss "what does proof prove," in terms of where a century's worth of critical reassessments in both disciplines have landed us with respect to the question of how well Homer, the Pentateuch, and other early traditions are likely to reflect real events or early realities, per the testimony of extraliterary evidence. And I will discuss "what can proof prove," what should it seem to mean today if a surviving text does, or does not, seem to have a significant relationship to early realities. And once again, we will see that what a combined approach can achieve has less to do with modifying the results of older scholarship than with reassessing the *purposes* of demonstrating the relationship between text and reality in a context where even the presence of a significant relationship between text and reality would mean much less than we once imagined.

Taking a Wrong Turn

Even as Julius Wellhausen was putting the finishing touches on his *Prolegomena,* a new world was growing up under his feet. In fact, though it would play little enough role in the scholarship of his day, Egyptian hieroglyphs had been deciphered already in the 1820s and '30s by Champollion, and Akkadian by Rawlinson in the late 1840s.[2] Austen Henry Layard

---

2. The Rosetta Stone had been discovered by Napoleon's armies in Egypt in the

would begin his famous excavations at Nineveh in the forties and fifties, and Paul-Émile Botta at Khorsabad. Palestinian archaeology would largely begin with Sir Flinders Petrie's excavations at Tell el-Hesi in 1890.[3] And a new age in scholarship would be explicitly heralded by the publication of George Smith's *Chaldean Account of Genesis* in 1876, based on the eleventh tablet of the Gilgamesh epic.[4]

In addition, as Wellhausen's work made its way to the printers, Heinrich Schliemann was already sinking shafts at Troy. At any rate, in 1878, he was digging at Hisarlik, the Turkish site that is still generally *believed* to be ancient Troy. In fact, this was already his second visit. The first excavation campaign had spanned from 1870 to 1873, and after this 1878–79 season, he would return twice more, in 1882 and 1890.[5] He had also begun at Mycenae in 1876, after a preliminary visit in 1874.[6] Schliemann himself was a lamentable archaeologist, and never really grasped what he had actually begun to uncover, beyond believing that he had found Homeric fantasy made flesh. But, as other excavations and studies would show—Wilhelm Dörpfeld at Pylos, Harriet Boyd at Gournia, Christos Tsountas in 1893's prescient *The Mycenaean Age*—there was certainly more *there* there than of the patriarchs, the exodus, or the conquest: "a brilliant and very distinctive [Greek] civilization around the Aegean *before the classical*," whose important centers actually featured in Homer's poems.[7] This was, to be clear, the world *of* Mycenae rather than of Homer, which is literary in character. But modern scholars had not met the Mycenaeans before. Soon, the same pattern would repeat in Crete, where the fact that Arthur Evans, who began excavating in 1900, was certain he had discovered the actual civili-

1790s but the language it held the key to would not be deciphered until the 1820s and '30s (F.L. Griffith, "The Decipherment of the Hieroglyphs," *JEA* 37 [1951], pp. 38-39). A dramatic account of how the British ended up with the Stone appears in Donald Malcolm Reid, "Rediscovering Ancient Egypt: Champollion and al-Tahtawi," in *Whose Pharaohs? Archaeology, Museums, and Egyptian National Identity from Napoleon to World War I* (Oakland: University of California Press, 2002), pp. 37-38. See also Donald Malcolm Reid, "Egyptology under Ismail: Mariette, al-Tahtawi, and Brugsch, 1850–1882," in *Whose Pharaohs?*, p. 114. As for Akkadian, "In 1846-1847 Henry Rawlinson published a transcription and translation of the whole Old Persian text of the trilingual cuneiform inscription of Darius I at Behistun, Persia. A decade later, Rawlinson and two other scholars triumphantly confirmed the decipherment of Akkadian" (Reid, "Rediscovering Ancient Egypt," p. 44).

3. Blenkinsopp, *The Pentateuch*, p. 9.

4. See the discussion in Blenkinsopp, *The Pentateuch*, p. 9.

5. William A. McDonald, *Progress into the Past* (New York: Macmillan Company, 1967), p. 14.

6. McDonald, *Progress into the Past*, pp. 49-50.

7. McDonald, *Progress into the Past*, pp. 12, 83, 116-69, 10.

zation of King Minos does not mean that he had not really begun to uncover what would later be called the Minoan civilization.[8]

Of course, even by the end of the nineteenth century, other discoveries still lay in the future. Ugarit—and Ugaritic, which would reveal the first complete narratives reflecting indigenous Canaanite traditions and myth—would not be discovered until the 1920s or deciphered until the early 1930s. For that matter, Linear B, the script of Mycenae, could not be read until the early 1950s.[9] But certainly the groundwork was being laid for quite a different kind of investigation, a kind that would come to dominate the twentieth century.

What happened next should, in my view, be regarded as something of a genuine surprise. At any rate, I think it is analytically useful to imagine being surprised by an intellectual history that may be too familiar to elicit it, whatever it deserves. But consider the broader picture here, including the discussions of the previous chapter. Around the turn of the nineteenth century, Wolf and de Wette had begun the process of historicizing the composition of the Homeric poems and the Pentateuch. Wolf argued that the original Homer, an oral poet, was beyond recovery and that the surviving text was essentially the work of Peisistratus, the sixth-century BCE Athenian tyrant. De Wette, among other contributions, noticed that no one in the books of Kings seems to act according to pentateuchal law, or even like they know about the Pentateuch, or even to mention it, while in the books of Chronicles, which we know to be late, a different situation prevails.

The result of these and other early efforts was that the nineteenth century saw the more or less complete replacement of uncomplicated assumptions of Homeric and Mosaic authorship with various models of how the final texts had come together in much later periods. Different Analysts, Unitarians, and Documentarians came to different conclusions about how ancient the core traditions were, and about the process, but by the late nineteenth century, both fields had landed in reasonably skeptical places.

---

8. "According to Evans," Cathy Gere notes, "Knossos was the true Cretan Labyrinth, the historical reality behind the myth of the virgin-devouring Minotaur" (Cathy Gere, *Knossos and the Prophets of Modernism* [Chicago: University of Chicago Press, 2009], p. 4). Gere also observes that, in Evans's *The Palace of Minos,* "Evans bequeathed to his war-torn age a scientific vision of life before the Fall—Minoan society reconstructed as Western civilization's earliest blossoming" (Gere, *Knossos and the Prophets of Modernism,* p. 4). McDonald refers to a speech Evans gave in 1937, upon his last visit to Crete: "We know now ... that the old traditions were true. ... It is true that on the old palace site what we see are only the ruins of ruins, but the whole is still inspired with Minos's spirit of order and organization and the free and natural art of the great architect Daedalos" (McDonald, *Progress into the Past,* p. 169).

9. For the former, see Peggy L. Day, "Dies Diem Docet: The Decipherment of Ugaritic," *Studi Epigrafici e Linguistici* 19 (2002), pp. 37-57. For the latter, Stephen V. Tracy, "The Acceptance of the Greek Solution for Linear B," *Hesperia: The Journal of the American School of Classical Studies at Athens* 87.1 (2018), pp. 1-16.

Before Schliemann, at any rate, many Homerists "believed that the *Iliad* and the *Odyssey* contained no historical truth, that Agamemnon and Pylos and the Trojan War had had no more real existence than Polyphemos or Lotus Land or the Council of the Gods on Mount Olympus."[10] Wellhausen, at nearly the same time, had concluded much the same thing: that the Pentateuch was *essentially* a late collection which did a far better job reflecting the realities of the era in which it came together than preserving the impression of real events.

In this context, we might well expect that the sudden emergence of new kinds of evidence and new kinds of investigations would *confirm* scholars in their skeptical priors. After all, as I will discuss below, many of the skeptical counter-arguments of the mid-twentieth century relied less on any new discoveries than on reassessing existing ones. Instead, the opposite happened. Scholars in both disciplines, broadly speaking, saw in this evidence dramatic confirmation of the basic historicity of the traditions they studied, and of their great antiquity. This, too, took different forms, and especially between American and European Hebrew Bible scholars. But on both sides of the Atlantic, text- and tradition-historical inquiries largely converged on arguments that were really remarkable. They did not explicitly replace the prior fruits of historical-critical inquiry per se, but, much more so than is often acknowledged, they purported to make them irrelevant.

In other words, the emerging view, in the first half of the twentieth century, that the Homeric poems reflected Mycenaean realities fairly well and that the Pentateuch either presented a literal or impressionistic vision of the actual experiences of Israel's ancestors was accompanied by the conviction that the poems *themselves* were essentially Mycenaean, that new ways of thinking about composition in performance obviated the need to explain the distance between its early formulation and later representation, and that the pentateuchal narrative had been completed in all its major particulars already in the premonarchical period or at latest in the very early monarchy. As a result, the processes through which the basic, original narrative grew into the familiar literary artifact could be interesting and useful for some questions but did not meaningfully describe the history of the narrative itself. Or, as Martin Noth would put it about the Pentateuch, "the essential point" of his and other contemporaneous studies was that "the decisive steps on the way to [its] formation ... were taken during the preliterary stage, and the literary fixations only gave final form to material which in its essentials was already given."[11] So it seemed to be for Homer, too, after the work of Nilsson and Parry.

10. McDonald, *Progress into the Past*, p. 4.
11. Martin Noth, *A History of the Pentateuchal Traditions* (trans. Bernhard W. Anderson; Chico, CA: Scholars Press, 1981), p. 1.

I think of this as a "great wrong turn" in the history of scholarship because, in the literal sense, I think it could easily have gone another way. This would, I think, have only been natural. It tends to happen that scholarship proceeds from less skeptical to more where the history behind traditions is concerned. And I think it not only should have happened here but easily could have. Indeed, one of the great innovations of this era, Albrecht Alt's "peaceful infiltration theory," was already premised on the recognition that archaeology could not support the historicity of one of the major chapters in the Hebrew Bible's vision, the Israelite conquest of Canaan.[12] It was a choice, not an inevitability, for Alt himself, and Noth after him, to offer an explanation for how Israel could, nevertheless, have entered Canaan from the outside in a way the preserved the possibility that earlier chapters in the narrative could reflect distorted memories of still earlier experiences rather than to grapple more seriously with the inaccuracy of such an important account.

Thus, that scholarship in both disciplines zigged into robust visions of the correlation between text and early reality, and text and early tradition, rather than continuing to zag into the kind of skeptical conclusion which would appear later in the century, and seem a more natural continuation of earlier arguments, is cause for reflection on its own. I consider it, above all, a testament to something I have been talking about throughout: just how much more *desirable* it seemed to many scholars to recover a particular kind of tradition—early, something like memory—than to study surviving texts. This desire, acting on new evidence, transformed that evidence so it appeared to be what it was useful for it to be: a tool capable of *rescuing* traditional preoccupations just when they seemed on the verge of falling away.[13]

As I mentioned above, however, I am not most interested in these over-bold claims about the age and reliability of traditions which, in any case, would be addressed before too long. I am interested in the fact that many of these scholars treated an earlier generation's assumptions and imaginations *about* early traditions, which were fundamentally flawed in various ways, as if they, too, could be proven by newly available evidence. Again, in some cases, these scholars acted as if proving one set of propositions *by itself* proved the other; if a tradition was early and somewhat reliable, it was also, surely, a collective production, essentially memory, the product of a heroic age and so on. As a result, the arguments that I have in mind not only

---

12. Albrecht Alt, *Die Landnahme der Israeliten in Palästina: Territorialgeschicht-liche Studien* (Leipzig: Druckerei dei Werkgemeinschaft, 1925); Albrecht Alt, *Die Staatenbildung der Israeliten in Palästina: Verfassungeschichtliche Studien* (Leipzig: Edelmann, 1930).

13. I discuss this issue of desire-led transformations at length in Tobolowsky, "On Comparison with Ancient Greek Traditions," p. 2.

revitalized an older set of conclusions, they resurrected a set of essentially Romantic assumptions as *if* they were empirical propositions. In the process, I would argue, they so obscured the Romantic roots of these visions that they preserved certain flawed assumptions and paradigms for decades to come. Quite a wrong turn indeed.

What Can Proof Prove? Part One

Many of the arguments I am critiquing here will be very well known to one set of readers or another. Still, the exigencies of trying to provide a useful guide for comparative work makes offering a brief sketch of major developments in the early to mid-twentieth century useful. In the previous chapter, I already discussed the work of Hermann Gunkel, who "rescued," in a sense, the idea that the Pentateuch was based on very early traditions that reflected real events and that could be recovered, with tools that hardly differed from those used by the folklorists in the early nineteenth century. But by the 1930s and '40s, the same sorts of conclusions, in both disciplines, would be placed upon new grounds, via new discoveries and new kinds of investigations.[14] In Classics, we can give the work of the likes of Schliemann and Evans, and that of the more enthusiastic scholars among their audiences, a similar turn-of-the-century role. And then there would be the arguments of scholars such as William Foxwell Albright, Martin Noth, Martin Nilsson, and Milman Parry.

Where the era I am interested in here is considered, I concede, of course, that a consideration of the work of four scholars cannot stand in for a full discussion of the nuances of this period or of decades of debate. Even so, where illustrating this scholarly era is concerned, we could do worse than considering these four in particular. They by no means present a monolith in their approaches or conclusions. But their arguments nevertheless tended to converge on the same points. Indeed, I would argue that focusing on some of the oft-mentioned differences can be misleading, especially between American and European Hebrew Bible scholars. It is true, for example, that Albright was convinced that "we may confidently assume that Moses was a Hebrew who was born in Egypt and reared under strong Egyptian influence" while Noth thought only that "the 'patriarchs' and Moses are to be reckoned as historical

---

14. For the study of the Hebrew Bible, a useful glimpse at more of what happened between the turn of the twentieth century and the 1930s can be found in two summary, state-of-the-field articles from this period, one by Rudolf Kittel in 1921 and another by Hugo Gressmann in 1924 (Rudolf Kittel, "Die Zukunft der Alttestamentlichen Wissenschaft," *ZAW* 39 [1921], pp. 84-99; Hugo Gressmann, "Die Aufgaben der alttestamentlichen Forschung," *ZAW* 42 [1924], pp. 1-33).

figures in the prehistory of the Israelite tribes."[15] And it is true that this difference is broadly representative of the kind of differences that existed between American and European arguments and conclusions in this era. Even so, they seemed far more important at the time than they actually are, and certainly in contrast to any genuinely skeptical argument. The "Altians," as they are sometimes called, after Noth's teacher Albrecht Alt, were still convinced that the "core traditions" of anything deemed "legend," or *Sage,* was based on historical fact, even if the fit was looser than the Albrightians supposed.[16] And Noth himself was quite convinced that the pentateuchal narrative—what he called the *Grundlage* or common basis of the documentary sources—was essentially premonarchical in origins. Few other European scholars offered much later dates.[17] Thus, in the early to mid-twentieth century, there was quite a general agreement, contra somebody like Wellhausen, that pentateuchal traditions in particular were heavily based on very early oral traditions that reflected real historical experiences, however more skeptical Europeans were about the nature of that reflection.

At any rate, Albright and Nilsson alike would work by cataloguing a series of seemingly robust correspondences between text and Bronze Age reality, as revealed by new material evidence, which suggested to them the essential accuracy of nearly the entire Pentateuch and the basic reality behind the Homeric poems. Here, too, there were differences. Albright was really far more convinced of the historicity of the traditions he studied than Nilsson, whom, incidentally, Albright misrepresented, and who considered the poems more like a reflection of Mycenaean culture than a more or less accurate record of a real event.[18] Even so, their most famous arguments proceeded along similar lines. Albright proposed a series of robust cor-

15. William F. Albright, *From the Stone Age to Christianity: Monotheism and the Historical Process* (Eugene, OR: Wipf & Stock, 2003), p. 196; Noth, *History of the Pentateuchal Traditions*, p. 257.

16. Megan Bishop Moore, *Philosophy and Practice in Writing a History of Ancient Israel* (New York: T. & T. Clark, 2006), p. 64. The Altians also believed that "stories reflective of the experience and beliefs of ... smaller groups were told at tribal gatherings. ... Eventually the nation that arose from these groups incorporated these traditions into their store of common tradition, the Bible" (Moore, *Philosophy and Practice in Writing a History of Ancient Israel*, p. 2).

17. Gerhard von Rad imagined that the earliest pentateuchal document had been worked out by the Yahwist only in the court of King Solomon, but even he supposed that "he found already made for him whole complexes of tradition, themselves the outcome of a long process of development" (von Rad, *The Problem of the Hexateuch and Other Essays*, p. 52).

18. It was not true, as Albright claimed, that Nilsson had demonstrated the "basic historicity" of the *Iliad*, or indeed, thought he had (Albright, *From the Stone Age*, p. 76).

respondences between the traditions of Genesis and the material record of early second-millennium Mesopotamia and between the exodus narrative and certain aspects of Egyptian and Palestinian realities in order to make the case that Abraham and Moses were real people who did essentially what the narratives claimed.[19] Following on the work of Kittel, anticipating the work of Cross, he even imagined, for a time, that the source documents of the Pentateuch must be "an old national epic, based on poems which came down ... from the Patriarchal Age."[20] Nilsson, meanwhile, expressed the similar view that the correspondences between the important centers in Homer (and other traditions about early Greece) and the actual centers of Mycenaean civilization not only proved the Mycenaean origins of the surviving poems themselves, but to some extent, of Greek mythology generally.[21]

Then Noth and Alt were, in Megan Bishop Moore's phrase, "early practitioners of sociological research into the biblical world" because their vision of early Israel, per "peaceful infiltration," was deeply influenced by the work of Max Weber among others.[22] It had been Weber who proposed, in what would be published in 1921 as *Das antike Judentum,* that early Israel had been a "covenant community" formed in the land. And it was his account that informed both biblical scholars' vision of "early Israelites as seminomads or transhumants."[23] Indeed, Noth's tremendously influential argument that early Israel had formed as an amphictyony, in the mode of ancient Greek amphictyonies, was of course his own in its particulars, but it mirrors Weber's vision in its general shape.[24]

Meanwhile, Parry's contribution was "oral-formulaic theory," essentially the idea that formulaic expressions, especially Homeric epithets, revealed the originally oral composition of the Homeric poems because they reflected the activity of a poet improvising a traditional tale for an audience, and using memorized formulae in the process to meet the meter. This argument he achieved by combining his prior studies of Homeric dialect and epithets with anthropological fieldwork researching the practices of South Slavic bards. The end result—one of the end results—would be "what would later be called the Milman Parry Collec-

19. For example, that "the latest discoveries at Mari ... have strikingly confirmed the Israelite traditions according to which their Hebrew forefathers came to Palestine from the region of Harran" (Albright, *From the Stone Age,* p. 179).

20. Albright, *From the Stone Age,* p. 183.

21. See in particular Martin P. Nilsson, *The Mycenaean Origin of Greek Mythology* (Berkeley: University of California Press, 1972), pp. 27-28.

22. Moore, *Philosophy and Practice in Writing a History of Ancient Israel,* p. 60.

23. Moore, *Philosophy and Practice in Writing a History of Ancient Israel,* p. 59.

24. Originally articulated in Martin Noth, *Das System der zwölf Stämme Israels* (Stuttgart: Kohlhammer, 1930).

tion of Oral Literature" at Harvard, including records of "around 700,000 lines of South Slavic song, more than 12,500 individual texts ... around 750 of them in oral form recorded on 3,580 aluminum disks," an invaluable resource even now.[25]

From this body of research, Parry would conclude that the *Iliad* and the *Odyssey* were themselves oral, traditional poetry, and that Homer himself was little more than a particularly skilled conduit through which it passed. "In a society where there is no reading and writing, the poet ... always makes his verse out of formula."[26] "The young poet learns from some older singer not simply the general style of the poetry, but the whole formulaic diction."[27] "The oral poet by no means limits his borrowing to the single formulae; rather he uses whole passages which he has heard. This is, indeed, his whole art: to make a poem like the poems he has heard."[28] "The good singer wins his fame by his ease and versatility in handling a tradition which he knows more thoroughly than anyone else ... but his poetry remains throughout the sum of longer and shorter passages which he has heard."[29] And so on.

Certainly, one thing we can say about all of these arguments is that they offer empirical propositions that can be tested and reassessed. Either the material evidence suggests a strong correlation between the Homeric poems and Mycenae, or Genesis and early second-millennium Mesopotamia, or it does not. Either sociological models justify concluding that Israel formed as a covenant community in the premonarchical period, or it does not; either the oral poet inevitably uses an inherited system of formulae to tell an already well-known story, or they do not. And so on. And in this regard, it is possible to say, nearly a century later, that future reassessments were not overly kind. Nilsson and Albright saw many more parallels than there actually are; there is no real justification for Noth's historical reconstructions. Neither Parry's vision of the oral poet as conduit or the universal applicability of oral-formulaic theory have stood the test of time.

Where the central question of this chapter is concerned, however, it is useful for us to imagine for a moment that it had gone the other way instead, and these early apprehensions had been substantially reconfirmed. What exactly would *we* think had been reconfirmed? Suppose that we could now

---

25. Steve Reece, "The Myth of Milman Parry: Ajax or Elpenor," *Oral Traditions* 331.1 (2019), pp. 118-19. Reece notes that the timing of Parry's visit was "felicitous," since it was late enough in time that recording equipment was available but early enough that a thriving oral tradition still existed.

26. Milman Parry, *Studies in the Epic Technique of Oral Verse-Making, II. The Homeric Language as the Language of an Oral Poetry* (Harvard Studies in Classical Philology, 43; Cambridge, MA: Harvard University Press, 1932), p. 6.

27. Parry, *Studies in the Epic Technique of Oral Verse-Making, II*, pp. 8-9.

28. Parry, *Studies in the Epic Technique of Oral Verse-Making, II*, p. 12.

29. Parry, *Studies in the Epic Technique of Oral Verse-Making, II*, p. 15.

say with confidence that the Pentateuch was essentially very early and based on real experiences. Would we also now agree with Albright's transparently Romantic (and supersessionist) proposition that the development of biblical traditions reflects a chapter in the process of development from "the savage mentality" through "half-savage" stages to "Judeo-Christian heights of spiritual insight?"[30] If the *Iliad* were a Mycenaean poem, would we still agree with Nilsson that the genre of epic must *by its nature* "originate in ... a heroic age ... praising the deeds of living men and describing contemporary events," just as certain nineteenth-century scholars imagined?[31] Would we agree, too, that "the great cycles of myths" *could* only have been products of a heroic age, that "the tragic poets hardly invent new myths but ... reshape old ones ... the same is to be said of the choral lyric poets?"[32] Would we think, like both Nilsson and Parry, that "the glory and fame of ancient poets depended not ... on their invention of something quite new and original, but rather on their presentation of the old traditional material in new and original fashion?"[33] Or would we *simply* believe that these stories had their roots in real events and formed at early times?

Just so, even if contemporary sociology validated Noth's vision of how early Israel had formed, what would justify his view that it was also the context in which the *Grundlage,* or "common basis" of the pentateuchal sources, emerged? What would justify his extraordinary argument that the *Grundlage* "had no particular 'author' or even 'authors' but rather emerged, developed, and was transmitted through the mouths of 'narrators' within the anonymous totality of the tribes?"[34] Folklore scholarship supposedly did, and especially the work of Axel Olrik and Andres Jolles, as well as the prior inquiries of Gunkel, discussed in the last chapter. But this is what I mean when I say that we are in the presence of a wrong turn. As John Van Seters would later point out, none of this work went unchallenged, even in the discipline of folklore itself at the time.[35] And someone who took their debt to studies of folklore seri-

30. William F. Albright, *Archaeology and the Religion of Israel* (Louisville, KY: Westminster John Knox Press, 2006), pp. 3-5.

31. Nilsson, *The Mycenaean Origin of Greek Mythology*, pp. 16-17. He would reiterate this point in *Homer and Mycenae* (*Homer and Mycenae*, pp. 208-209).

32. Nilsson, *The Mycenaean Origin of Greek Mythology*, pp. 1-2.

33. Nilsson, *The Mycenaean Origin of Greek Mythology*, pp. 1-2.

34. Noth, *History of the Pentateuchal Traditions*, p. 44.

35. Van Seters details the dependence of the Alt-Noth school on folklore scholarship that had first been deployed by Gunkel, especially Olrik's *Epic Laws of Folk-literature*. In addition, Jolles's view that "family sagas," like the one in Genesis, tend to be the oldest by their very nature was very influential. Thus, "In the works of Alt, Noth and von Rad ... it was largely considered established that the narrative basis of Genesis was an oral tradition of ancient *Sagen,* and their scholarly interest shifted from a literary criticism of the written source to a history of the pre-literary stage of the legend-traditions" (John Van Seters, *Abraham in History and Tradition* [New Haven, CT:

ously enough could just as easily have known, instead, that "the older ideal of a folk community preserving its traditions faithfully over the centuries could no longer be substantiated," a view that had appeared in folklore scholarship as early as the 1910s and '20s.[36] As for Parry, there is quite a substantial difference between the idea that the presence of formulaic expressions indicates an originally oral composition and his various conclusions about how little freedom, or desire, the oral poet had to alter the stories they knew or come up with new ones. And there is one of equal magnitude between his apprehensions of how South Slavic oral poets of the early twentieth century operated and his conviction that here he had discovered how *all* oral poetries work, a position that would be greatly extended by his one-time assistant, Albert Lord, in 1960's famous *Singer of Tales*. In short, in the twenty-first century, even if proof could prove—so to speak—that Homer was much earlier than the Homeric poems, and based on a real Trojan War; that the Pentateuch was based on the early experiences of the Israelite nation in and before their era of national origins, we would not now think that this validated the Romantic models of collective authorship and linear inheritance that are at the heart of all of them.

If not, then, from the evidence they were using itself, where did the larger shape of their arguments come from? As I have already intimated, they come from the then-recent past. In other words, in resurrecting the idea that the Pentateuch and Homer were the early traditions of Israel and Greece—and more or less accurate reflections of early experiences—these scholars also recreated a vision of a set of early traditions that serve as the collective memory of the group, are handed down in linear fashion, and persist ever after as the central charter traditions. And by offering these recreated Romantic assumptions in connection to professedly, and essentially empirical inquiries, they reinvented them as if they were empirical too, as if they could be proven by the same evidence that could demonstrate whether or not a story was largely true, and particularly old. But the opposite of the observation at the end of the last paragraph holds as well as it does. These conclusions did not come from any of the evidence that seemed to prove the extraordinary age and basic reliability of the traditions

---

Yale University Press, 1975], p. 132). The problem, however, is that greater attention to folklore scholarship itself would have revealed that Jolles's views received "severe criticism ... [from] folklorists working in this field," and in many cases "it was rejected from the start" (Van Seters, *Abraham in History and Tradition*, pp. 135-36). The same was broadly true of Olrik's. See also Patricia G. Kirkpatrick, *The Old Testament and Folklore Study* (JSOTSup, 62; Sheffield: Sheffield Academic Press, 1988), pp. 43-44.

36. Kirkpatrick, *The Old Testament and Folklore Study*, p. 45; R.H. Lowie, "Oral Tradition and History," *Journal of American Folklore* 30 (1917), pp. 161-67; F.C. Bartlett, "Some Experiments on the Reproduction of Folk Stories," *Folklore* 31 (1920), pp. 30-47.

in question. No evidence that only concerns how old a story is, or what its relationship to reality was can. Really moving past Romantic assumptions means recognizing that a story can be early and accurate—whether or not these are—without being a collective productive or reflecting real memories any better than later.

It is not entirely clear whether all of these scholars, or others like them, were consciously aware of the blending that was going on between proposition and assumption. Certainly, aspects of early twentieth-century Hebrew Bible scholarship suggest that the scholars just discussed were less aware even than some of their classical contemporaries of the challenges that had been raised to the basic models they espoused. Albright, who spoke without hesitation of the "savage mind," falls into this camp, even if his view that the presence of such a thing had now been validated by the work of "cultural anthropologists, social psychologists, sociologists, and philosophers" fits into the overall picture I am sketching.[37] In fact, he was so sure of his psychology-based rebuttal of Wellhausen that he claims to have seriously considered seeking "the collaboration of a professional psychologist" for his *Archaeology and the Religion of Israel*.[38] Noth's claims about what folklore scholarship had demonstrated, despite other folklore scholarship that denied the same, is another example.

In Classics, however, both Parry and Nilsson show a keen awareness of earlier shifts in assumptions that might plausibly have put their conclusions out of reach. Parry, for one, knew perfectly well that his understanding of oral traditional poetry was very similar to the older idea of "Natural poetry," or what the Grimms had called *Naturpoesie*.[39] And he knew, too, that the idea of *Naturpoesie* had long since been "given up largely because of the romantic notions of those who sought to apply it."[40] Likewise, he acknowledged that "the Romantic opinion that the poetry in question was more natural than other poetry was, as we can now see with our greater anthropological knowledge, little more than the first fancies about the thought of civilized man."[41] He argued, however, that the first proposition had since "been revived in a much sounder way in a late study of the psychological processes of poetry."[42] As for the second, "when Jousse,"

37. Albright, *Archaeology and the Religion of Israel*, pp. 3-4.
38. Albright, *Archaeology and the Religion of Israel*, pp. 3-5.
39. Parry himself was a warm supporter of the Great Divide model of tradition production in which the advent of writing was "the great cultural happening" that "account[s] for the loss of the primitive" and "the growth of a new form of society in which there is no longer any place for the old heroic ideal" (Milman Parry, "Whole Formulaic Verses in Greek and Southslavic Heroic Song," *TAPA* 64 [1933], p. 181).
40. Parry, "Whole Formulaic Verses," p. 180.
41. Parry, "Whole Formulaic Verses," p. 181.
42. Parry, "Whole Formulaic Verses," p. 180.

Marcel Jousse, a scholar of oral traditions, "after dividing poetry into the oral and the written, explains his reasons for thinking the thought of oral poetry the more spontaneous, he is working on much sounder ground."[43] The doubled reference to a "sounder" way makes the point. Some of these scholars actively believed that newly available proofs had now provided a secure foundation for what they knew had been only Romantic intuition: that older assumptions not only deserved to be preserved but had now been placed firmly on an empirical basis.[44]

As for Nilsson, his work offers quite a useful illustration of my contention that other scholars of his day, especially Hebrew Bible scholars, could certainly already have been aware of the outdated nature of some of their ideas, that the commitment of certain scholars to Romantic assumptions is more than merely a natural consequence of the era in which they were working. For one thing, he knew that that there is something of "mysticism" in the "romantic idea of popular collective poetry which cannot be ascribed to the interference of any individual but ... grows up unconsciously as a product of the collective mind of the people" *at the very same time* that Noth was articulating precisely this "mystic" vision of his *Grundlage*, and, in fact, earlier.[45] Likewise, he had an almost modern skepticism about the stability of oral tradition over time, noting that if certain stories "were ... handed down by oral tradition, it is difficult to imagine that they survived more than two or at most three generations."[46] And he acknowledged other cautions as well: that "if good historical tradition is to be preserved, an undisturbed life both in regard to setting and to civilization is an absolute condition, but the downfall of Mycenaean civilization was a most stormy and turbulent age."[47]

43. Parry, "Whole Formulaic Verses," p. 181.

44. Likewise, Albert Lord would later argue that "the whole body of verse that we have now agreed to designate as oral has been called by many names. . . . Those who call it 'folk epic' are carrying on a nineteenth-century concept of composition by the 'folk' which has long since been proved invalid." However, he believed "it was looking in the right direction," even though "its theory of composition was invalidated, because no one could show how the people as a whole could compose a poem." In addition, Lord's main objection here seems to be that these epics were actually "more often ... aristocratic and courtly" than the product of actual folk authors, not the idea that they express collective understandings; and he is actually quite convinced that the stories preserved in tradition represent an entire nation's most central ones (Albert B. Lord, *The Singer of Tales* [Cambridge, MA: Harvard University Press, 1960], p. 6).

45. Noth, *History of the Pentateuchal Traditions*, p. 44; Nilsson, *Homer and Mycenae*, p. 12. The German version of Noth's *History* mentioned here was published in 1948, while Nilsson's *Homer and Mycenae* and *The Mycenaean Origin of Greek Mythology* came out in 1933 and 1932 respectively.

46. Nilsson, *The Mycenaean Origin of Greek Mythology*, pp. 11-12.

47. Nilsson, *The Mycenaean Origin of Greek Mythology*, pp. 3-4.

It might, then, even seem surprising that he *reached* the conclusions that he did, which was the result of taking these skeptical apprehensions to the opposite extreme. In other words, he concluded that because oral tradition is so fallible, because it is precisely the material conditions described in a narrative that are most "liable to be altered and changed through assimilation to the conditions prevailing at the time when the poems were composed," the only way for the authors to have gotten so much right is *if* the text and narratives were essentially Mycenaean.[48] But then we can ask whether it is even possible for someone who was already convinced that epics must inevitably be contemporaneous with the events they describe, that poets simply pass on what they receive, and that the heroic period is the only period that sees genuine mythological invention to come to any other conclusions, regardless of what the evidence showed.

Indeed, the dynamic of blending I am interested in here is particularly well reflected in Nilsson's own summary of his main argument:

> My proof is nothing more than the constant application of this principle, a thorough-going comparison of the cities to which mythological cycles are attached with the cities where finds from the Mycenaean age have been made. If the correlation is constant; i.e., if we find that the cities to which the mythological cycles are attached were the centers of the Mycenaean civilization also, this constant correlation ... will prove the connection between the mythological cycles and the Mycenaean civilization; i.e., that the mythological cycles in their chief outlines go back into the Mycenaean age.[49]

He consciously presents each of these conclusions as nothing more than the neutral working out of a scientific principle. The modern reader, however, can see just how much difference there is between the proposition on one side of the second "i.e." and the other. In other words, if we agreed that the Mycenaean geography of the *Iliad* proves some form of "connection between the mythological cycles and the Mycenaean civilization" we would, or should, still think we needed to do much more work before concluding that the "chief outlines" of this story went "back into the Mycenaean age." And so, the scientific formula is more than simply science after all.

Ultimately, the blend of empirical propositions and essentially Romantic assumptions that emerged from this period had, in my opinion, significant

---

48. "The unavoidable conclusion is that the earliest poems incorporated in the Homeric poems and utilized in their composition cannot be more than a century or a little more older than the Homeric poems themselves" (Nilsson, *The Mycenaean Origin of Greek Mythology*, p. 12). Even so he acknowledged that "the gap between the earliest and latest elements in Homer comes nearer to a whole millennium than to a half-millennium" (Nilsson, *The Mycenaean Origin of Greek Mythology*, p. 14). See also Nilsson, *The Mycenaean Origin of Greek Mythology*, p. 24.

49. Nilsson, *The Mycenaean Origin of Greek Mythology*, pp. 27-28.

consequences for the debates of the rest of the century. In one sense, as we will see, the wrong turn was reversed. Starting, for the most part, in the 1950s in Classics and the 1970s in Hebrew Bible, a series of critical reassessments returned, or produced, significant skepticism to the enterprise of assessing the historicity of the traditions in question and of their absolute antiquity. At the same time, the ongoing inheritance of flawed assumptions about early traditions and accurate traditions—not to mention, as time would tell, the value and feasibility of reconstructing early historical realities in the first place—largely kept these critiques from operating on another, still essential level. The question of *what* it tells us about a tradition that it either is, or is not, based to some extent on real events was not interrogated in a meaningful way until much more recently. In other words, the focus of the dramatic reassessments of the rest of the century on what the available proof proved if *not* what these early forays suggested left ghosts alone that ought to have been expelled.

The Era of Critical Reassessments

Again, between the 1950s and 1970s, the robust reconstructions of the antiquity and reliability of ancient traditions that had dominated the early twentieth century were repeatedly reassessed and found wanting. Nilsson's, which was really among the most careful and skeptical, was, nevertheless, one of the first to receive this treatment. Moses Finley's 1954 study *The World of Odysseus* looked at the same evidence that had so convinced the older scholar and saw, almost contemporaneously with the decipherment of Linear B, something very different.[50] What he emphasized is the extent to which Nilsson *et al.* had allowed what was really only suggestive evidence to seem to be absolute proof. He acknowledges that Schliemann had really found Troy but notes that:

> nothing he or his successors have found, not a single scrap, links the destruction of Troy VIIa with Mycenaen Greece, or with an invasion. ... Nor does anything known from the archaeology of Greece and Asia Minor or from the Linear B Tablets fit with the Homeric tale of a great coalition aligning against Troy from Greece.[51]

---

50. Michael Ventris, with the help of John Chadwick, deciphered the language in the early 1950s, though their edition, *Documents in Mycenaean Greek,* would not be published until 1956—after Ventris's untimely death in a car accident. According to Finley, Homer's "arms bear a resemblance to the armor of his time, quite unlike the Mycenaean, although he persistently cast them in antique bronze. ... His gods had temples, and the Mycenaeans built none, whereas the latter constructed great vaulted tombs ... in which to bury their chieftains and the poet cremates his" (Moses Finley, *The World of Odysseus* [New York: New York Review of Books, 2002], p. 39).

51. Finley, *The World of Odysseus*, p. 37.

As for the correspondences between text and reality that had so occupied Nilsson, Finley pointed out that even the *existence* of the Linear B tablets was proof of the inaccuracy of Homer's vision of a world "without writing or record-keeping ... [and] one in which the social system was too simple and the operations too restricted, too small in scale, to require either the inventories or the controls recorded on the tablets."[52] Finley's critiques have not all stood the test of time. He thought the "World of Odysseus" was really the ninth century BCE, a century before the poet's day, while now the consensus is that the poems preserve "an amalgam of different layers that range from the Mycenaean to the Archaic age," alongside important later developments.[53] But others would come to similar conclusions, in terms of their skepticism about the background of the poems, in the sixties and seventies with a certain regularity.[54]

As for Parry's oral-formulaic theory, it has, in some ways, fared the best of any of the arguments described above, though it has been repeatedly qualified, decade to decade. But first it would take on new scope in Albert Lord's famous *The Singer of Tales,* published in 1960.[55] Lord, once Parry's assistant, would really transform the theory by making it essentially universal, hunting for proofs of oral composition in the written literature of a great many different cultures.[56] But in the 1970s, Ruth Finnegan would explore, through anthropological work in Africa, whether oral cultures really do tend to compose in more or less the same way as each other, and whether they feature the same set of relationships between storyteller and story. And, of course, this is no minor matter, since Parry's original argument required that the practices of twentieth-century South Slavic bards be directly applicable to the study of a pair of very ancient Greek poems, and Lord's reformulation required much more.

52. Finley, *The World of Odysseus*, p. 40.

53. Jonas Grethlein, "From 'Imperishable Glory' to History: The Iliad and the Trojan War," in *Epic and History* (ed. David Konstan and Kurt A. Raaflaub; The Ancient World: Comparative Histories; Oxford, UK: Wiley Blackwell, 2010), pp. 126-27.

54. Bernard Knox, in the introduction to the 2002 edition of *The World of Odysseus*, notes that Finley considered himself part of a "heretical minority" at this time, while the decipherment of the Mycenaean tablets initially birthed the same parallelomania that Near Eastern sources did in the study of the Hebrew Bible. However "it soon became apparent that the decipherment of Linear B, far from confirming the thesis that the Homeric poems were a reflection of Mycenaean society, had in fact dealt that thesis a fatal blow" (Bernard Knox, "Introduction," in *The World of Odysseus*, by M.I. Finley [New York: New York Review of Books, 2002], p. xiii).

55. Lord, *The Singer of Tales*.

56. "The impact of *The Singer of Tales* (1960) has ... been enormous. ... It will always be the single most important work in the field, because, simply put, it began the field as we now know it" (Foley, *The Theory of Oral Composition*, p. 41).

Yet, as Finnegan would show, not only did the African groups she studied compose oral traditions differently from the South Slavs, they did so differently from one another. The "Chopis singers" have "long-considered and rehearsed [oral] compositions," while the "leader in a boat- or dance-song" displays "facile improvisation."[57] The "Limba story-tellers" practice "the combination and recombination of known motifs into a single unique performance."[58] Some stories are spoken, but others, like "the Southern Bantu praise poems ... [and] the Yoruba hunters' *ijala* poetry are chanted in various kinds of recitative."[59] And many stories, in many places, feature a constellation of different relationships between written and oral storytelling.[60]

Indeed Finnegan, unlike many of the scholars discussed in this chapter, actually did take aim at the Romantic assumptions *animating* the counter-arguments she encountered.[61] As she correctly observes,

> Various questionable assumptions about the nature of oral tradition and so-called "folk art" among non-literate people have not made matters any easier ... they include such ideas as that "oral tradition" ... is passed down word for word from generation to generation and thus reproduced

57. Ruth Finnegan, *Oral Literature in Africa* (Oxford: Clarendon Press, 1970), pp. 7-8.

58. Finnegan, *Oral Literature in Africa*, pp. 7-8.

59. Finnegan, *Oral Literature in Africa*, p. 4. As J.B. Hainsworth put it in a review of John Miles Foley's 1988 study, *The Theory of Oral Composition*, "It is easy to see now that an ancient tradition represented by a corpus of two texts of unknown provenance and a few fragments is not the best material from which to evolve a theory" (J.B. Hainsworth, "Oral Poetry and Homer," *Classical Review* 40.1 [1990], p. 2).

60. This includes both written compositions that are most often performed orally and texts that are clearly based to some extent on oral performance. In general, as Foley put it, Finnegan's work evinced "a pluralistic model of oral literature," which is to say, a model that engages with the actual diversity of oral composition, and through it, the need for an "Oral Theory that faithfully treats the complex mass of materials that have heretofore too easily been forced into the simplistic oral-versus-written dichotomy" (Foley, *The Theory of Oral Composition*, pp. 102-103). It is worth noting a tendency to critique Finnegan excessively when the plain meaning of her work—that oral poets often work very differently from each other—is centrally important, and a necessary intervention in previous work. Foley's comparatively gentle criticism—"although the literary specialist may find fault with the lack of philological underpinning" in her work—is coupled with a more sophisticated understanding of how significant her contribution was against, say, Nagy, who accuses Finnegan of "misreading Parry's concept ... at the very point where it attempts to undermine its validity" (Foley, *The Theory of Oral Composition*, p. 102; Gregory Nagy, *Homeric Questions* (Austin: University of Texas Press, 1996), p. 23).

61. "The variability typical of oral literary forms has tended to be overlooked by many writers. This is largely because of certain theoretical assumptions held in the past about the verbatim handing down of oral tradition supposedly typical of non-literate societies" (Finnegan, *Oral Literature in Africa*, p. 9).

verbatim from memory throughout the centuries; or, alternatively, that oral literature is something that arises communally, from the people or the "folk" as a whole, so that there can be no question of individual authorship or originality.[62]

Someone who is well aware of the failure of these propositions will, more or less inevitably, be more interested in "the actual contemporaneous performance, variations, and the role of the individual poet or narrator in the final literary product" than someone who, ideologically, thinks the storyteller has no meaningful role.[63]

In addition, and even as Lord himself would largely continue to defend Parry's original formulation, oral-formulaic theory would be qualified in other ways by the likes of Cedric Whitman and Gregory Nagy.[64] Then, near the turn of the twentieth century, it would be dramatically updated by John Miles Foley. This he did both structurally and practically. Structurally, he published an annotated bibliography of oral-formulaic theory in the mid-eighties, and founded the journal *Oral Tradition*.[65] Practically, he was more clear-eyed about all the qualifications necessary when applying oral-formulaic theory to oral storytelling than most, referring to the need to "allo[w] each oral poetic tradition its idiosyncratic features," to recognize the presence of "verbal art" even in the use of formulaic expressions, to pursue "greater precision in comparison," and so on.[66]

In a later chapter, I will discuss other aspects of Foley's work: his concept of "traditional referentiality," for example, which helped break oral-formulaic theory out of the stranglehold of the vision of an oral poet who is merely a vector for an old story told anew.[67] For now, however, it is enough to say that it is characteristic of Foley's approach not to consider a given

62. Finnegan, *Oral Literature in Africa*, p. 14.

63. Finnegan, *Oral Literature in Africa*, p. 14.

64. Whitman, e.g., emphasized the individuality of Homer as an artist and, against Parry, the meaningfulness of formulae even as he concluded that "there is no evidence at all that the poet of the *Iliad* invented a single character or episode in his whole poem. He may not even have invented a single phrase" (Whitman, *Homer and the Heroic Tradition*, p. 14). Nagy has made many contributions, but has particularly emphasized the importance of repeated key words and themes to understanding the whole of the Homeric poems—and to what makes Homer's supposed version Homer's. See especially Gregory Nagy, *The Best of the Achaeans: Concepts of the Hero in Archaic Greek Poetry* (Baltimore, MD: Johns Hopkins University Press, 1979).

65. John Miles Foley, *Oral-Formulaic Theory and Research: An Introduction and Annotated Bibliography* (New York: Garland, 1985).

66. Foley, *The Theory of Oral Composition*, pp. 109-11.

67. "Tradition elements reach out of the immediate instance in which they appear to the fecund totality of the entire tradition ... and they bear meanings as wide and deep as the tradition they encode.... Traditional referentiality, then, entails the invoking of a context that is enormously larger and more echoic than the text or work itself"

story, such as the *Iliad* and the *Odyssey,* as an "artifact" of an earlier age, but an "instance" of a living tradition.[68] This tradition is something the storyteller draws from in a more complicated fashion than is allowed for in Parry's vision of an oral poet telling a single, familiar story in a new way as well as possible.

As for Noth, it would really take quite a long time before his vision of the *Grundlage* of the amphictyony so much as faced challenges, but when that happened, it would be, of all of these arguments, the easiest to dismiss.[69] The amphictyonic aspect of the argument in particular was based on a fallacy. His conviction was that the number twelve (or six) was both traditional and functional, because it allowed amphictyonies to serve their sanctuaries in an orderly monthly or bimonthly "rota."[70] Unfortunately, easily accessible classical sources—Strabo for example—explicitly mention odd-numbered amphictyonies, and there is no evidence that the number of amphictyons is really meaningful for their operation.[71] Nevertheless, it took nearly thirty years before the comparative evidence was so much as seriously revisited, even though Noth's case was built on almost nothing else, and so much was built on Noth's case.[72] Albright for one, whatever he thought of some of Noth's other arguments, was quite sure that "the central religious institution of Israel after the Conquest was the system of twelve tribes grouped around a central shrine."[73] But there was really nothing to it, and it should have been easy to realize as much.

(John Miles Foley, *Immanent Art: From Structure to Meaning in Traditional Oral Epic* [Bloomington: Indiana University Press, 1991], p. 7).

68. John Miles Foley and Justin Arft, "The Epic Cycle and Oral Tradition," in *The Greek Epic Cycle and its Ancient Reception* (ed. Fantuzzi and Tsagalis), p. 78.

69. I discuss this in Tobolowsky, "On Comparison with Ancient Greek Traditions," pp. 6-10.

70. Martin Noth, *The History of Israel* (New York: Harper & Row, 2nd edn, 1960), p. 88.

71. Strabo describes the seven-member Kalaurian amphictyony (Strabo 8.374).

72. C.H.J. de Geus notes that the amphictyony hypothesis "dominate[d]" visions of early Israel for a period of thirty years, starting with the publication of 1930's *Das System* (C.H.J. De Geus, *The Tribes of Israel* [Studia Semitica Neerlandica, 18; Assen: Van Gorcum, 1976], p. 40). For Noth's eventual critics, see Harry M. Orlinsky, "The Tribal System of Israel and Related Groups in the Period of the Judges," in *Studies and Essays in Honor of Abraham A. Newman* (ed. Meir Ben-Horin, Bernard D. Weinryb, and Sol Zeitlin; Leiden: E.J. Brill, 1962), pp. 375-88; Bruce Donald Rahtjen, "Philistine and Hebrew Amphictyonies," *JNES* 24.1/2 (1965), pp. 100-104; Niels Peter Lemche, "The Greek 'Amphictyony'—Could It Be a Prototype for the Israelite Society in the Period of the Judges?," *JSOT* 2.4 (1977), pp. 48-59; Frank Crüsemann, *Der Widerstand gegen das Königtum: Die antiköniglichen Texte des Alten Testamentes und der Kampf um den frühen israelitischen Staat* (Neukirchen-Vluyn: Neukirchener Verlag, 1978).

73. Albright, *Archaeology and the Religion of Israel*, p. 102.

Finally, where Albright himself was concerned, a similarly simple set of refutations would emerge in the mid-1970s, especially in the work of John Van Seters and Thomas L. Thompson.[74] Albright and the Albrightians had built their case primarily on the same kind of correspondences that so occupied Nilsson. Like Nilsson, they drew attention to the fact that many of the cities mentioned in Genesis actually were important in the second millennium period in which the patriarchs would have to have lived, and, in addition, the presence of many familiar personal names at places like Mari suggested to them the basic accuracy of biblical memory. The problem, as Thompson and Van Seters would point out in nearly contemporaneous studies, is that correspondences at least as strong as those the Albrightians regarded as decisive existed in first-millennium materials as well, which is to say, the era when biblical texts were actually being written.[75]

So, for example, it is true that patriarchal-type names appear at Mari, a Semitic settlement on the upper Euphrates, with records from the eighteenth century BCE. But, as Van Seters and Thompson both pointed out, it is also true that these names *remained* popular into much later periods, including the main eras of biblical composition.[76] It is true that Ur and Harran, the Mesopotamian sites connected to Abraham in Genesis, were important enough in the early second millennium BCE. But they were at least as important, if not more so, in the middle first millennium. In fact, the famous "Ur of the Chaldeans" from which Abraham sets out is a name that assumes the *presence* of the people called Chaldeans, a group that would not arrive in the region until the first millennium, gaining prominence through the "Chaldean dynasty" of Babylon in the late seventh and sixth centuries BCE.[77] As for Harran, it was an important site in the last days of the Neo-Assyrian Empire, in the late seventh century BCE. And it would also be received in the mid-sixth century, during the reign of the last Chaldean king, Nabonidus, who was born there.[78]

74. Thomas L. Thompson, *The Historicity of the Patriarchal Narratives: The Quest for the Historical Abraham* (Berlin: de Gruyter, 1974); Van Seters, *Abraham in History and Tradition*.

75. Thompson, *The Historicity of the Patriarchal Narratives*; Van Seters, *Abraham in History and Tradition*.

76. Thompson observes that "names directly parallel or identical to ... Abram are found from the second half of the Second Millennium until long after the Genesis traditions had been formed," and "Jacob is one of the most common West Semitic names used in the ancient Near East and it is found in the records of almost every century from the Old Babylonian period ... to early post-Christian times" (Thompson, *The Historicity of the Patriarchal Narratives*, pp. 317-18).

77. Van Seters, *Abraham in History and Tradition*, p. 23.

78. Amélie Kuhrt, *The Ancient Near East c. 3000–330 BC*, vol. 2 of *Routledge History of the Ancient World* (London: Routledge, 2003), pp. 545, 600.

In addition, we could raise a quibble, which perhaps has not been sufficiently raised even now, with a hallmark of Albrightian scholarship that I
tend to think of as "piecemeal proofs." In a nutshell, what we find in these
studies is a tremendous willingness to see the reflection of biblical episodes in the experiences of virtually *any* Semitic group in the entire region,
and over more or less the entire second millennium BCE. In other words, a
typical Albrightian case can refer, at once, to supposed correspondences
between biblical episodes and an Amorite migration in the nineteenth century, the onomasticon of Mari in the eighteenth century, the prominence
of the Hyksos in Egypt in the seventeenth and sixteenth centuries, the
experiences of the Semites who remained in Egypt *after* the expulsion of
the Hyksos in the fifteenth and fourteenth centuries, the religion of the
Midianites, and the history of the mysterious 'Apiru besides.[79] The idea
that all of these different groups could somehow represent the ancestors of
the Israelites *simultaneously*, or peoples who were encountered by them, is
seldom even justified in this scholarship beyond references to the idea that
Israel took shape as a mixed multitude.

At any rate, the end result of these and other inquiries is that scholarship
in both disciplines entered the 1980s and '90s in a much more skeptical
place than it began in the second half of the century. Serious questions had
once more been raised about the accuracy of any of these traditions, and
about their true antiquity. The question we could ask, however, is simple:
what did these reassessments do, and what *didn't* they do? Though they did
challenge the empirical claims made by earlier scholarship, they did not
often address the spirit that motivated them. And again, my view is that this
has significant consequences for the study of these traditions even today.

Toward a New Model

As we zero in on the question of how a combined approach can point the
way to a more sophisticated understanding of the relationship between
traditions and pasts, we can consider again the idea of a wrong turn: that
early twentieth-century scholarship was on some level *more* off-base than
it had to be, that it is not, therefore, analytically useful to explain its major
features merely as a reflection of the norms of the era in which it was

79. So, the excavations at Mari "strikingly confirmed the Israelite traditions
according to which the Hebrew forefathers came to Palestine from the region of
Harran," *while* the entry and exit of the Hyksos from Egypt had an "obvious relation"
to the biblical account of Joseph's life—and *while* "the 'king who knew not Joseph'
and who oppressed the Israelites should be a pharaoh of the New Empire, after the
expulsion of the hated Asiatics from Egypt," even though that meant the Israelites were
at once the Semitic people who entered and conquered Egypt *and* the ones left behind
when they were repulsed (Albright, *From the Stone Age*, pp. 180, 150, 184).

conducted.[80] And I think the easiest way to make this case is simply to point out that it is actually odd that some of these arguments were not only made, but succeeded for decades, even given what was knowable at the time. Why *should* Noth, for example, have been able to claim that Israel formed as an amphictyonic organization because of the correspondences between twelve-tribe Israel and the Delphic amphictyony when all anyone had to do was look at Strabo or other easily accessible sources to see that the number "twelve" did not have the significance Noth attributed to it? And why, since the claim was so easily refuted, was it essentially dominant for at least three decades?[81]

Likewise, in the face of the Albrightian claim that the true antiquity of Genesis was attested to by the correspondences between the text and early second-millennium realities, it might well have seemed *obvious* to investigate whether that was unique to the era in question, which did not happen until the seventies. It might well have seemed obvious to Lord *et al.* to investigate more deeply whether all oral poets compose like either the South Slavic or hypothetical ancient Greek bards before describing the theory as more or less universally applicable. Why did it take until the 1990s before Rosalind Thomas successfully made the point that there are formulaic expressions even in poetry that was originally composed in writing, *and* oral poetry without formulae?[82] Why shouldn't that have been one of the first questions asked?

Meanwhile, I have already mentioned the fact that folklore scholars knew as early as the late 1910s that "the older ideal of a folk community preserving its traditions faithfully over the centuries could no longer be substantiated," even as Noth *et al.* reproduced precisely this model of the history of the pentateuchal narrative, ostensibly under the influence *of* folklore scholarship.[83] I have pointed out that Nilsson already knew what Noth did not: that societies do not compose traditions collectively. And I was particularly struck, in researching this chapter, by the fact that Ruth Finnegan, in her path-breaking and too-long-ignored study of oral traditions in Africa, could already quote at length from a 1913 study by Henri-Alexandre Junod, who was aware that the perceived "antiquity" of traditional tales among the Thonga is only

80. Though, I suspect this argument will land the same way that other attempts to diminish the power of the idea that past individuals were simply products of their time have. It will, in other words, be sympathetic to some readers and not others.

81. I discuss this issue in greater detail in Tobolowsky, "On Comparison with Ancient Greek Traditions," pp. 7-10.

82. Rosalind Thomas, *Literacy and Orality in Ancient Greece* (Cambridge, UK: Cambridge University Press, 1995), pp. 42-43.

83. Kirkpatrick, *The Old Testament and Folklore Study*, p. 45; Lowie, "Oral Tradition and History"; Bartlett, "Some Experiments on the Reproduction of Folk Stories."

relative; that is to say they are constantly transformed by their narrators and their transformations go much further than is generally supposed, further even than the Natives themselves are aware of. ... It would be a great error to think that, writing a story at the dictation of a Native, we possess the recognized standard form of the tale. There is no standard at all! ... *New Elements* are also introduced ... the *contents of the stories themselves* are changed by oral transmission, this giving birth to numerous versions of a tale, often very different ... sometimes hardly recognizable.[84]

For that matter, Parry's *guslars* never told the same story twice either.[85] Rather, when he asked them, they often insisted they were telling the traditional story just as it was, but the record revealed something different.[86] And this is a crucial point Rosalind Thomas would make much later: that the fervent belief that tradition and memory function totally differently in oral societies than in more literate ones, even among many scholars, is to some extent an illusion *produced* by orality. Or, as Thomas herself put it, "a shallow, unchanging past can be the effect of the oral tradition, not a fundamental characteristic of oral societies."[87] When we can check, however, the evidence is clear, "orally transmitted accounts are inevitably unstable"; and so the correct conclusions could also have been clear very early in the century.[88] Parry knew it, if he admitted it; Junod knew it well before. As a result, it is the case that nothing about the evidence available at the time stopped early twentieth-century scholars from following where their own,

84. Henri Alexandre Junod, *The Life of a South African Tribe, 2* (2 vols.; Neuchâtel: Attinger, 1913), pp. 198-200; Finnegan, *Oral Literature in Africa*, pp. 8-9.

85. Robert Kanigel, *Hearing Homer's Song: The Brief Life and Big Idea of Milman Parry* (New York: Knopf Doubleday, 2021), pp. 179-80.

86. A recent biography describes an early effort to record the work of the *guslar* Nikola Vujnović. By chance, Nikola started the story "Marko and Musa," but stopped in the middle, only to let Parry write down the rest later that evening. "Sometime later, Parry asked Nikola to again sing 'Marko and Musa,'" which he told very differently—so much so that a Russian companion tasked with keeping track of variations "was swamped. Even Nikola was surprised by the many discrepancies" (Kanigel, *Hearing Homer's Song*, pp. 176-77).

87. Basically, we can think that oral cultures zealously safeguarded their original traditions because this is what oral practitioners claim, and we *cannot check their compositions against earlier ones* the way we can when stories are written down. "It has sometimes been thought, for instance, that primitive cultures (which would lack writing) do not change. But this image of oral culture as totally static, often undermined by archaeological excavations, has surely been fostered by the fact that no written evidence has survived from the past to contrast with the present. The slow, subtle changes in customs and habits are the last things such societies would try to remember in their oral traditions" (Thomas, *Literacy and Orality in Ancient Greece*, p. 7).

88. Mait Koiv, *Ancient Tradition and Early Greek History: The Origins of States in Early Archaic Sparta, Argos and Corinth* (Tallinn: Avita, 2003), p. 14.

more skeptical, scholarly forebears had already begun to lead rather than reversing this progress to re-found Romantic models.

Certainly, in surveying the landscape of the early to mid-twentieth century we see a great many examples of the strong tendency to attempt to find a way back by new means—so strong, in fact, as to transform any newly available evidence *so that it looked like* corroborating evidence. And the exercise of this tendency certainly includes more recent arguments, like Frank Moore Cross's that the Pentateuch was based on an Israelite epic that was perfectly analogous to a Homeric epic.[89]

After all, it should have been very hard to make this argument, especially by the time Cross made it. The Homeric poems are, well, epic poems, and, in addition, are concerned with the deeds of legendary heroes at one specific legendary time and place, just one small part of the Trojan War, just Odysseus's journey home. The Pentateuch is a prose narrative concerned with very different protagonists, stylistically speaking, over quite a long span of time, offering an account of how a family grew into a great nation over centuries and approached the land of its destiny. But what Cross's view was shaped by, presumably quite unconsciously, was the fact that the analogy would allow him to rescue the idea that the Pentateuch was "the traditional narrative cycle of an age conceived as 'normative,' the events of which give meaning, self-understanding to a people or a nation," and "a 'national' composition."[90] This is what he imagined epics to be on a definitional level, also incorrectly.[91] So it was appealing to him as a possibility, and it was appealing to others. The power of that appeal reshaped the evidence until it seemed to be what it was useful for it to be. There are many even more recent examples.

89. This idea itself has a longer history, which is laid out in Charles Conroy, "Hebrew Epic: Historical Notes and Critical Reflections," *Bib* 61.1 (1980), pp. 1-30. And I discuss it at greater length in Tobolowsky, "On Comparison with Ancient Greek Traditions," pp. 10-20. I also discuss this aspect of Cross's program, and its similarities with Gunkel's acts of rescue, in Tobolowsky, "The Hebrew Bible as Mythic 'Vocabulary.'"

90. Frank Moore Cross, "The Epic Traditions of Early Israel," in *The Poet and the Historian* (ed. Richard E. Friedman; Chico, CA: Scholars Press, 1983), pp. 18-19. As Van Seters observes, "The reason for proposing the scheme of an original poetic epic behind the sources of the Pentateuch is to argue for the great antiquity of its 'history' through a long stage of oral tradition. But the scheme proposed by Albright"—who originated, but later moved away from the idea—"on the supposed Greek model cannot be demonstrated from the Greek sources or from the Old Testament" (John Van Seters, *In Search of History: Historiography in the Ancient World and the Origins of Biblical History* [New Haven, CT: Yale University Press, 1983], p. 30). See the discussion in Tobolowsky, "On Comparison with Ancient Greek Traditions," pp. 15-20.

91. In other words, Homer, too, and certainly any oral traditions Homer's poems are based on, are neither *the* traditional narrative cycle of an age nor a "national" composition in the sense of being a representation of collective memory.

Here, however, the question of why this desire to return exists is second-ary to *how* it continues to exist, and, as in the first chapter, I am offering an argument based on the failure to confront not claims, which is to say empirical claims about the age and reliability of the traditions in question, but assumptions, imaginations, paradigms. We might put it this way: both nineteenth- and twentieth-century inquiries into the history behind tradi-tions were motivated, to some extent, by "historicism" itself, a complicated term, and more complicated all the time, but one that boils down to a desire to describe the past "as it really was."[92] And this is because it is considered valuable to describe the past as it really was because the history of peoples, events, and institutions is supposed to explain those peoples, events, and institutions. Indeed, much of the first two chapters of this book actually offers an exercise in historicism, attempting to explain the existence of a set of scholarly problems to solve by describing their roots and how they became embedded in these disciplines.

One of the issues I will discuss below is that both the feasibility and value of historicist investigations, at least where efforts to *write* history are concerned, have quite reasonably been called into question in recent decades. I will begin, however, with a different point. The early- to mid-twentieth-century arguments discussed above successfully presented themselves as historicist in character, and, indeed, more successfully than their predecessors in certain ways because their mode was different. As I said at the beginning, the pretense that the use of what I am calling "proof" in arguments makes those arguments objective has done quite a lot of work on their behalf. There is of course something to this, and something to the claim that in combining archaeological, epigraphic, and anthropologi-cal inquiries with textual inquiries, these early twentieth-century schol-ars were *actually* doing better work than their predecessors, who had to content themselves with tools like the "generic method," discussed in the previous chapter, for want of better ways to assess the relationship between text and reality. There is simply *also* an element that I have referred to as *transformation*: that these arguments, by being couched in the language

---

92. See, e.g., Georg G. Iggers, "Historicism: The History and Meaning of the Term," *Journal of the History of Ideas* 56.1 (1995), pp. 129-52; Ethan Kleinberg, "Deconstructing Historicist Time, or Time's Scribe," *History and Theory* 62.4 (2023), pp. 1-18. Iggers traces the term back to Schlegel and Novalis in addition to the usual figures—Leopold von Ranke in particular. Von Ranke's conviction of the "necessity of proceeding from a critical reconstruction of the past" emerged from his belief that, through such a reconstruction, "the great forces which shaped history would become apparent" (Iggers, "Historicism," p. 131). Kleinberg is eloquent on the subject of what has brought historicism into less repute in recent years—especially that it makes "time, not the historian ... the basis for historical explanation" (Kleinberg, "Deconstructing Historicist Time," p. 3).

of empirical inquiry, transformed the appearance of inherited, essentially Romantic assumptions about where traditions come from, and how they are handed down, into apparently empirical propositions themselves.

Thus, the problem for us is that the critiques of the mid- to late-twentieth century were *also* mainly historicist in character. This may or may not be a problem in and of itself, for reasons I will discuss below. But it was problematic to the extent that these were intended to serve as an antidote to the flaws of earlier inquiries. Briefly, these studies did a much better job in assessing what the available evidence really suggested about the historicity of surviving traditions, what had "really happened," and the likely antiquity of the narratives in question, given the instability of narratives over time. But in interacting with these early arguments primarily *by* reassessing their empirical claims, subsequent challenges actually left their other, more Romantic claims intact. At least, they left the possibility that those claims could still be validated, one way or another, or even that they could still be viewed as a natural outcome of proving that the tradition corresponded to the evidence. As we will see, this would continue to be a pattern throughout the century: increasing skepticism about what proof can prove, and not enough attention to the question of what it would mean even if it did. And so, later scholarship in both disciplines would consistently land in ever more reasonable places with respect to what available extraliterary proofs *do* prove but often without seriously investigating what it *could* prove, even in the most extreme cases.

Thus, it is interesting to consider for a moment what the progress of scholarship might have looked like if the fluidity and instability of oral traditions were embraced in early periods *as they well could have been* instead of the Parry-Lord model of general stability in the study of ancient traditions. It is interesting to consider how they would have gone differently if the discontinuities espied by the likes of Finley, Van Seters, Thompson, and others were as visible in the early twentieth century as they would become later on. What if it had been Finley, rather than Nilsson, who set the tone for assessing the nature of the correspondences between the *Iliad* and the material record of Mycenae? And so on.

The more important point, however, is that the authors of these critical studies often did not notice, or at least often discuss, the stakes of the question of how well texts preserve early realities or early traditions, only whether or not they actually did. And so, even as scholars grew more skeptical about the accuracy of biblical and Greek depictions of early events, it still seemed possible late into the twentieth century that if you *could* prove a surviving text preserved an early reality or even just an early tradition you could therefore prove that it was the kind of tradition that nineteenth-century scholars had imagined stood on the other side of the Great Divide, even though it should already have seemed impossible to believe as much.

Thus, the tendency to arrive at more conservative conclusions about what traditions preserve and reflect than a neutral reading of the evidence allows remained strong into very recent times.

Therefore, as we turn our attention to the central question of the chapter, the question of what a combined approach can tell us about what should happen next that might be less obvious in either discipline alone, we arrive at a moment of reckoning with the two questions I have been gesturing at throughout. There is still the question of what the last twenty years of inquiry have suggested about "what does proof prove," which is to say, what today, after still more reassessments, seems most likely to be true about the relationship between traditions about great events like the Trojan War, the era of the patriarchs, the exodus, and so on and historical reality? Yet we also have to discuss the question that has only recently begun to be broached consistently: What *can* proof prove? What *would* demonstrating the existence of even a substantial set of correspondences between ancient texts and early realities or early traditions seem to mean today, if we successfully divorce ourselves from inaccurate assumptions about early traditions? What would it tell us about these texts; what would it tell us about early realities; what do we achieve when we prove that the material record, or the tradition historical record or anthropological inquiries, has resonances with what a text describes? And this is where a combined approach has the most light to shed.

What Does Proof Prove?

One thing we can say with some certainty is that, exceptions aside, prospects indeed seem quite dim for establishing any kind of robust correspondence between ancient Greek traditions about early Greece generally and historical reality, and for the Hebrew Bible, the same, even up to at least the period of the United Monarchy.[93] Where the latter is concerned, we are the heirs, here, of the so-called minimalist–maximalist debate of the 1990s. This was a dramatic reassessment of the historicity of biblical traditions construed in terms of the question of how the Hebrew Bible is best used as a source when writing scholarly histories. In other words, should scholars rely on it "maximally" whenever there is no good reason to think a story *isn't* true? Or "minimally," only when scholars have good reason, from extrabiblical sources, to believe that a story *is* true.[94] The

93. In the latter case, I discuss the development of historiographical techniques and opinions in Andrew Tobolowsky, "Israelite and Judahite History in Contemporary Theoretical Approaches," *CBR* 17.1 (2018), pp. 33-58.

94. Prominent scholars regarded as minimalists include Philip R. Davies, Niels Peter Lemche, Thomas L. Thompson and Keith Whitelam. Occasional "maximalist" histories continue to appear, too, e.g., Iain Provan, V. Philips Long and Tremper Long-

minimalists were generally regarded as quite radical at the time, and in some ways they were, or, at any rate, some were and are; and far from all histories of Israel have arrived at the same pitch of historicist skepticism even today. But they also made a critical mass of scholars finally acknowledge how little evidence there is for so many of the great events of the Hebrew Bible's narrative, from at least Genesis into the books of Judges, and virtually all contemporary histories of Israel are indeed different as a result.

This is not to say that there are no arguments out there today that are maximalist, we might say, even to the point of absurdity. As I write this, for example, a controversy has erupted over a "curse tablet" supposedly found on Mt. Ebal from the twelfth or even thirteenth century BCE, which is all of forty letters.[95] Every aspect of the interpretation of this find seems dubious in the extreme, including its supposed date and translation. But the more important point is that one of the arguments being made on its behalf, an argument that was actually once fairly common, is ridiculous anyway, no matter what is true about the tablet itself: that since it is supposed to have a few literary flourishes, it proves there was enough literary ability in the time period in which it was supposedly written to compose other biblical texts, which is supposed to mean, all by itself, that other biblical texts, even the whole Hebrew Bible, *was* written in that period, and is therefore very early and very accurate.

Other arguments in the same vein, if more sympathetic, continue to be made about figures like David, too, who may well have existed, but whose mighty United Monarchy seems like a fantasy, at least *where* its might is concerned. We can consider, as an example, the idea that activity at a copperworks at Khirbet en-Naḥas might prove the accuracy of the biblical account of a Davidic empire of sorts.[96] Both the appeal and the problem of this evidence is that Khirbet en-Naḥas is in what would later be biblical

man III, *A Biblical History of Israel* (Louisville, KY: Westminster John Knox, 2003). See the discussion in Tobolowsky, "Israelite and Judahite History in Contemporary Theoretical Approaches," pp. 34-36.

95. See the discussion in Nathan Steinmeyer, "An Early Israelite Curse Inscription from Mt. Ebal?," *Biblical Archaeology Society*, 25 April 2022, https://www.biblical archaeology.org/daily/biblical-artifacts/inscriptions/mt_ebal_inscription/.

96. See Thomas E. Levy *et al.*, "Lowland Edom and the High and Low Chronologies," in *The Bible and Radiocarbon Dating: Archaeology, Text and Science* (ed. Thomas E. Levy and Thomas Higham; Oxfordshire: Routledge, 2005), pp. 129-63; Thomas E. Levy and Mohammad Najjar, "Some Thoughts on Khirbet En-Naḥas, Edom, Biblical History and Anthropology—A Response to Israel Finkelstein," *Tel Aviv* 33.1 (2006), pp. 3-17; Neil G. Smith and Thomas E. Levy, "The Iron Age Pottery from Khirbat En-Nahas, Jordan: A Preliminary Study," *Bulletin of the American Schools of Oriental Research* 352 (2008), pp. 41-91.

Edom, not Israel, and nothing at the site remotely ties it to Israel, except the biblical claim that the United Monarchy was supposed to have conquered Edom (2 Sam. 8.14). Thus, the scholars who make this case must make a circular argument: that since *if* a big United Monarchy existed, it would make sense for it to have operated this installation, *therefore* the installation is proof of such a United Monarchy.[97]

Even so, as a general rule, both the nature and results of historicist inquiries have changed dramatically over the last few decades. They have certainly moved ever further from using ancient texts as uncomplicated sources for the reconstruction of real events in the context of scholarly attempts at historiography. We might say that the common *range* of opinions has shrunk considerably. As we have seen, arguments about the historicity of something like the exodus were once conducted between those who believed that it had really happened or that only something *like* it had happened. But now, for the most part, the poles of the debate are those who still argue that some enslaved Semites escaped Egypt and came to Canaan in the era of early Israel where, joining this community, their story was transformed into part of the familiar all-Israel epic, and those who consider it pure fiction.[98]

Similarly, someone who wanted to point to the historical existence of a King David, who is not mentioned in any record contemporaneous with his likely reign, could still refer to epigraphic evidence such as the Tel Dan Stele and, perhaps, the Mesha stele. The former is an Aramean stele that seems clearly to refer to Judah as the "house of David," from perhaps the mid-ninth century, a century or so after David is supposed to have lived.[99] The second is a Moabite inscription that may well do the same.[100] If outsiders thought David had founded the Judahite kingdom not so long after he would have to have done so, it seems reasonable evidence that he actually did, without telling us anything about how powerful it was or much else about his real career.[101] And this is, broadly, where the majority of scholars

---

97. Tobolowsky, *The Sons of Jacob and the Sons of Herakles*, p. 26.

98. See the discussion in Megan Bishop Moore and Brad E. Kelle, *Biblical History and Israel's Past* (Grand Rapids, MI: Eerdmans, 2011), pp. 83-95.

99. See, e.g., Avraham Biran and Joseph Naveh, "The Tel Dan Inscription: A New Fragment," *IEJ* 45.1 (1995), pp. 1-18.

100. André Lemaire, "The Mesha Stele and the Omri Dynasty," in *Ahab Agonistes: The Rise and Fall of the Omri Dynasty* (ed. Lester L. Grabbe; LHB/OTS; London: T. & T. Clark, 2007), pp. 135-44.

101. See, e.g., the various essays in Amihai Mazar and Israel Finkelstein, *The Quest for the Historical Israel: Debating Archaeology and the History of Israel* (ed. Brian B. Schmidt; Atlanta, GA: Society of Biblical Literature, 2007). These contain essays from two prominent archaeologists known for disagreeing with each other, but in evidence-based ways, organized into a survey covering the whole scope of early Israelite history.

differ, but not a great deal. That is, I think most still believe that he was a real person and king; but the skeptical pole is that he was quite a local leader, and the less skeptical pole is that he ruled some form of United Monarchy that was nevertheless much smaller and less powerful than the one the text depicts.

A similar dynamic, and history of development, is reflected in what has sometimes been called the "New Battle of Troy." Basically, the debate over the historicity of the *Iliad*, or at least of a Trojan War, was reinvigorated in 2011 by an exhibit of Trojan artifacts touring museums in Germany.[102] This exhibit, which largely reflected the views of the German scholar Manfred Korfmann, described Late Bronze Age Troy as a mighty city and a worthy opponent of Mycenae.[103] In response, some scholars, such as Joachim Latacz, latched on to Korfmann's archaeological reconstruction to make the argument that we should indeed, as Jonas Grethlein put it, "take the epic poem at face value, that is, to read it as a source for an actual war."[104] Others, such as Frank Kolb, thought there was very little to the Trojan City in that era, and, consequently, that the Homeric poems were largely fantasy.[105]

Broadly speaking, scholars today seem to lean far more to Kolb's side than Latacz's, but here, too, the typical range has gotten much smaller. The chief evidence for the historicity of the event, whatever one makes of the nature of Mycenaean reflections in the poems, is references in what are sometimes called the Ahhiyawa Letters to past unpleasantness between "Wilusa," ancient Troy, and "Ahhiyawa," likely the Achaeans of Homer's poems.[106] Few scholars imagine these alone could mean that there were certainly mighty coalitions of Greeks and Trojans facing off against each other, but they vary on the question of just *what* it means for the historicity of the story in the *Iliad*. In short, once again, most scholars differ on whether the relevant stories are loosely based on a real event or not based on one at all, with a few major exceptions in each.

102. Christian Baier, "Homer's Cultural Children," *History and Memory* 29.2 (2017), p. 49. See, e.g., Dieter Hertel and Frank Kolb, "Troy in Clearer Perspective," *Anatolian Studies* 53 (2003), p. 71.

103. Baier, "Homer's Cultural Children," 49.

104. Grethlein, "From 'Imperishable Glory' to History," p. 124. See, among others, Joachim Latacz, *Troy and Homer: Towards a Solution of an Old Mystery* (trans. Kevin Windle and Rosh Ireland; Oxford: Oxford University Press, 2004).

105. Baier, "Homer's Cultural Children," pp. 49-50.

106. See generally Gary Beckman, Trevor Bryce, and Eric H. Cline, *The Ahhiyawa Texts* (Leiden: E.J. Brill, 2012). In their view, "this discussion is more than merely an academic one because the texts, at least indirectly, may shed light on various aspects of the Trojan War, or at least on the kernels of truth that seem to underlie the story as told to us by Homer" (Beckman, Bryce, and Cline, *The Ahhiyawa Texts*, p. 1).

Yet we now indeed face new questions. These certainly include how practical, or useful, it is to write traditional historiographies in the first place, how well any such history represents the typical experience of ancient realities, and especially how well the premise of objective, proof-based inquiry actually stands up when we consider all the subjectivities inherent in choosing what to use and how to interpret it. But the more central concern is whether it is useful and meaningful to describe any of the traditions considered here *as* a representation of a real event, even if we think they do represent them to some extent; and it increasingly seems the answer is no.

What Can Proof Prove? Part Two

When it comes even to the writing of historiographical accounts of the ancient world, or attempting to demonstrate the true antiquity of surviving traditions, there are a number of new practical issues to consider in the use of what I have called "proof." First and foremost, we can no longer consider the use of such proofs as objective and scientific in the way that was common throughout much of the twentieth century, and especially not as an objective *alternative* to mere literary musings. Consider, for example, the "New Battle of Troy." The argument that something like the Trojan War had happened after all was presented as the neutral, obvious outcome of new archaeological discoveries, but it is typical of these kinds of reassessments that the nature of the discovery would hardly seem to suggest anything like the conclusions built on top of it without subjective interpretation.

In this case, as we saw above, the key fact seems to be that new finds and interpretations supposedly reveal the wealth and might of Wilusa in the relevant era. Obviously, even if we agreed that this was proven beyond all doubt, we would not necessarily agree that it proved *as well* that this meant the Achaeans had fought a mighty Troy. Indeed, if we chose to emphasize some other aspect of the evidence—"the insignificant number of arrow heads recovered from the site," for example—we could wonder whether this mighty Troy was ever even captured.[107] If we decide it was, it is still true, as Finley knew decades ago, "there is still no evidence that the attackers were Greeks."[108] As for the Ahhiyawa Letters, "Latacz adopts the thesis that Wilusa, Taruisa, and Ahhiyawa, mentioned in Hittite documents, are identical with Ilios, Troy, and Achaeans. ... Even if we agree ... all we are left with is that the Hittites had contact with Troy and that Achaeans had some influence in the area."[109] The enterprise of deciding what to make of the combination of archaeological proofs of a mighty Troy with more sug-

107. Grethlein, "From 'Imperishable Glory' to History," p. 125.
108. Grethlein, "From 'Imperishable Glory' to History," p. 125.
109. Grethlein, "From 'Imperishable Glory' to History," p. 125.

gestive proofs that *something* happened between Mycenae and Troy is still subjective in its essence, even if predicated on objective evidence.

In other words, as Grethlein points out, the supposedly "'objective data' presented by Korfmann and Latacz turn out to be the outcome of a specific interpretation."[110] Someone else looking at the exact same evidence could easily come to a different conclusion. And what this makes visible is another stumbling block in the way of traditional approaches to writing historiography: the fact that the *veneer* of scientific and empirical proof can actually be used, consciously or unconsciously, to costume the role of interpretation in revealing what the evidence proves.[111] In other words, the idea that if an argument uses archaeology and epigraphy it is therefore objective can really give a boost to arguments that, in fact, rely on very subjective interpretations indeed. And this was certainly as true for Albright *et al.* as it is today. Similarly, and especially in the study of the Hebrew Bible, the sheer paucity of evidence means that marshalling the material evidence can sometimes tell us a lot less than we think. Barstad, for one, refers to "the arbitrariness" of what we find and do not find. "The amount of work done on textual discoveries like those of e.g., Kuntillet Ajrud or Tel Dan may not at all be in proportion to the relative historical value or the representativeness of those texts."[112]

In addition to issues of this sort, we now also have to grapple with decades worth of challenges to the usefulness and feasibility of the enterprise of representing the past "as it really was" in a more general sense. Here, one of the more striking (and telling) things about episodes like the minimalist–maximalist debate is actually how late they happened. This was, as Megan Bishop Moore has observed, quite a modernist argument decades after postmodernism had at least reshaped how conversations about historiography proceeded in a great many other fields.[113] In other words, the minimal-

110. Grethlein, "From 'Imperishable Glory' to History," p. 125.
111. "Korfmann and Latacz, however, insist on the objectivity of archaeological data while at the same time promoting a rather slanted interpretation. ... The thesis that Troy was a major trading port not only rests on shaky ground but it also runs the risk of falsely projecting modern notions of trade onto an archaic system based on the exchange of goods. ... Moreover, the archaeological evidence does not necessarily indicate that Troy VII was destroyed by a single attack" (Grethlein, "From 'Imperishable Glory' to History," pp. 124-25 [124])
112. Barstad, *History and the Hebrew Bible*, p. 12.
113. Moore notes that "antirepesentationalists argue that the conventions of representation, particularly language, interfere with one's ability to know or express anything about an object such as the past," and that contemporary historiographers tend to seek "a middle ground. ... Holding on to the idea that representation is possible, they use insights from antirepresentationalism to mediate potentially oversimplistic notions of representation" (Moore, *Philosophy and Practice in Writing a History of Ancient Israel*, p. 12). Moore's treatment of this topic is overall excellent. Note Barstad's addi-

ists and maximalists shared a goal: they wanted to write the best possible traditional historiographies, and they disagreed on how useful the Hebrew Bible could be toward that end.[114] But since at least the sixties and seventies, there have been those who have wondered both whether a representation of the great events of national history meaningfully reflects how many people in that nation understood their own past—if a farmer's life does not change much during the Assyrian conquest, is it really a great event in their sense of history, for example—and whether past events fit as neatly into cause-and-effect-style narrative accounts, as we have long believed.[115]

Thus, Barstad for one has argued that the problem with the supposed radicalism of the original minimalists and historiographical skeptics since is that "their very concept of history ... is wrong."[116] He begins by acknowledging that we seem to have an addiction to the question of "what really happened" that we are not going to shake no matter what theoretical advances have to say about its importance.[117] A lot of the anxiety about whether we can prove the accuracy of aspects of surviving traditions surely comes from there. But, drawing on the work of Hayden White among others, he notes that the Hebrew Bible's narratives, as of course the Homeric poems as well, are "literary, not 'historical' texts," which is to say they are not modern historiographical inquiries; they are stories about the past.[118] And while their authors might well have believed they were *true* stories about the past, to them, "there is no difference between the 'historicity' of, for instance, the Primeval story"—Adam and Eve and so on—"and of other stories in the Hebrew Bible." Thus, "the process of cutting out bits and pieces of these stories in order to evaluate these as 'true' or 'not true' ... is not only very unfair to the integrity of ancient texts, but also highly

tional comment that self-references to "paradigm shift" by certain more skeptical scholars may reveal a lack of awareness "that what we may call a conventional concept of history today is highly problematic, still working within the parameters of historical-critical research, assuming that history is a science and that one must work with the 'hard' facts" (Barstad, *History and the Hebrew Bible*, p. 12).

114. A colleague, Daniel Pioske, points out that one of the underappreciated side effects of this debate is that few non-archaeologists even attempt to write histories of ancient Israel anymore.

115. A classic early treatment of this set of concerns can be found in Louis O. Mink, "Narrative Form as a Cognitive Instrument," in *Historical Understanding* (ed. Brian Fay, Eugene O. Golob, and Richard T. Vann; Ithaca, NY: Cornell University Press, 1987), pp. 182-203.

116. Barstad, *History and the Hebrew Bible*, p. 8.

117. Or, as he puts it, we have imbibed "a tendency to classify all written material in categories of true = historical, and not true = fictional" and "no 'post-modernist' thinker can stop this" (Barstad, *History and the Hebrew Bible*, p. 15).

118. Barstad, *History and the Hebrew Bible*, p. 20.

anachronistic."[119] In other words, even if we, today, can prove a story is true or partially true, that does virtually nothing to explain its ancient impor- tance—among people who embraced stories that are clearly are not true in just the same way.

Thus, Barstad concludes (correctly in my view) that efforts to employ biblical traditions, and in my opinion also ancient Greek traditions, as sources for the reconstruction of ancient realities results in efforts that have a very hard time being anything other than "various forms of a retelling of the biblical stories [or classical stories], diluted with sparse, desultory, ana- lytical remarks, not seldom with disparate references to archaeology."[120] In other words, scholars go through the narratives, labeling diverse episodes true, not true, mostly true, or partially true, and use primarily this to cre- ate historiography. My sense is that I attribute more value to the effort to know what really happened as far as possible, and especially to know what really did not happen, which is the topic critiques since the mid-twentieth century have most profoundly influenced discussions of, than Barstad and certain others do. But there are serious questions to be asked about what the purpose of offering aspirationally representational histories of ancient Israel in particular is, as something that is not only quite apart from the biblical vision but quite apart from how ancient Israelites and Judahites understood their own past. Writing the "real" history of ancient Israel and Judah would appear to be much more analogous to something like writing a history of Edom, Ammon, or Moab than we have imagined, something we could see intellectual value in, but which nevertheless few seem motivated to perform.

We are not, however, most concerned with the writing of historiograph- ical accounts of ancient Israel and ancient Greece. We are not most con- cerned with *whether* traditions can be sources of historical fact, although the answer seems to be "sometimes, but not reliably, and much less so than we used to imagine." We are interested in what any imaginable rela- tionship to historical events, or to much earlier traditions, means for the study of *traditions* themselves. In other words, what, today, are the stakes of demonstrating even significant correspondences between surviving texts and early historical realities? What are the stakes of demonstrating that they really reflect or preserve much older traditions, through the type of anthropological inquiry that produced oral-formulaic theory or any other approach? Why, in short, does it matter how true a given story is?

Here I remind readers that the point I have been making throughout is that in the nineteenth century, and for much of the twentieth, there seemed to be

119. Barstad, *History and the Hebrew Bible*, p. 8.
120. Barstad, *History and the Hebrew Bible*, p. 9.

clear answers to these questions about stakes *that are no longer clear.* When someone believes that an early tradition is fundamentally different from a later, proving greater antiquity is about identifying which is which. When someone believes that some traditions are the distorted, collective memory of the ethnic nation and some are not, proving that a story is accurate or somewhat accurate also identifies which is which. When someone believes that a specific kind of tradition can survive as the singular charter tradition of that nation for its entire history, when someone has reason to believe that some traditions, and some modes of tradition, can escape the vicissitudes of change over time that are the common lot of stories—because of fantasies about the difference between oral culture and literate cultures, or the ancient world and the modern world—the search for correspondences between text and reality is, ultimately, a search for the *kind of tradition* that has always been privileged, since the very early days of both modern disciplines.

This kind of tradition has gone by different names: terms like *Natur-poesie*, collective memory, or, in more recent years, "genuine," as opposed to "invented" tradition.[121] Indeed, it is worth noting that, even today—a topic I will discuss at greater length later on—"memory" is far too often used "as a simple substitute or synonym for older notions of 'tradition,' 'folklore,' *'Märchen,' 'Heldensagen,'* or *'Geschichts-Legende'* once common to biblical historians."[122] But outside the realm of historiographical inquiry, the importance of these investigations into the roots of surviving stories has historically been inspired by this hunt for distinctions between tradition and tradition. When we do not think these distinctions exist or, at least, are meaningful for understanding the fundamentals of any given story, we have to ask again why they matter at all. In other words, even in a case where we feel that correspondences are significant, should we now think that the events a tradition was once based on are really significant for understanding the version that survives? Do we think the original importance of the event itself is a sufficient explanation for the ongoing importance of the tradition? And so on.

Ultimately, like Barstad, I do not think that ancient peoples actually saw a difference between stories that we think of as mostly true or mostly false, because I do not think they typically knew the difference. A centrally important tradition in a given period was, no doubt, regarded the same way, and believed in just as much whether an outside observer could, with research, determine that it was actually based on real events or not. And

121. A topic, again, introduced in particular in the work of Eric Hobsbawm (Eric Hobsbawm, "Introduction: Inventing Traditions," in *The Invention of Tradition* [ed. Eric Hobsbawm and Terence Ranger; Cambridge, UK: Cambridge University Press, 1983], pp. 1-14).

122. Daniel Pioske, "Retracing a Remembered Past: Methodological Remarks on Memory, History, and the Hebrew Bible," *BibInt* 23.3 (2015), p. 294.

if we dispense with all the flawed explanations for why some traditions would be preserved essentially intact over time while most changed constantly, as inherently inadequate, there is no reason to think that a mostly true tradition and a mostly false tradition have different *lives* from each other after they appear. Both will change in various ways. And, finally, there is no reason to think a story based on a real event has an advantage, over time, compared to one that does not, in terms of its survival and the maintenance of its original importance. In other words, both the "true" story and the invented one survive because they are believed and will survive further only if useful and relevant, and not otherwise, which is to say, even a story that originated in an early formative experience can lose traction if the nation re-forms differently in some later era.[123] And they will be reshaped in the same ways and for the same reasons over time and arrive in a place as different from where they began as each other.

Thus, no matter what the relationship between story and reality is, there is no very good reason to think the early reality or tradition is very responsible for the later version, or that the importance of an early event can explain more than where the basic facts of the tradition originally came from. This relationship cannot explain or predict the form the story will take later on, or, indeed, in an era before scientific historiography existed, aspects of the form it originally took. Instead, all ancient traditions that purport to describe the past are to be regarded as representations of past events that are shaped by the literary form that the representation is executed in, what Ian Douglas Wilson calls the "discursive horizon" in which it emerged, and the purposes to which it is put in a given context.[124]

Barstad offers an example, the biblical account of the building of King Solomon's temple in the books of Kings. If Solomon really built the temple, this story would be based on a real event, and if not, not. But either way, he suggests, the text itself participates in a "Building Genre. ... When the story of a king's building activities was recorded, this genre was always used."[125] Thus, the story, regardless of its basis, is so shaped

---

123. Pioske offers an elegant discussion of "growing discontent with the broad generic designation of 'history' or 'historiography' to categorize those narrative works included within the Hebrew Bible," referring to various studies by Mark S. Smith, Philip Davies, Jens Bruun Kofoed and others (Pioske, "Retracing a Remembered Past," pp. 293-94).

124. Wilson, *Kingship and Memory in Ancient Judah*, p. 10. Malkin describes the typical valence of the term "representation" in recent studies of historiographical theory, referring to Stephen Greenblatt's idea of representations as "engaged," "relational," "local," "historically contingent" and "interdependent" with historical contexts—descriptions of past events gain meaning from how and where they are used (Malkin, *The Returns of Odysseus*, p. 23).

125. Barstad, *History and the Hebrew Bible*, p. 20.

by "literary conventions" that it cannot be used to reconstruct the actual process of building that temple, even if we knew for sure that happened.[126] Other scholars, in other periods, have concerned themselves mainly with the question of whether the biblical tradition is based in historical reality. We need to be the ones to recognize that it is still a literary text even if it does describe something that, on some level, really happened. And, of course, later references to the building of the temple by Solomon have a variety of purposes, especially tying the prestige of the temple to Israel's golden age and most powerful king, which explain the presence and nature of the reference much better than the real event could, even if there was one.

Irad Malkin discusses a similar issue in the study of the tradition known as the "Return of the Herakleidae," which, because it depicts the Herakleid conquerors leading an army of Dorians, has often been regarded as a memory of a real "Dorian invasion." I will discuss the question of the historicity of this event at greater length in a later chapter; but, regardless, Malkin counsels studying its diverse "representations," which is to say, how the story is actually told in different contexts in which it is used: "at one point in terms of continuous validation of the Spartan royal houses," who were supposed to be descended from the Herakleidae; "at another in terms of its impact on and use for legitimating the attempts of the Spartan Dorieus"—a self-identifying Herakleid descendant—"to settle in western Sicily ... at a third in terms of its relationship to the religious festival of the Karneia," and so on.[127] Nothing about the fact that the narrative might, or might not, be based on a real event explains its use in any of these contexts nor predicts what shape it will take to serve any of these roles. And, anyway, regardless of its historicity, it still seems like the most robust claim one could actually make on behalf of the role the event plays in the formation of the story is that the narrative inclusion of a Dorian army was *inspired* by an actual fact. And the most a historiographer could do with this story is discover a historical possibility to investigate further by other means. They could not use any of its details to flesh out what actually happened.

Indeed, points like these are central to Malkin's overall argument, which has been tremendously influential in the study of ancient Greek traditions: that "'historicizing' myths, myths which explain a present situation in historical terms, are often of little use as evidence for events. In and of themselves ... they are 'facts' firmly interwoven into the context of the period in which they are written." In other words, they are "fact[s] of *mentalité*," facts that reveal primarily how their authors imagined the past, even

---

126. Barstad, *History and the Hebrew Bible*, p. 20.
127. Malkin, *The Returns of Odysseus*, p. 22.

if some aspect of that imagination has a kernel of truth.[128] He gives an example: when Tyrtaios, the seventh-century Spartan poet, "proclaimed in Sparta that 'Zeus himself … has given this land to the Herakleidai, with whom we [Dorian Spartans] lefty windy Erineos'" the idea that such a story could be used "as direct evidence for the Dorian invasion would be highly problematic."[129] This is true *even if* it happened. Tyrtaios is describing it because he believes it happened—but, then again, no historian can prove that Zeus gave Sparta to the Herakleidai for obvious reasons. So, the significance of the event for Tyrtaios is beyond the realm of proof altogether.

Likewise, Daniel Pioske observes, in conversation with the work of Mark S. Smith, that "significant cultural memor[ies]" like the Sinai theophany can be "'remembered' differently over time in response to new social contexts and changing theological sensibilities," an example that fits nicely within a larger effort to trace "the long-term transformations of particular religious and national memories within a given community or region."[130] Eva Mroczek has shown how traditions about biblical and extrabiblical figures continued to have dynamic lives in early Judaism in ways that demonstrate, much more clearly than the sparse evidence from the biblical period can, how the inherited past is constantly made new for new realities.[131] These kinds of developments not only cannot be explained by any relationship we propose between tradition and reality, but provide a context in which that relationship can hardly be regarded as relevant. Ruth Scodel has compared the transmission of traditions over time to "Darwinian natural selection," where mistakes, successful alterations, and changing conditions all produce the next generation of storytelling.[132] These further remove the impression of real events from them, and give the events less and less explanatory power, either for what the story is, or for any importance it has in new cultural contexts.

128. Malkin, *Myth and Territory in the Spartan Mediterranean*, p. 3.

129. Malkin, *Myth and Territory in the Spartan Mediterranean*, p. 3.

130. Pioske, "Retracing a Remembered Past," p. 296; Mark S. Smith, *The Memoirs of God: History, Memory, and the Experience of the Divine in Ancient Israel* (Minneapolis, MN: Fortress, 2004), pp. 140-52.

131. Mroczek, *The Literary Imagination in Jewish Antiquity*.

132. Ruth Scodel, *Listening to Homer: Tradition, Narrative and Audience* (Ann Arbor, MI: University of Michigan Press, 2002), p. 17. She also notes that "traditions as a whole change to meet changing conditions," citing as an example the Song of Roland where "the skirmish with Christian Basques" that stands behind it "becomes an immense battle with Saracens, and although the fight still takes place in a rugged mountain pass, the knights fight as if on a plain. Near the poem's end, the trial of Ganelon addresses problems of the poet's own time" (Scodel, *Listening to Homer*, pp. 17-18).

Thus, once again, we have to confront an era long before scientific, objective historiography emerged, in a context where it is not possible to determine which traditions are really *Naturpoesie*, because there is no such thing. We have to realize that, when dealing with ancient traditions, it is not possible to identify a tradition that reflects collective memory in the sense of a collectively produced memory, because there is no such thing. We have to realize the question of which traditions are "genuine" and which are "invented" has no real importance, because ancient audiences showed no preference—they equally embraced and equally believed the traditions they thought were true regardless of their real history. As a result, what we have to acknowledge, hard as it may be, is that even the identification, through "proof," of a great many correspondences between story and reality *makes very little difference* where the study of traditions is concerned. The original inspiration for the story neither defines nor explains its later form. Even if the identification of these correspondences helps us flesh out scholarly historiographies, whatever value we attribute to writing them, this will largely be useful *for* those historiographies, not for defining or explaining the tradition.

Another crucial point, however, is that this does not mean that we cannot extract interesting and useful historical information from surviving texts. It means that this will be a different kind of information than some are used to valuing, and a kind which is, in fact, as accessible even in complete fictions as it is in more accurate accounts.[133] As Barstad observes, for example,

> Novels may provide us with some valuable insights here. No one, hopefully, would deny that from reading D.H. Lawrence, *Sons and Lovers* (1913) we learn a lot about what it is like to grow up in a mining village in Nottinghamshire around the turn of the century.[134]

Someone confronted with the biblical account of the building of Solomon's temple in 1 Kings 6 for the first time could, similarly, learn all kinds of interesting and useful historical things: that the authors worshiped YHWH as chief god, and perhaps the only god, a little of what ancient Israelite temples looked like, the prestige of cedar wood, cypress, and gold, the expectation of both inner and outer spaces and more. They simply would not learn about how the temple in Jerusalem was actually built, and, again, even if Solomon really was the one to build that temple. Someone who studies

---

133. "In the future we shall, irreversibly, have to adjust to a different view on history from that of historical-critical methods of the nineteenth century: A history with different 'truths' that are much less (when at all) the result of scientific analyses of empirical data. A history whose epistemic standing should no longer be regarded as part of science, but much more as a part of culture" (Barstad, *History and the Hebrew Bible*, p. 13).

134. Barstad, *History and the Hebrew Bible*, p. 22.

the various representations of the Return of the Herakleidae will not learn very much about a Dorian invasion, even if there was one, but can learn all kinds of other useful things instead. Someone who studies the traditions of King David will learn, above all, of the terrific importance David held in Judahite historical memory.

Similarly, there has already been a tendency in recent years to see "Homer"—whoever Homer was or however many authors were Homer— as fundamentally a product of his time, *even if* the story he told has a relationship of sorts to much earlier traditions and perhaps earlier realities. The *Iliad,* for one, "may not simply be a mirror of historical society, but it gives us interesting insights into social and cultural history."[135] More than one scholar has now suggested that the particulars of the war fought in the *Iliad* were actually inspired by the *ruins* of Mycenae and Troy in the Archaic Age. As Kurt Raaflaub puts it,

> whatever traditions survived from the Bronze Age and however old Greek epic song may have been ... the great war celebrated by the singers became precisely a war between Troy and Greeks under Mycenaean leadership for no other reason than that the giant ruins of Troy and Mycenae were the most magnificent remains of a heroic age for which only Homer's recent ancestors had developed a fascination.[136]

This would mean that the story *was* inspired by Mycenaean reality and, indeed, by its material culture, without being mainly memory at all. The ancients also occupied a world that was already ancient.

Meanwhile, the famous boar's tusk helmet, which Nilsson described as clear evidence of Mycenaean origins, is, as Grethlein observes, "mentioned in part of the *Iliad* that is considered particularly late," and he wonders whether "ancient objects were integrated into the epics as relics that were familiar to the bards and their audiences."[137] In other words, a very early artifact can appear in a late text *to make it look authentic.* As he also notes, the correlations that have typically been used to date the tradition to earlier periods can actually work in the other direction. Latacz argues that epic fighting looks like archaic fighting, but then again, archaic fighting might consciously be ordered on an "epic model."[138]

135. Grethlein, "From 'Imperishable Glory' to History," p. 126.

136. Kurt A. Raaflaub, "Epic and History," in *A Companion to Ancient Epic* (ed. John Miles Foley; Malden, MA: Blackwell Publishing, 2005), p. 60. Grethlein adds that we might understand "the *Iliad* itself as an act of memory," which "supports the thesis that the rise of the Greek epic was inspired by the Mycenaean ruins that were still visible in the Archaic Age" (Grethlein, "From 'Imperishable Glory' to History," p. 132).

137. Grethlein, "From 'Imperishable Glory' to History," pp. 125, 128.

138. Joachim Latacz, *Kampfparänese, Kampfdarstellung und Kampfwirklichkeit in der Ilias, bei Kallinos und Tyrtaios* (Munich: Beck, 1977); J.P. Crielaard, "Past or

Thus, the *Iliad* too might be best used as a historical source that can

> provide us with important insights into the social and cultural history of
> the time of their fixation ... as part of history, particularly as the attempt
> to cope with immense social ruptures and changes ... the embedded past
> in the Iliad mirrors the heroic past as seen by the Archaic Greeks. Epic
> poetry is a source not only for history, but also for the history of history,
> revealing a distinct idea of history.[139]

And it is likely more the latter than the former, revealing, most of all, an
Archaic Greek idea of history rather than an actual Bronze Age historical
episode. It may be built, perhaps, with some Bronze Age materials, but to
Archaic Age specifications. And so, once again, the possibility that there was
anything like a real Trojan War can remain *without telling us anything really
useful about the Iliad.* And the *Iliad* can tell us a lot of interesting historical
facts if we do not demand they be about the Bronze Age. Why shouldn't we
want to learn what later Greeks believed, valued, and even experienced just
as much if not more than we want to know about the Trojan War?

Another way to put it is that the correlations between the *Iliad* and the
Mycenaean world, however robust a given scholar determines them to be,
may actually nevertheless be a reflection of the effort to *symbolize* a past in
which a Trojan War might have happened, or even *convey a sense of past-
ness.* This would be because the elements so deployed were known to be,
generally, places and artifacts of a prior age *in the age when the text was
written.* And this possibility might well provide a genuine microcosm of
the typical nature of the relationship between a tradition and the real past.
The point is not that there is none; so proving that there is changes little.
It is that the inherited past will, more or less inevitably, serve as a set of
ingredients for the making of a new vision of the past all the same.[140]

In other words, the past has a role to play in new stories, whether it has
some connection to real events or not, whether it is reflected in genuinely
ancient tradition elements or not. A story inspired by the ruins of an actual
place, say, has its basis not in the past but in the image of the past in the
present, or even an image of the past that is sprung from the present. That
the artifacts were real, that the ruins were cities, that the new vision of the
past may be anchored to the real one by half-glimpsed and half-remem-

Present? Epic Poetry, Aristocratic Self-Representation, and the Concept of Time in the
Eighth and Seventh Centuries BC," in *Omero Tremila Anni Dopo* (ed. Franco Montanari and Paola Ascheri; Rome: Edizioni di Storia e Letteratura, 2002), pp. 259-62.

139. Grethlein, "From 'Imperishable Glory' to History," p. 134.

140. This and other discussions of "ingredients" in this book are inspired to some
extent by a memorable description of the elements of a myth as a "soup cube," which is
boiled up into various different soups in Wendy Doniger's *The Implied Spider,* without
intending to reiterate her argument there (Wendy Doniger, *The Implied Spider: Politics
and Theology in Myth* [New York: Columbia University Press, 2011], p. 105).

bered things tells us very little other than what was to hand for the fashioning of something new. And all the reasons to privilege the search for the real past over the imagined past have dwindled with time.

Toward the Future

I have two final points to make. First, I would say the endurance of many less-than-useful concerns for so long has something to do with the historical lack of diversity in the field. I am painfully aware that I myself am by no means giving a kaleidoscope view of the arguments of a century in two disciplines. I am hoping that what I have discussed, and will discuss, seems like a usefully representative sample of the most visible trends of the periods under consideration. But this is part of the problem; the historical visibility of arguments is itself not a neutral feature of scholarship. Nearly all the scholars I have discussed so far were white, male Protestants because the structure of religious studies academia was such that these were bound to be the prominent voices. A more meritocratic structure might have resulted in very different arguments and trends emerging throughout the century. If, for example, the perfectly apt critiques of Ruth Finnegan were taken more into consideration in the seventies and eighties when they were made, the future study of Homer might have proceeded very differently.

More generally, it is not hard to imagine that an academic community that featured a greater diversity of religious perspectives would presumably have had more scholars who did not feel personally invested in the question of whether pentateuchal traditions reflected the actual experiences and practices of the early Israelites or not and were therefore able to operate more dispassionately. A more culturally diverse community would presumably have had more, too, who did not find the idea of accessing the supposedly ancient race memories of European peoples like the Greeks so tantalizing that they got carried away as, it is fair to say, Milman Parry sometimes did. These scholars might have brought more skeptical approaches to bear, earlier, because they might have had less reason to object to the simple facts of the case as they now appear to be to us. And there were trailblazers of course. I mentioned Harriet Boyd, who excavated the important (Minoan) site of Gournia, on Crete. In biblical archaeology, there was Kathleen Kenyon, who excavated at numerous sites, especially Jericho, and who largely argued the Albrightian line, but often with more skepticism and discernment.[141] Alice Kober contributed materially to the

---

141. For example, she agreed with Albright that the correspondences between biblical and Bronze Age names were telling enough "that it was to the Amurru or Amorite setting" of second millennium Mesopotamia "that the Patriarchs belong." However, she could also acknowledge that "there is no archaeological evidence" that supports

decipherment of Linear B, and so on. Umberto Cassuto also deserves mention here as a rare prominent Jewish voice, someone who contributed significantly to the study of Ugaritic, even as anti-Semitism forced him from the Italian universities he spent much of his career working in. But there can be no question that historical gatekeeping has robbed us of many valuable contributions and continues to do so today.

Second, I would simply reiterate that the main takeaway from this chapter, in my view, is that the primary importance of the effort to establish the rootedness of surviving traditions in earlier realities is an outmoded relic of a paradigm in which earlier traditions had greater value than later ones. There are very, very few cases where an ancient tradition might be enough like modern historiography that the actual events they purport to describe have any explanatory value for why the tradition looks the way it does: Thucydides, the books of Kings, perhaps a few others. And even then, we have to work very hard not to imagine a modern historian employing modern historiographical techniques so that, almost always, the biases and emphases of the author are the historical realities that will emerge most clearly from the work.[142] This means that the study of, especially, traditions that describe early periods and the use of extraliterary evidence to reconstruct early realities really are largely separate. Traditions can tell us, sometimes, what we might look for in the extraliterary evidence; the extraliterary evidence can tell us if it is there. But something *being* there doesn't really explain the tradition at all.

Yet looking at the larger picture of these first two chapters, and the intellectual history they explored, there is an additional takeaway as well. We can, in general, think of the paradigm I am criticizing as a set of explanations for why those who inherit traditions could neither change them too greatly nor create their own of exactly the same sort, quality, and importance. Moving on from this paradigm—exorcising the ghost—means realizing that none of these explanations are valid, and that no exception or principle or belief in a distinction between oral and written, or ancient past and present, can resurrect it. This is a trend that, at least in the study of the Hebrew Bible, began with Gunkel's efforts to overcome the harsh logic of a Wellhausian chronology by arguing that even the oral precursors of sur-

---

Albright's position that the patriarchal age was between the twentieth and eighteenth centuries BCE, and expressed her own preference for a "seventeenth or sixteenth century" date for the patriarchs also "without strong grounds and only because I would prefer to reduce the length of period in which traditions had survived" (Kathleen M. Kenyon, *The Bible and Recent Archaeology* [Atlanta, GA: John Knox, 1978], pp. 8, 10).

142. An account of the colonial overtones of applying modern notions of historiography to ancient stories can be found in Uriah Y. Kim, *Decolonizing Josiah: Toward a Postcolonial Reading of the Deuteronomistic History* (Sheffield: Sheffield Phoenix Press, 2005).

viving traditions were accessible despite both the late debut of the textual account and the supposed enmity of the Priestly authors to the spirit and character of all that came before. It is reflected in all the efforts to construct exceptions and apply piecemeal proofs, or to put the Great Divide on new, "sounder ground," so that the recovery of oral traditions actually meant the recovery of early and more representative traditions rather than just oral traditions, full stop.

When, however, we recognize the utter failure of this framework, hierarchy, paradigm, we need to think differently about the *value* of discovering earlier elements, not just in this chapter but in chapters to come, where we will see that older approaches that focused on the recovery of kernels of truth are also in tension with later understandings of how traditions are used as a medium for expressing contemporary concerns and agendas. And this intellectual move will, hopefully, dispense with a certain amount of wishful thinking where their study is concerned. When an argument is not just wrong in certain particulars but *premised* incorrectly, we are better off starting over than salvaging them. There is no need to stand on the shoulders of giants when they are walking the wrong way.

Or, perhaps, we might put it this way: stories about real events sometimes do get handed down, with the connection between story and event faring sometimes better, and sometimes worse. We can, sometimes, use extraliterary evidence to show that this has happened. But the downfall of our linear models of tradition inheritance and identity require certain recognitions nonetheless, most especially about the creative agency of every generation and, indeed, every author. Thus, an early tradition, if we can identify it, still tells us primarily about early historical memory, social realities, and the intentions of early authors in the same way that later traditions tell us those things about later periods. And any correlations between these traditions and the testimony of archaeological, epigraphic, and anthropologic research reveals, largely, where some portion of the grist for the mill of memory came from, nothing more.

3

GENEALOGIES

In a way, the idea for this book first grew out of my study of genealogical traditions. There are a number of reasons why, including the fact that here, of all the topics I discuss, we come closest to having a genuinely shared genre rather than a roughly similar set of narratives. That is, we might well say that both ancient Israel—and Judah—and ancient Greece had "founding traditions," the topic of the next chapter. But this is a way of gesturing at the fact that both groups have stories that explain the foundation of cities, religious sites, and other institutions, *not* an expression of the belief that authors in each context had the same literary conventions in mind when writing them. This is why my focus is on comparing scholarly *approaches* to problems and questions that are genuinely shared rather than primary sources whose similarities can be misleading. Still, "segmented genealogical traditions," traditions that trace the descent of contemporary groups from legendary figures along multiple genealogical lines and describe the activities of multiple generations, are not only apparently structurally identical in both contexts, they are rare in the rest of the ancient Near East and Levant. Which is to say, the genealogical traditions of the Hebrew Bible are fundamentally *more like* the traditions of ancient Greece than they are those of Mesopotamia or of other Levantine cultures, which makes them the *most* instructive direct comparison for each other.

Second, however, this is simply where I started my own work on comparisons between the Hebrew Bible's traditions and those of ancient Greece, years ago.[1] And anyone who has done the same will quickly realize that, here in particular, scholars in each discipline really do study essentially the same kind of traditions very differently. Certain recent efforts aside, Hebrew Bible scholars still generally approach genealogical traditions, especially those concerning the twelve tribes of Israel, as the fossilized memory of real social and political arrangements in very early periods.

---

1. Tobolowsky, "Reading Genesis through Chronicles"; Tobolowsky, *The Sons of Jacob and the Sons of Herakles*; Tobolowsky, "The Problem of Reubenite Primacy"; Tobolowsky, *The Myth of the Twelve Tribes of Israel*.

Contemporary scholars of ancient Greek traditions, by contrast, are much more likely to display an awareness that the relationships presented in later genealogical narratives tend to reveal the operation of ideological agendas rather than schematize early historiographical realities. As a result, both the nature of these investigations and the significantly more expansive evidence they are predicated on can indeed provide useful suggestions for the study of the Hebrew Bible's traditions, more than the other way around. And this chapter, in that sense, offers the *beau idéal* of the combined approach I am advocating here.

In what follows then, I will first show how and why approaches in each discipline evolved in different directions, with particular attention to a now familiar pattern. Here, too, Hebrew Bible scholarship has showed a stronger tendency to, in a sense, repeatedly rescue outdated approaches from obscurity than scholars of ancient Greek traditions by means of finding supposedly new justifications for old conclusions. Since, however, the inadequacy of those original conclusions actually stems not from the flaws of prior argumentation but from the flawed assumptions that inspired them in the first place, they *cannot* be rescued in any real way. And this recognition will allow us to discuss, next, how scholars in both disciplines can use the actual evidence for how segmented genealogical traditions are adapted and reused to break the influence of these outdated assumptions and reach conclusions that better reflect what we actually see and what it means. Here too, we have a context where it is less practical, less useful, and, in my view, less interesting to ask what surviving texts preserve than how their authors use what was handed down to them, and awareness of that should shape approaches to the study of these texts.

Finally, I will begin to lay the groundwork for some of the larger conclusions of this study by using the topic of genealogical traditions to discuss the *general* nature of tradition inheritance. Broadly speaking, even many scholars whose work is path-breaking in other ways—where the study of how familiar figures, events, and concepts are used and adapted in new stories is concerned—continue to insist on an essential conservatism to the process. In a nutshell, they believe that there are certain rules that the heirs of traditions cannot break. I will argue, however, that the persistence of this belief is actually the result of confusing the *usefulness* of redeploying familiar materials in service to innovation for the necessity of keeping to established patterns. In other words, I will argue that genealogists and other storytellers do very often attempt to give their innovations a boost by clothing them in the authority of better-known stories, but that this is indeed not necessary, and that the phenomenology of genealogical traditions reveal as much. Thus, the variety we see in the actual practice of inheriting and adapting genealogical traditions reveals that genuinely disruptive innovations that nevertheless come to achieve a significant authority are perfectly possible. And we will see the same in the next chapter's study of foundation traditions, just as we have in previous chapters.

Kernels of Truth

In a previous study, I described the traditional approach to interpreting the data of genealogical traditions as an attempt to break a kind of "code," a term actually used in Abraham Malamat's *History of Biblical Israel*.[2] In his view, and certainly not his alone, genealogical accounts—who was descended or related to whom—represented a "schematisation" of "internal tribal structures" and "inter-tribal relations and groupings." As a result, different versions of, say, the genealogy of Jacob could reveal "the complex processes involved in the rise and decline of the specific sub-units within the ... framework ... the continual fluctuation of dissolution and eventual unification," and much else besides.[3]

Others have referred to these supposedly coded messages as "kernels of truth," which in my view is, in and of itself, already a reflection of the Romantic assumptions that animated the early search for them. After all, why not just "truths," simple representations of real relationships? But the idea here developed out of the vision, discussed in Chapter 1, of early authors as little more than vessels of a sort for a collective understanding of the ethnic nation but possessed of a divine simplicity that kept them from being either proper historians or pure storytellers, in the sense of inventors. They, therefore, somehow managed at once to channel the real past, or the past as they understood it, almost completely accurately—but into representations that were so vague and impressionistic they require extensive scholarly interpretation even to understand the basics of what they are supposedly trying to represent.

Thus, the attempt to study genealogical traditions for what they revealed about early relationships and realities was indeed a fixture in both disciplines under consideration here, and a part of a much more general phenomenon. This certainly included the study of what is usually called *Völkerwanderung,* a Romantic vision of ancient people movements as a supposed cause for the formation of nations, traditions, and much else besides.[4]

2. Tobolowsky, *The Myth of the Twelve Tribes of Israel*, p. 32.

3. Abraham Malamat, *History of Biblical Israel* (Leiden: E.J. Brill, 2001), pp. 47-48.

4. As Felix Wiedemann recently put it, "In the late nineteenth and early twentieth centuries, certain fields of ancient and classical studies in particular, such as archaeology, prehistory, and ancient Near Eastern studies, focused on questions relating to the origins and the wanderings of certain peoples, races, and nations. Anthropology and archaeology were dominated by contemporary approaches ... which put forth the 'wanderings of people'—as general explanations for cultural and historical change" (Felix Wiedemann, "Migration and Narration: How European Historians in the Nine-

At any rate, as Jonathan M. Hall observes, all kinds of "myths of ethnic origins" were supposed to preserve "a hazy and refracted recollection of genuine population movements," in this case of the Bronze Age, which the scholar uses as a basis for revealing "what actually happened."[5] The genealogical kind of these traditions was typically held to preserve the original relationships between the groups that participated in these movements, or in the formation of the early *ethnos*.

A case in point that I discussed in a previous study concerns the tribe of Reuben, whose biblical descriptions offer us a kind of mystery. On the one hand, Reuben is described as Jacob's eldest son, a position of prominence that it is easy to suppose reflects a historical prominence as well. But nothing about biblical depictions of the tribe of Reuben suggest that it was ever more than a marginal tribe. To an earlier generation of scholars, operating from a kernels-of-truth perspective, it seemed obvious that the explanation must be that the genealogical traditions, which were mostly written down in rather late periods, somehow preserved a memory of early realities *better* than any other text. Reuben's prominence in the genealogical traditions reflected an "age of preeminence," otherwise forgotten, and now "overlain by a patina of traditions stemming from later centers of power and prestige, in Joseph and in Judah."[6]

Similar arguments were long advanced in the face of the extensive Greek genealogical system that presents the eponymous ancestors of many Greek groups as close relatives. Walter Burkert, for example, described the fact that Doros and Aeolus are Hellen's sons, while Ion and Akhaios—the ancestors of the Dorians, Aeolians, Ionians, and Akhaians—are only grandsons, as an example of "mythical thinking." That is, it supposedly revealed that, in early periods, the "Ionians and Achaians [were] ... closer to each other," compared to other Greeks.[7] Others have long made similar claims about these kinds of details, and also, the unusually large set of narratives and genealogical structures that provide the Greeks with foreign founders—Cadmus the Phoenician, Danaos the Egyptian, and so on.

Here, taking a page from Irad Malkin, discussed below, we can consider the instructive example of the Bérards, father and son. They were among many throughout even the twentieth century who wrote actual histories of

teenth and Early Twentieth Centuries Told the History of Human Mass Migrations or Völkerwanderungen," *History and Theory* 59.1 [2020], pp. 42-60).

5. Hall, *Ethnic Identity in Greek Antiquity*, p. 41. As Hall notes, ancient historians sometimes did much the same thing.

6. Cross, *From Epic to Canon*, pp. 28, 56. See the discussion in Tobolowsky, "The Problem of Reubenite Primacy."

7. Walter Burkert, *Structure and History in Greek Mythology* (Berkeley: University of California Press, 1979), p. 25.

ancient nations largely through the supposed science of extrapolating kernels of truth. Victor, the elder, was still reporting it as fact that Thebes was founded by Cadmus, a Phoenician stranger, just as in the familiar myth, in 1902.[8] Jean, his son, was as keen to follow the path of genealogical links to half-remembered influences as William Foxwell Albright, and around the same time. Indeed, for the book as a whole, it is worth reflecting a moment longer on the similarities in approach between someone like Bérard *fils* and someone like Albright, in the sense that they often made not just structurally similar arguments, but ones that were mutually exclusive, about the same world historical events.

For example, Bérard attempted to connect the Greek tradition of Phaeton to the biblical account of Joseph's time in Egypt, just as Albright suggested "the obvious relation in which the Joseph story and the later history of Israel in Egypt stand to the Hyksos movement."[9] Where Albright thought the end of Hyksos rule is what cast the Israelites down into Egyptian slavery, for Bérard, the significance lay in his belief that it sent the descendants of Io, "les dernier Hyksôs," the last of the Hyksos, fleeing toward Greece.[10] In other words, just as the story of Io, the Argive princess who arrived from afar was supposed to correspond to the sudden appearance of foreign rulers in Egypt, so their removal saw "le retour en Grèce de Danaos et de Cadmos," the return to Greece of both Danaos and Cadmus to found their Greek cities.[11] All this was an expression of Bérard's belief in "le substrat de réalité historique que ... recouvrent les legends," the "substrate of historical reality that covers the legend."[12] Albright would and, of course, did say much the same. But if both were right, the Hyksos would be both Joseph and the Danaans; their arrival would be that of Io and Joseph, their expulsion of Moses and the mythological founders of Argos and Thebes.

8. Victor Bérard, *Les Phéniciens et l'Odyssée* (Paris: Armand Colin, 1902), p. 225. For an early rebuttal of the historical roots of the Cadmus tradition see A.W. Gomme, "The Topography of Boeotia and the Theories of M. Bérard," *The Annual of the British School at Athens* 18 (1911), pp. 189-210; A.W. Gomme, "The Legend of Cadmus and the Logographi," *JHS* 33 (1913), pp. 53-72.

9. Albright, *From the Stone Age*, p. 184.

10. Jean Bérard, "De la légende grecque à la Bible. Phaéton et les sept vaches maigres," *RHR* 151.2 (1957), pp. 221-22.

11. Albright, *From the Stone Age*, p. 184; Bérard, "De la légende grecque à la Bible," p. 222.

12. Bérard, "De la légende grecque à la Bible," p. 221. As Malkin notes, this was also true of Bérard's influential history of colonization in the Mediterranean which typically "explains cults identified with Greek heroes as necessarily originating in prehistorical (e.g. Mycenaean) contacts" (Malkin, *The Returns of Odysseus*, p. 22). See Jean Bérard, *La colonisation grecque de l'Italie méridionale et de la Sicile dans l'antiquité: l'histoire et la légende* (Bibliothèque des Ecoles françaises d'Athènes et de Rome; Paris: Ed. de Boccard, 1941).

And I think the fact that they performed the same logical deductions and arrived at the same basic conclusions, but for totally different groups, is more than a little telling.

Above, I mentioned Malkin, who refers to the later Bérard to say that he—Malkin—will, in his work, champion a "myth as history" approach, too, but only after turning the former's understanding of the concept "on its head: I study myths as an integral part of the history of the period in which they were told."[13] I, of course, am doing much the same. But it is worth asking why this belief in "kernels of truth" was so prominent for so long in the first place, and is still not uncommon today. After all, consider what would have to be true for genealogical traditions to, *as a rule,* describe only the actual relationships between early groups and the pattern of their engagement. We would need, first, a guileless narrator who had no ambition beyond mapping the actual social relations in their era, but, for some reason, could only do it in a form of code. There would be no ideology here, only fact and its schematic representation. Then, what they did would simply be passed on unthinkingly even by those who no longer had any idea what they were preserving and had no agenda of their own—so that even much later compositions could be nothing more than these coded representations of early realities.

When we have to put it this way, going through the motions of actually describing what would have to have happened, we can recognize the existence of a fundamental relationship between the hunt for kernels of truth and the "Great Divide" discussed in the first chapter. That is, and especially because we actually know that genealogical traditions were used in later periods for the pursuit of agendas of all sorts, we cannot adopt the kernel-of-truth approach without the idea that once upon a time storytelling worked differently than it does in any period we can actually study. In one era, it was pure representation; in another, pure repetition. We see the relationship between this understanding of genealogical traditions and the "linear models" described in the first chapter, that surviving genealogical traditions are always the reflection of original genealogical traditions, which scholars can work back to, and that each ethnic group understands its origins and descent in the same way throughout the course of its history. And this is simply not how it works. Identity changes. Traditions change. And there was never an era when traditions were simply a reflection of the actual experience of the ethnic nation. This is a fantasy with no real evidentiary support.

So, once again, one of the problems I will discuss below is a kind of confusion. It is not that it is impossible to prove that some details of sur-

---

13. Malkin, *The Returns of Odysseus,* p. 22.

viving genealogical traditions are early; it is that there is a continued mis-
understanding about what it means when they are. And this confusion
is to some extent a consequence of the typically binary framing of the
debate about whether traditions do or do not preserve, the idea that if we
can prove they preserve something, we will validate earlier conclusions.
But the downfall of the linear model means that even if a text preserves an
earlier tradition, that tradition might be one of many conflicting traditions
in its time, and the only one to survive for reasons that are unrelated to
its initial popularity. The downfall of the Great Divide framework means
that even an earlier tradition is not a collective production, not a distillation of what "the" Israelites or "the" Greeks believed, or understood, or
experienced, an idea that never had much basis beyond the Herder-Rous-
seau equation between primitive man and an idealized vision of childhood
within the developmental model.

So, in a nutshell, there is often no reason to doubt that a detail such as the
aforementioned fraternal relationship between Doros and Aeolus indeed
appeared early in the development of the basic genealogical tradition so
many later efforts would build on; that seems to be precisely the case. As a
result, it will, of course, reveal *an* early reality. I would never deny that the
expression of genealogical relationships between real groups in a genealogical narrative is meaningful. The question is *what kind of early reality*
should we expect to find buried in the details? And again, I think the idea
that early traditions more or less must preserve distorted historiography
even while we know that later texts offer mainly ideological adaptations
has no basis outside of the idea that early and later authors compose according to fundamentally different modes.

Thus, we should instead conclude that early traditions can reflect social
and political realities, but also ideological agendas as easily as later ones,
and, above all, the impression of what the individual author *believed* to
be true or *wanted* to be true. In any given case, this may also have been
a popular impression—or not. It may have reflected the way things were,
of long duration or short. And then again, it may represent nothing more
than an ambition for a reality that never was. And above all, as in the first
chapter, there is no reason to think the possibility that surviving texts may
preserve the impression of early realities *or* early agendas is more interesting than the impression it preserves of the agendas of its author; there is no
reason to think we are going to be that good at extricating the early reality when we have lost the context that produced it; and there is genuinely
no justification for thinking that what is preserved is distorted memory in
particular. And if one question is why this imaginary was so popular in the
first place, another is why it has survived so much better in the study of the
Hebrew Bible than elsewhere.

The Hebrew Bible

Where the study of the genealogical traditions of the Hebrew Bible are concerned, we once again see, in the historical development of approaches, an element of *rescue*. In other words, as an early and more transparently Romantic approach to genealogical traditions as the distilled memory of the early nation met a series of challenges in the mid-twentieth century, Hebrew Bible scholars found a new set of apparently empirical justifications and plunged ahead. And today, rather than re-engaging with these traditions in a way that responds to what was wrong with early twentieth-century approaches, the most common methods of analysis, even in otherwise skeptical cases, involve advancing similar kinds of conclusions to those of a century before, only more cautiously and speculatively.[14] Thus, the original inaccurate assumptions survive, cautiously and speculatively. No decisive break with the past has been made.

I have described the history of approaches to genealogical traditions before, but will do it again, simply, for the sake of the comprehensiveness of the investigation here.[15] The central figure where the study of the Hebrew Bible's genealogical traditions is concerned is Martin Noth. This is not to say he bears sole responsibility for what was quite a common way of thinking about these kinds of traditions, but his formulation of the history of the tribes and the relationship of that history to the various representations of the tribes in biblical texts stands behind later studies most directly. It was his view that diverse tribal groups, with diverse traditions reflecting their diverse experiences, had come together in a premonarchical "amphictyony." There, they had combined their traditions together to form a single charter myth, a *Grundlage,* which was the "common basis" of the pentateuchal sources.

In other words, this was a vision in which a number of different ethnic groups, independently preserving the memories of the group in the form of traditions, had, upon joining with others, created the pentateuchal narrative by combining these memories together.[16] What could be more natural than the view that the history and prehistory of the amphictyony itself was hidden away in this final account? Thus, Noth's *History of Israel* is drawn, in part, from arguments like his claim that Genesis 29–30, the birth narrative of the tribal ancestors, was really a representation of the processes through which pre-Israelite tribal groups had joined together. In particular, he

---

14. Tobolowsky, *The Myth of the Twelve Tribes of Israel*, p. 35.

15. Tobolowsky, *The Myth of the Twelve Tribes of Israel*, pp. 27-44.

16. As he put it, "It goes without saying that the tribes had a history of their own before they entered Palestine and in the Old Testament certain tribal traditions from that early period have been preserved. ... On the other hand, these traditions were first given their definitive form within an Israel that was already united in Palestine and they were conditioned by its point of view" (Noth, *The History of Israel*, p. 53).

argued that the fact that the tribes have four different mothers here reflects the pre-existence of four different communities. The fact that Leah was both the elder sister and first wife and that she had six of Jacob's children reflected the existence of a six-tribe league that predated the formation of the twelve-tribe league in Canaan.[17] And so on.

Other details, in other texts, helped flesh out Noth's history. The well-known fact that some tribal lists contain Levi and Joseph, but others Ephraim and Manasseh, was, in his view, similarly pregnant with meaning; they represented an early development in which Levi ceased being regarded as a secular tribe because of its priestly status, and Joseph was divided into two, Ephraim and Manasseh, to maintain the traditional number of twelve.[18] The prominence of not just Judah but Issachar in some lists suggested that these were among the first to settle in the region, while the story of the Judahite Caleb reflected the fact that the Calebites lived in the southern mountains. All of this was written out of what the *relationships* between groups described in biblical genealogies supposedly reflected.[19]

The amphictyonic hypothesis, again, fell apart between the late 1960s and mid-1970s. Yet this method of analyzing the data of genealogical traditions, which I have called the "preservative method" because it focuses on what these traditions preserve, survived.[20] In this case, it did so particularly through the agency of two new comparisons, especially as presented in the work of Robert Wilson and Malamat:[21] first, with the genealogical "king-lists" of ancient Babylon and Assyria, some of which had only recently been translated;[22] second, with the oral genealogical traditions of various African communities, especially the Nuer, generally as discussed in

17. Noth, *The History of Israel*, pp. 86, 89; Tobolowsky, *The Myth of the Twelve Tribes of Israel*, p. 33.

18. Noth, *The History of Israel*, p. 85.

19. See, generally, Tobolowsky, *The Sons of Jacob and the Sons of Herakles*, pp. 48-50; Tobolowsky, *The Myth of the Twelve Tribes of Israel*, pp. 27-44.

20. Tobolowsky, *The Myth of the Twelve Tribes of Israel*, pp. 27-44.

21. Once again, see Tobolowsky, *The Sons of Jacob and the Sons of Herakles*, pp. 48-50; Tobolowsky, *The Myth of the Twelve Tribes of Israel*, pp. 27-44. For important early studies, see Robert R. Wilson, "The Old Testament Genealogies in Recent Research," *JBL* 94 (1975), pp. 169-89; Wilson, *Genealogy and History in the Biblical World*; Wilson, "Between 'Azel' and 'Azel'"; Abraham Malamat, "King Lists of the Old Babylonian Period and Biblical Genealogies," *JAOS* 88.1 (1968), pp. 163-73; Abraham Malamat, "Tribal Societies: Biblical Genealogies and African Lineage Systems," *European Journal of Sociology* 14.1 (1973), pp. 126-36.

22. Ignace J. Gelb, "Two Assyrian King Lists," *JNES* 13.4 (1954), pp. 209-30; Jacob J. Finkelstein, "The Genealogy of the Hammurapi Dynasty," *Journal of Cuneiform Studies* 20.3/4 (1966), pp. 95-118.

studies that were already three decades old.[23] The former was supposed to show that the early Israelite community *could* or *would* have composed genealogical traditions because their "Amorite" ancestors had.[24] The other revealed that oral genealogical traditions indeed reflect the social and political structures of tribal societies.[25] Thus, together, they seemed to substitute for Noth's Romantic vision of an early charter tradition that was a collective production, and therefore bore the impression of formative experiences, a much better founded argument that arrived at the same conclusions. If oral genealogical traditions reflect social and political realities, and surviving pentateuchal accounts of tribal Israel are based on early oral traditions, then indeed they will preserve a record of early social and political realities.

There are, however, many problems with this conclusion. In other studies, I have focused on the fact that these were the wrong sorts of comparisons. The genealogical traditions of the Hebrew Bible are, obviously, *not* oral, like the African tribal comparisons. The genealogical traditions of Mesopotamia, Amorite or otherwise, are, for the most part, "linear" not segmented, which is to say they mainly follow the descent of individuals in a single line from father to son or mother to daughter.[26] These comparisons will, therefore, only prove instructive for the written, segmented genealogies of the Hebrew Bible under two conditions. First, that the Pentateuch is primarily a reflection of *early oral* traditions, a common view in the early- to mid-twentieth century, but not now. Second, that the early Israelites are Amorite enough that we can assume they engaged in writing *any* kind of genealogical traditions, even without evidence, simply because their ancestors had written a *different* kind of genealogical composition. Here, of course, are echoes of an ethnic essentialism over time that also belongs to a different age.

Meanwhile, as not only I but others before me have noted, the conclusion simply falls apart with the *right* comparisons.[27] The problem is that the

23. Specifically, the work of Evans-Pritchard, in E. Evans-Pritchard, *The Nuer* (Oxford: Clarendon Press, 1940).

24. Wilson, "The Old Testament Genealogies in Recent Research," p. 175; Wilson, "Between 'Azel' and 'Azel,'" pp. 3, 14.

25. Malamat, "Tribal Societies'; Malamat, *History of Biblical Israel*, p. 48; Wilson, *Genealogy and History in the Biblical World*, pp. 11-55.

26. Wilson, *Genealogy and History in the Biblical World*, pp. 57-64, 122-32.

27. Van Seters, *Prologue to History*, pp. 199-206; Knoppers, "Greek Historiography and the Chronicler's History: A Reexamination'; Guy Darshan, "The Biblical Account of the Post-Diluvian Generation (Gen 9:20–10:32) in the Light of Greek Genealogical Literature," *VT* 63.4 (2013), pp. 515-35; Guy Darshan, "The Story of the Sons of God and the Daughters of Men (Gen 6:1-4) and the Hesiodic Catalogue of Women," *Shnaton, an Annual for Biblical and Ancient Near Eastern Studies* 23 (2014), pp. 155-78; Tobolowsky, "Reading Genesis through Chronicles'; Tobolowsky, *The Sons of Jacob and the Sons of Herakles*; Tobolowsky, "The Problem of Reubenite Primacy';

idea that the largely later corpus of biblical genealogical traditions mainly reflects early realities requires a fluidity in their oral phase that is *not* present in their written phase. In other words, we would have to presume that tribal traditions were fluid enough, in the oral period, to reflect multiple stages of changing social realities, but then static enough ever after that even much later tribal compositions went on reflecting diverse early realities, and nothing much else. In addition, we would have to presume that early authors never represented anything we know that later authors represented, like ideological agendas that were entirely aspirational.

Yet the Hebrew Bible's traditions *are*, as I say, written and segmented, not oral, wherever they originally came from, and so are those of ancient Greece. And, a centerpiece of this chapter, the ancient Greek corpus reveals that genealogical traditions were altered and reinvented almost continuously even after they were written down, and perhaps especially. As Robert Fowler argues, "the world of myth" in these genealogical traditions is not a preserved memory of an era otherwise almost beyond recall, it is "a mirror and projection of the present world; through one, the Greeks explored and gave meaning to the other."[28] This they did, among other methods, by adapting these genealogical traditions to match the needs of the present.

Thus, it has not often been realized that the Wilson–Malamat model proposes a binary that simply does not exist. Wilson, for one, quite accurately acknowledged the fluidity of genealogical traditions over time, so much so that he regarded them as a "major formal characteristic" of genealogies. He knew that the fact that genealogies can act as a charter for social arrangements means that they "must change in order to mirror alterations" in society; that when disputes arise, "alternative genealogies may appear"; that "genealogies that have no function," are no longer used, and so on.[29] He even concluded, therefore, that oral genealogies cannot function as historical records *because* they are primarily used to "legitimize contemporary lineage configurations" so that the "accurate information" they contain is about the relations that exist *at the time* they are composed.[30] More recent and more sophisticated discussions of African tribal genealogical traditions

Mark McEntire and Wongi Park, "Ethnic Fission and Fusion in Biblical Genealogies," *JBL* 140 (2021), pp. 31-47.

28. Robert L. Fowler, "Genealogical Thinking, Hesiod's Catalogue and the Creation of the Hellenes," *Proceedings of the Cambridge Philological Society* 44 (1999), p. 17.

29. Wilson, *Genealogy and History in the Biblical World*, pp. 27, 40, 46.

30. Wilson, *Genealogy and History in the Biblical World*, pp. 54-55. He adds, "A society may knowingly manipulate a genealogy, and rival groups within the society may advance conflicting tendentious genealogies" and so on, with the result that societies are always in the process of redetermining which is the true version of the tradition.

have only underscored their essential fluidity and multiplicity.[31] Wilson simply thought all of this was only true when genealogies were oral, that the oral phase of pentateuchal genealogies occurred in the premonarchical period, and that the advent of writing—and the monarchy—froze them in place.[32] And this is precisely the premise that the more accurate Greek comparisons teach us to reject.

Thus, genealogies do reflect realities to an extent, those of the era in which they were written, *and*, I freely confess, of the eras in which whatever relationships exist in surviving texts were first worked out. But they are not history, and they are not memory. They are not a representation of social and political relationships as "they really were." Still less are they the submerged reflection of *Völkerwanderung,* put by a natural and untutored generation into a symbolic language that those who passed the traditions on did not even understand. Instead, they are, as in any era, a schematization of society as *one* author thought it was or, just as likely, wanted it to be. If we can acknowledge that, in a later era, Reuben might have been elevated by a Reubenite partisan for some reason or another, against the evidence of actual realities, we can acknowledge that this could have happened in early periods, too. And then, by some quirk of fate, it could have been this partisan's efforts that were adopted and handed down. Or the idea of Reubenite primacy could have been introduced in literally any era.

But here is the pattern I have made so much of all along, the second step in a familiar two-step move. Contemporary Hebrew Bible scholarship is, generally speaking, as aware of some of the flaws in the arguments of the mid- to late-twentieth-century studies mentioned above as those making these arguments were of the flaws in Noth's more Romantic approach. But they, too, perform an act of rescue. Rather than acknowledging the bankruptcy of the *premise* that early genealogical traditions encode a neutral, collective representation of social realities, many scholars simply heavily qualify similar conclusions.[33] A recent study, by quite a good and insightful historian, contains many caveats and forthrightly acknowledges just how frequently manipulated genealogical traditions can be. However, it also asserts, without evidence, that "the representation of social relations

---

31. See especially J. Teresa Holmes, "When Blood Matters: Making Kinship in Colonial Kenya," in *Kinship and Beyond: The Genealogical Model Reconsidered* (ed. Sandra Bamford and James Leach; Oxford: Berghahn Books, 2009), pp. 50-83. Malkin notes the struggles of "the British in Nigeria who invested enormous effort in putting the genealogies in order, only to find them changing even before their registration books were complete" (Malkin, *Myth and Territory in the Spartan Mediterranean,* pp. 17-18).

32. Wilson, *Genealogy and History in the Biblical World,* p. 193.

33. Tobolowsky, *The Myth of the Twelve Tribes of Israel,* pp. 34-49.

in a genealogical form is typical of the Iron Age."[34] Where could we even find the evidence for such a conclusion without proving it first *on* the traditions we have in mind here? Another study, which also deems the twelve tribes tradition in its final form essentially an invention, nevertheless refers to the preservation of an early core of genealogical traditions in the "palace schools of Samaria and Jerusalem."[35] Certainly, these might have existed, but we have no direct evidence they did, and none about what was in them. And if early traditions were preserved there, we would still need to explain why they did not experience the destiny of early Greek genealogical traditions which were so frequently *re*made over time. Perhaps there is something about Levantine scribal culture that is different enough that such an argument could be made; but that is the point, we need to ask the question.

In other words, if we are to establish, today, that biblical genealogical traditions are fundamentally different from ancient Greek ones, we cannot do it simply by insisting that older conclusions have a limited validity instead of a robust validity. We have to *start over.* I think when we do that, especially with the comparison produced below in view, we will indeed come to different conclusions altogether. And here of course we re-encounter the purpose of this book. When it comes to segmented genealogical traditions that connect the familiar worlds of antiquity to their own heroic ages, scholars of ancient Greek traditions not only face the same problems and questions because they have such similar traditions. In this case, they also have them from more or less the same period, looking back more or less the same amount of time. On both sides, the vast majority of surviving texts are mid-first-millennium compositions looking back at events that, if historical, we would have to place in the second millennium BCE.

As a result, classical examples do not only suggest the world of the possible where the question of how people inherit and adapt earlier genealogical traditions is concerned, but specifically what we can expect of authors working with heroic traditions in the mid-first millennium BCE, looking back at an imagined era of heroic origins. Again, in a period where so little evidence of any sort survives, comparison offers the opportunity to expand the useful corpus tremendously. And again, this is the particular value of comparisons with ancient Greece in particular, where there are so many

---

34. Mario Liverani, *Israel's History and the History of Israel* (London: Routledge, 2005), p. 42. He notes that "whole tribe[s] might be invented," and that the familiar concept of the twelve tribes of Israel may not have existed before the sixth century BCE (Liverani, *Israel's History and the History of Israel*, pp. 59-60; Tobolowsky, *The Myth of the Twelve Tribes of Israel*, pp. 35-36).

35. Ernst Axel Knauf and Philippe Guillaume, *A History of Biblical Israel: The Fate of the Tribes and Kingdoms from Merenptah to Bar Kochba* (Sheffield: Equinox, 2016), p. 45.

more ancient Greek genealogical traditions to study, and so many more visible interactions between later authors and earlier sources to consider.

Ancient Greek Genealogies

Again, not so long ago, scholars of ancient Greece sieved genealogical traditions for kernels of truth about early realities as avidly as any. Today, however, a much more dynamic approach to what the details of these ancient texts preserve is increasingly common in that field while Hebrew Bible scholars still often pursue a modified kernels-of-truth approach. If there is a practical explanation, it is, once again, simply the weight of evidence. And here I refer to the fact that scholars of ancient Greece have a great many more examples to work with and have had to grapple with such recognitions as the fact that the most familiar articulation of Greek identity in genealogical terms, the Panhellenic genealogy, was itself a later invention.[36] How late remains a debated topic, but "no one argues for a mature Panhellenism in the *Iliad* (or in the late Dark Age or early Archaic period more broadly)" today, the key word being "mature."[37] Thus, the corresponding recognition that later genealogical constructions, those that charter Panhellenism, are *of necessity* inventions has long since spurred a greater scholarly openness to the presence of invention.[38]

In other words, once we know that the surviving representations of the relationships between Ion, Doros, Akhaios, *et al.* were created to establish a Panhellenic vision of the past, we *cannot* imagine they, in their present form, mainly tell us what the original set of relationships between these groups was, long ago. And this recognition opens the door for another. It turns out that, after its invention, the Panhellenic concept,

---

36. "Most nineteenth-century scholars treated the Greeks as a distinct, discrete people from the beginning," as McInerney notes, though there were some—like Karl-Otfried Müller and Ernst Curtius who thought that "the Greeks" were "the biological and cultural fusion of two Unterstämme, Ionians and Dorians, whose innate genius determined the cultural flowering of the Classical age." However, Numa Denis Fustel de Coulanges "and most of the historians who came after him championed the notion that the turning point for the Greeks came not in the blending of two subdivisions of the Greeks but in the founding of cities." Which is not to say that Fustel de Coulanges was any less convinced that Greek "tribes existed before the emergence of the fully developed city-states of the Classical age," who were still members of the unified Greek nation (Jeremy McInerney, "Ethnos and Ethnicity in Early Greece," in *Ancient Perceptions of Greek Ethnicity* [ed. Irad Malkin; Washington, DC: Center for Hellenic Studies, 2001], pp. 52-53). Thus, the recognition that there was no early Panhellenism was an important one that distanced later research from earlier.

37. Shawn A. Ross, "Barbarophonos: Language and Panhellenism in the Iliad," *Classical Philology* 100.4 (2005), p. 302.

38. Ross, "Barbarophonos," p. 302.

along with its basic genealogical framework, served as a constant source for efforts to make and remake the present through altering the organization of the past. This, in its turn, reveals the fallacy of imagining that any set of relationships presented in surviving texts is necessarily a coded message about a distant era of origins, let alone a neutral representation of the historiographical realities of that era. As above, so below; even the early versions of these traditions were likely representations of ideological imaginings.

Thus, scholars of ancient Greece, more so than of ancient Israel and Judah, have had to accept that genealogical traditions, as an inherited form, generally serve as the *medium* through which different groups pursue ideological agendas in a way that, of course, only compounds over time. So, for example, it is likely enough that the Athenians, originally, were genealogically disadvantaged. Notoriously marginal in the Homeric poems, despite the Bronze Age origins of their city, early traditions linked the Athenians to the autochthonous Erechtheus. Genealogically speaking, this is a problem: people born out of the ground have few relatives.[39] At some point, however, the Athenians seem to have reinvented themselves as Ionians, while never precisely divesting from their myths of autochthony. At any rate, Solon supposedly referred to Athens as the "eldest country of Ionia," likely in the early sixth century BCE.[40] Ultimately, since Ion would be described as the son of Xuthus, grandson of Hellen, and Creusa, the daughter of the Athenian culture hero Erechtheus, this development attached Athens's native genealogical traditions to the evolving Panhellenic framework.

Then, once Athenian traditions had been placed in this framework, the framework itself of course became the basis for subsequent claims and interpretations. Early on, the assertion of Ionian identity might have played a role in Athens's quest to acquire the island of Salamis.[41] And as time went on, this Ionian identification would feed additional Athenian attempts to assert hegemony over the Ionian city states of Asia Minor, which they attempted to help in the Ionian Revolt of 499 BCE, the act that precipitated the Persian Wars a decade later.[42] Still later, however, Ionian identity would

39. See the excellent summary in Timothy Gantz, *Early Greek Myth* (Baltimore, MD: Johns Hopkins University Press, 1993), I, pp. 233-47. Gantz also observes that Hesiod "makes no mention of any early figures from Athens, save for Pandion" (p. 233), and that other early figures such as Kekrops and Erichthonios are also described as autochthonous.

40. J.P. Crielaard, "The Ionians in the Archaic Period: Shifting Identities in a Changing World," in *Ethnic Constructs in Antiquity: The Role of Power and Tradition* (ed. Ton Derks and Nico Royman; Amsterdam Archaeological Studies, 13; Amsterdam: Amsterdam University Press, 2009), p. 42.

41. Patterson, *Kinship Myth in Ancient Greece*, p. 72.

42. See the discussion in Tobolowsky, *The Sons of Jacob and the Sons of Herakles,*

be central to Athens's claim to leadership of the Delian League, which was the counterpart of the Peloponnesian League helmed by (Dorian) Sparta in the Peloponnesian War.[43] In other words, the centrality of Ionian identity waxed and waned in Athens to some degree in response to its political usefulness in a given context; but as time went on, it acquired many different uses.

Indeed, subsequent alterations could change the status of Ion himself, with corresponding effects on the self-presentation of these Ionians, however defined. A case in point is Euripides's play *Ion,* which contends, or reveals, that Ion's father was not Xuthus after all but Apollo himself, obviously elevating the lineage of the Athenians in the process.[44] In addition, the play also offers a number of other genealogical justifications for the Athenian present and future, again linking the Ionians of Athens with the Ionians of Asia Minor.[45] Another play, Sophocles's *Ajax,* makes "the Salaminians of the chorus ... autochthonous Athenians" and attempts in various ways to navigate around inconvenient details, such as the fact that the titular Ajax, who was king of Salamis, is *not* an Ionian but an Aeacid.[46] Demetra Kasimis has also pointed to the way that Euripides's play justifies the unequal treatment of Athenian metics, a free immigrant class, because of their lack of a blood connection to the Athenian nation.[47]

Then, while the discourse surrounding the Persian War tended toward expressing the unity of Ionian Athenian and Dorian Spartans in the face of the Persian threat, Peloponnesian War discourses were sometimes built around reasserting the crucial difference between the two.[48] In other words, the fact that Ion and Doros were brothers could serve as a means of assert-

---

pp. 101-102. See also Hall, *Hellenicity*, pp. 27, 68-70; Crielaard, "The Ionians in the Archaic Period: Shifting Identities in a Changing World," pp. 40-41.

43. Christoph Ulf notes that it was the Ionian cities themselves who asked whether the Athenians rather than the Spartans might want to lead them—and just as "the term 'Dorian' allowed Sparta to build up its area of dominance, which comprised a large area of the Peloponnese" ... "Athens used the name 'Ionian' in order to justify its position in the Delian-Attic league" (Christoph Ulf, "The Development of Greek Ethnê," in *Politics of Ethnicity and the Crisis of the Peloponnesian League* [ed. Nino Luraghi and Peter Funke; Hellenic Studies, 32; Cambridge, MA: Center for Hellenic Studies, 2009], p. 235).

44. Tobolowsky, *The Sons of Jacob and the Sons of Herakles*, pp. 101-102.

45. Hall, *Ethnic Identity in Greek Antiquity*, p. 56.

46. Ruth Scodel, "Aetiology, Autochthony, and Athenian Identity in Ajax and Oedipus Coloneus," *Bulletin of the Institute of Classical Studies. Supplement* 87 (2006), p. 65.

47. Demetra Kasimis, "The Tragedy of Blood-Based Membership: Secrecy and the Politics of Immigration in Euripides's Ion," *Political Theory* 41.2 (2013), pp. 231-56.

48. Hall, *Ethnic Identity in Greek Antiquity*, p. 37; Ulf, "The Development of Greek Ethnê," p. 235.

ing their closeness to each other, *or* their separateness, depending on circumstances. Elsewhere, K.F.B. Fletcher has drawn attention to the way Apollodorus, in attempting to offer a systematic vision of the whole course of Greek tradition, actively attempts to disassociate Greece from Rome on a genealogical basis.[49] Generally, Fletcher sees Apollodorus creating "a series of genealogies connecting Greeks with their Mediterranean neighbors" but purposefully excluding Rome in the process.[50] Someone else could have or might have done it differently.

In short, much more than we see the preservation of early genealogical details over time, and, with them, coded information about the actual relationships between early groups, we see nearly constant processes of dynamic adaptation. We see how genealogies are used to make claims and respond to them, and how change begets change over time. We see how they are rearranged to license new ethnic formulations or to invent charters for new ethnic constructions, and how that, too, merely provides the starting point for the next round of developments and responses.

In addition, it is perfectly clear that later authors did not only manipulate the parts of the genealogy that were nearest in time to their own. Quite the opposite; it was the era of the origins that most often served as a platform for new claims. And the vast majority of changes seem ideological in character. Thus, if Ion was originally the son of Xuthus and became the son of Apollo, it does not mean that Ion and Xuthus reflect a real historiographical reality while Ion and Apollo are an invention. Xuthus might, and likely did, already have some significance in earlier Athens that made the development of his relationship to Hellen meaningful in early periods, in much the same way a relationship with Apollo would be later. Thus, excavating the earlier layer does not reveal the unvarnished truth but simply an earlier layer of discourse.

The question, and it is an important one, is whether all this is really applicable to the study of the Hebrew Bible's genealogical traditions. On the one hand, what seems to be true about ancient Greek genealogical traditions seems to be true of *segmented genealogical traditions* generally. As Bruce Lincoln put it, "Basic to the segmentary pattern is the principle of fission and fusion, whereby the members of a total social field can recombine at different levels of integration to form aggregates of varying size."[51] In other words, the simple fact that segmented genealogical tradi-

---

49. K.F.B. Fletcher, "Systematic Genealogies in Apollodorus' Bibliotheca and the Exclusion of Rome from Greek Myth," *Classical Antiquity* 27.1 (2008), p. 60.

50. Fletcher, "Systematic Genealogies in Apollodorus' Bibliotheca," p. 60.

51. Bruce Lincoln, *Discourse and the Construction of Society: Comparative Studies of Myth, Ritual and Classification* (New York: Oxford University Press, 1989), p. 19. In his view, society is a "synthesis" of parts in which the parts are divided by "cleavages" which are "only imperfectly and precariously bound together by the officially sanctioned sentiments of affinity that coexist with, and partially mask, the disin-

tions purport to represent the nature of the connection between *separate* groups means that both connection and separation are constantly available as options for those who use those traditions to make claims, and construct different constellations of connection and separation as well. This means that if it is really the case that the biblical representation of the twelve tribes of Israel only ever served as a means of articulating the connectedness of all Israel, that would, in fact, be quite unusual.

At the same time, the development of Panhellenism itself would appear to be quite a particular event for which there might be no parallel in the history of Israel and Judah. And the world inhabited by the people of ancient Israel and Judah was likely, in most cases, much smaller and less complex than that embraced by Greek colonization. Still, just as in every chapter in this book, while what *is* true in one context should never be regarded as proof of what happened in the other, it can provide us the means to ask the question *whether or not* it might be true in the other, which can be very useful indeed.

Genealogical Manipulation in the Hebrew Bible

Personally, I think biblical "Panisraelitism" was indeed invented in much the same way Panhellenism was, and perhaps even around the same time. And I am not the only one. There simply are not nearly as many good reasons to think the Judahites thought of themselves as Israelites in early periods as has long been assumed. It may be then, as many now argue, that the Judahites only came to understand themselves as Israelites in later periods. As a result, the genealogy of the sons of Jacob would be very much like the genealogy of the sons of Hellen, building a new identity out of sub-identities by constructing a genealogical framework in which they could coexist. I mentioned above that the majority of Hebrew Bible scholars still embraced a "preservative" method of interpreting the details of the Hebrew Bible's genealogies, but there is indeed a growing fondness for a "cultural invention" method that interrogates when and how a "Panisraelite" vision of Israel might have developed, by scrutinizing tribal lists and reconstructing the possible history of Panisraelitism.[52]

Yet here we return to a discussion from the first chapter. Contemporary theories of ethnicity actually do not require us to make a distinction between "real" and "invented" ideas. More simply, for the general question of what

tegrative ... sentiments of estrangement" (Lincoln, *Discourse and the Construction of Society*, pp. 10-11). Thus, segmented genealogical traditions are a literal representation of this synthesis across cleavages, for which see Lincoln, *Discourse and the Construction of Society*, pp. 18-19.

52. Tobolowsky, *The Myth of the Twelve Tribes of Israel*, pp. 45-52.

genealogical traditions preserve, it just does not matter whether Panisraelite identity was "invented" or there from the very beginning. After all,
whether descended biologically from the early Israelites or not, the Judahites would still constantly have been in the business of redescribing their
Israelite identity, because that is what identity is. Israelite identity encountered different circumstances in ancient Judah than ancient Israel regardless. And, the Judahites had segmented genealogical traditions, which are
remarkably easy to use to make the past something new. How could genealogical manipulation in service to diverse agendas not have happened, even
without changing many of the details of the basic tradition? Genealogical
representations of identity present a set of contents, organized into a set of
relationships, but there are many different possible ways of interpreting
what those relationships mean and justify. The Ionians and Dorians are an
obvious case in point. It can be most important in one context that they are
both descended from Hellen, and in another that they are separate entities.
The same is surely true of Judah and Benjamin, say.[53]

So, there may or may not be significant differences between when and
how the *concepts* of Panhellenism and Panisraelitism emerged; one may or
may not be considerably more ancient than the other. But, as I argued in the
first chapter, the development of the concept was surely only the starting
point for the processes of continual reinvention that are part and parcel with
what ethnic identity is either way. Thus, Panhellenism, the framework,
became the source for any number of visions of Panhellenism in different
places, for different reasons. And "the" Panhellenic genealogy was always
in flux as a result as different actors sought personal and national prestige, new relationships, justifications for conflict, and much else besides
by changing the details of the inherited tradition in various ways. There
is no reason to doubt that the same is true of Panisraelitism, whenever and
however it emerged.

If this is true, it is also very likely true that the genealogical traditions
that provided the charter for Panisraelitism were a major medium through
which it was constantly reinvented, because of the nature of the segmented
form. In recent years, a few scholars, among whom I count myself, have
begun to explore the ramifications of this recognition. Indeed, an article
by Mark McEntire and Wongi Park makes the point I am also making
about the fundamental link between "primordial theories … [the idea
that] ethnicity is a naturally occurring phenomenon rooted in the real
lives of ancestors" and the "traditional understanding" that the Hebrew
Bible's genealogical traditions "preserve Israelite ancestry in genealogi-

53. For a discussion of this topic, see Andrew Tobolowsky, "Benjamin and the
Anonymous Ten Tribes of Israel: A Holistic Approach to Tribal Confusions," *VT* 73.3
(2023), pp. 426-44.

cal form."[54] As I have insisted throughout, it should be the case, and has not been the case, especially in the study of the Hebrew Bible, that *as soon* as we recognize the constant fluidity of ethnic identity, we need to recognize the corresponding fluidity of traditions that provide charters for identity. They are not fossilized artifacts reflecting what the ethnic nation was in its early days; they are the arena in which the ongoing "strategic negotiation of identity" occurs.[55] And this is true whether the identity concept that is being negotiated is already very ancient, as Panisraeliteism might or might not have been in fifth-century BCE Judah, or not, as Panhellenism, which was developed around this time, was not—which is to say that those who inherit identity frameworks continue to adapt them in the same ways and to the same extent, continually, wherever they originally came from. Yet the older model hangs on, preserved, in my view, almost exclusively by an anxiety about what we lose if these traditions do not primarily preserve what we are used to having, and protected by the scholarly ability to acknowledge concerns with one hand and open a narrow way to preserve a premise with the other.[56]

Thus, in the end, the necessity of leaving an old paradigm behind and moving on to a new one does not come from any radical revision of the history of biblical genealogical traditions. And it does not come from the growing recognition that the Panisraelite genealogy may be "invented" rather than "genuine." It comes, very simply, from the fact that the old idea of a people preserving its original traditions, which were collectively produced from generation to generation, is wrong. It comes from recognizing how identity actually works, and how traditions develop as a result. And what all of these mean together, is, simply, that scouring the details of genealogical traditions not for deep memories of early arrangements but for the traces of ideological agendas is the way to go. And when we do, I think we quickly find a number of examples that prove the point.

For one thing, in my work, I have often tried to draw attention to the sheer scale of genealogical discourse in the Hebrew Bible, and to the particular era in which most of it seems to have been composed. In other words, there are an extraordinary number of descriptions of twelve-tribe Israel, and no one really doubts the vast majority of them are from the sixth and fifth centuries BCE, or, for that matter, that they are mostly written by Judahites.[57] Nor do the majority of scholars think, any longer, that

54. McEntire and Park, "Ethnic Fission and Fusion in Biblical Genealogies," p. 33.

55. McEntire and Park, "Ethnic Fission and Fusion in Biblical Genealogies," p. 33.

56. McEntire and Park's article contains many useful examples of efforts to renegotiate "ethnic fission and fusion," as the title suggests.

57. That is, there are around twenty-six different lists, fifteen in the Pentateuch alone, and six in the books of Chronicles, and most are believed to have been written by the Priestly author or the Chronicler.

the late debut of so many texts is meaningless because of the supposedly early origins of the traditions they reflect. Thus, whatever is true about the history of tribal concepts, we still have to ask why so many different authors were suddenly so interested in describing Israel in genealogical, or tribal terms. Certainly, the plethora of genealogical compositions does not serve a clear narrative purpose. No one would ever need to describe, for example, the arrangement of the tribes in the wilderness camp as many times as we see in the book of Numbers. So, at the very least, we should conclude that these diverse and numerous depictions reflect what they are, a number of relatively late Judahite efforts to describe and redescribe tribal Israel—which, therefore, most reflect a late *enthusiasm* for redescription. And it is hard to believe this has any other cause than the one that motivated the similar interest that flourished at the same time in ancient Greece.

As for specific examples of genealogical adaptation, we can consider the fact that the most extensive genealogical effort in the Hebrew Bible, an apparent attempt to recapitulate the history of Israel in genealogical form spanning the first nine chapters of Chronicles, shows numerous signs of the author actively aggregating and organizing traditions within an encompassing genealogical framework that are neither aggregated nor organized elsewhere. So, for example, a figure such as the judge Othniel, who is only described in the Primary History as a son of Kenaz and Caleb's brother, gets a full genealogical context in 1 Chronicles 4. Now he is the son of Kenaz, the brother of someone named Seraiah, the father of Hathath and Meonothai, the grandfather of Ophrah, the uncle of Joab, and the great-uncle of Ge-Harashim (1 Chron. 4.13). He has gone from a lone figure to one embedded in a genealogical superstructure.

Indeed, we can start from the beginning here. The text 1 Chronicles 1, on the whole, does little more than combine the genealogies of Genesis to create a comprehensive account of Israel's descent from Adam through Abraham. It invents no details that are not to be found elsewhere. It is, however, interesting that such a comprehensive picture is never actually given in Genesis itself and that the author of this text has combined the genealogical traditions in the *form* we find them in Genesis. In other words, Genesis 5 presents the genealogy of Adam and Noah as a linear genealogy; Genesis 10 presents the genealogies of Noah's sons, Shem, Ham, and Japheth, in segmented form; and Gen. 11.10-25 completes the picture by describing the descent of Abraham from Shem in a linear fashion. And in the process of combining these descriptions together, 1 Chronicles 1 retains these differences. Here, too, the ancestors mentioned in Genesis 5 are listed in linear fashion, followed by a segmented genealogy of Shem, Ham, and Japheth like Genesis 10, and then once again a linear account of the genealogy from Gen. 11.10-25. Thus, it reproduces in one chapter what takes six in Genesis, but in a way that reveals its direct dependence on either the Genesis texts or Genesis's own source materials.[58]

Other parts of the genealogy surely show creative adaptation. Repeatedly, "loose" figures such as Heman, Kalkol, and Darda, which is to say figures who are mentioned in Genesis through Kings but are never described in enough detail to extract genealogical information, get the familiar genealogical treatment of being aggregated within an existing system. In 1 Kgs 4.31 they, along with Ethan the Ezrahite, are only mentioned as the sons of Mahol, and as men Solomon is wiser than. In 1 Chron. 2.6, all four now appear among the five sons of Zerah, son of Judah through Tamar. Most strikingly, some figures—notably Samuel—actually have their background redefined within this genealogical structure. Samuel, "an Ephraimite in Samuel and Kings, becomes here not just a Levite but a Kohathite," presumably to better conform to how the role he plays in the book of Samuel was understood by the time of the Chronicler.[59] In other words, since Samuel is largely a religious leader in his eponymous book, and performs sacrifices and so on, it makes sense that he would seem to be a Levite once the notion that these things were specifically the job of Levites took root. The genealogy simply shifted to match.

Others of my studies have explored additional examples of genealogical manipulation. I have investigated even the possibility that the Jacob tradition and the Israelite tribal tradition evolved separately from each other in the same way that traditions of Hellen originally circulated apart from many figures who would come to be regarded as his family.[60] The idea that Abraham, Isaac, and Jacob were not originally family but instead more local figures who were eventually knit together is quite an old one now, but it has recently been reopened in Panisraelite scholarship as a way of thinking about how Israelite and Judahite traditions may have been brought together in the first place.[61] Casey Strine has suggested that, whatever the history of the Jacob tradition, it was reinvented to allow him to serve as a mediating figure of sorts for Israelite refugees to Judah after the Assyrian conquest of Israel.[62] Nadav Na'aman has given more weight to the idea that

---

58. Tobolowsky, "Reading Genesis through Chronicles," pp. 159-61.

59. Tobolowsky, "Reading Genesis through Chronicles," p. 164.

60. Tobolowsky, *The Sons of Jacob and the Sons of Herakles.*

61. See, e.g., Ernst Axel Knauf, "Bethel: The Israelite Impact on Judean Language and Literature," in *Judah and the Judeans in the Persian Period* (ed. Manfred Oeming and Oded Lipschits; Winona Lake, IN: Eisenbrauns, 2006), p. 292.

62. Casey Strine, "Your Name Shall No Longer Be Jacob, but Refugee: Involuntary Migration and the Development of the Jacob Narrative," in *Scripture as Social Discourse* (ed. J.M. Keady, T.E. Klutz, and C.A. Strine; London: T. & T. Clark, 2018), pp. 51-69.

Jacob became the familiar Panisraelite figure only in Judah in relatively late periods.[63] None of this would mean that Jacob himself was not an early figure of Israelite myth, only that the role he played expanded considerably over time.

In addition, a number of biblical narratives can at least potentially be read as the product of struggles between families of priests: the curse on the line of Eli, for example, to which Jeremiah may have belonged; or the destruction of the Korahites in the wilderness, who, nevertheless, survived (Num. 26.11) and are described as having important duties at the temple in later periods (1 Chron. 9.19; 12.6; 26.1, 19; 2 Chron. 20.19; Psalms 42; 45; 46; 47; 48; 49; 85; 87; 88). Perhaps even the disappearance of the line of Moses from the text after Jonathan son of Gershom should be explained in terms of genealogical competition (Judg. 18.30).[64] Where systematic issues are concerned, I have suggested that the removal of Levi from membership in the tribal system to be replaced by Ephraim and Manasseh, typically explained as a result of Levi's redefinition as a priestly tribe, may instead be a Priestly—capital letter—"idea," in that it often appears in narratives in which the other tribes are actually honoring Levi in some way.[65] And both the account of the split of the United Monarchy into two kingdoms and of the conquest of Israel in Kings seem rather unclear on whether there are one or two tribes in Israel, presumably an indication of some sort of competition between tribal partisans, conducted through revisions of the past.[66] In still other cases, an approach that imagines an equivalence between these authors in different parts of the Mediterranean rim offers a better explanation for certain aspects of biblical genealogical discourse than anything the "preservative" model might suggest. To go back to the examples I started with, Noth was certainly working too hard when he attempted to explain the prominence of the tribe of Judah, in a book that was largely put together in Judah, by suggesting it mainly reflected the early arrival of Judahites in the region of Israel in the Late Bronze Age.[67]

In my view, then, the combination of all these different kinds of genealogical manipulation, and potential instances of genealogical manipulation, with the sheer volume of sixth through fourth century BCE genealogical

---

63. Na'aman, "The Jacob Story and the Formation of Biblical Israel."

64. In 1 Sam. 22.6 Saul has the priests of Nob killed, except for Abiathar who returns to Anathoth, and Jeremiah is apparently a priest from Anathoth (Jer. 1.1).

65. Tobolowsky, *The Myth of the Twelve Tribes of Israel*, p. 56.

66. Among other issues, 1 Kgs 12.20 states unequivocally that "only the tribe of Judah" remained loyal to Rehoboam but 12.21 has him mustering an army of Judahites and Benjaminites while 2 Kgs 17.18 is equally explicit that after the Assyrian conquest "only the tribe of Judah remained." See the discussion in Tobolowsky, "Benjamin and the Anonymous Ten Tribes of Israel."

67. Tobolowsky, *The Myth of the Twelve Tribes of Israel*, p. 55.

compositions, gives us every reason to believe that biblical authors who made use of segmented genealogies were up to the same kinds of things as Greek authors, and around the same time. This would mean that the kind of agendas we find reflected in the shifting data of Greek genealogical traditions—Athens pursuing Salamis, elevating itself against its rivals, pursuing both alliance and war—are the kind we should expect to find in biblical genealogical traditions as well. And in both, we are perfectly justified in regarding these traditions as what David Litwa calls "rhetorically engineered products designed to generate social effects."[68] We can, I imagine, study the "social effects" of many different eras through them, if we do not hang on to old approaches and old priorities too tightly.

On Tradition Inheritance

Because the study of genealogical traditions represents what I have described as the *beau idéal* of the phenomenon I am interested in—a truly clear example of how the work of scholars in each discipline can illuminate possibilities in the other—the three-step organization of every chapter is especially clear and straightforward here, too. I have discussed how approaches in each discipline came to differ, and what one, therefore, can offer the other. And now, according to the program, I turn my attention to what contemporary debates suggest about the *future* of investigating genealogical traditions.

In particular, I am interested in how the phenomenology of inheriting and repurposing genealogical traditions can shed light on just how inventive the inheritance of traditions can be. Here I am referring to the still common conviction, in both fields, that there is an innate conservatism in how the reuse of inherited traditions can be conducted, even to the point of a kind of iron law of inheritance. I refer to the position, and variations on it, articulated by Margalit Finkelberg this way: "even a falsification of one's genealogical position could not be carried out arbitrarily, that is, without making it consistent in terms of the universally agreed upon system."[69] As I say, this is a subset of a widely accepted view in the study of ancient traditions of all sorts. Malkin, for one—for the most part, one of the most insightful analysts of how traditions are adapted in different contexts—cites, approvingly, Fritz Graf's gloss: that "a myth is not a specific poetic text, it is the subject material, a plot fixed in broad outline and with char-

---

68. M. David Litwa, "Genealogy," in *How the Gospels Became History: Jesus and Mediterranean Myths* (ed. Dale B. Martin and L.L. Welborn; New Haven, CT: Yale University Press, 2019), pp. 80-81.

69. Margalit Finkelberg, *Greeks and Pre-Greeks: Aegean Prehistory and Greek Heroic Tradition* (Cambridge, UK: Cambridge University Press, 2005), p. 28.

acters no less fixed, which an individual poet is free to alter only within
limits."[70] Thus, Malkin himself suggests, "If the poem is about Odysseus,
the hero must come to Ithaca and nowhere else."[71] The existing authority
of the known story, supposedly, constrains anyone who would try to tell
it from making changes that are too radical. And if someone makes up
a genealogical detail that is inconsistent with the system, it, supposedly,
could not possibly be effective in achieving its ends.

Limiting our discussion to genealogy alone, we can certainly say that
what these scholars, and many others, refer to is an accurate characteri-
zation of most forms of genealogical manipulation. Generally, ancient
genealogies operated in such a way that one of the most prominent formal
characteristics of genealogical traditions tends to be what Malkin calls the
"tension between fixity and fluidity."[72] A genealogist, most often, will not
suggest that it was actually Herakles who was the ancestor of Doros, Ion,
etc., not Hellen. They will instead invent a new sibling, or child, or nephew
for Hellen, or tell a story in which suddenly, even though we have been told
that Hellen is the father of Doros, ancestor of the Dorians, actually Doros's
real father was a Macedonian interloper who had an affair with Hellen's
wife Orseis, and so on. The fixity, the most familiar portions of the genealogy, becomes the stage upon which fluidity is enacted.

Most often, however, is not always, and unlikely is not impossible. The
idea that a genealogist *cannot* successfully introduce a radical innovation or
a dramatic change is one that deserves attention. After all, what would have
to be true for this to always be the case? Every single successful genealogist
would have to be governed, somehow, by invisible laws that they instinctively know, that no one disobeys even by accident. It would have to be the
case that no accidents ever defy the gravity of how things usually work to
become authoritative after all. The laws of inheritance would have to work
mystically and collectively, and quite differently than the act of retelling can
operate today. We can put it this way. In Finkelberg's formulation, there is
a "universally agreed upon system." Even limiting the scope to a literate
elite, how exactly does the widely spaced "universe" of Greek settlements
agree in such a way that not only the relationships but their significance will
always stay the same? Even when they try, they might well fail, and there is
no good reason to believe that every relevant author was trying.

I would argue that scholars have confused a strong *tendency* for an iron
law. And I think this is because there has been a general misapprehension
about why genealogists tend to make changes that are "consistent in terms

70. Malkin, *The Returns of Odysseus*, p. 50; Fritz Graf, *Greek Mythology: An Introduction* (trans. T. Marier; Baltimore, MD: Johns Hopkins University Press, 1993), p. 2.
71. Malkin, *The Returns of Odysseus*, p. 50.
72. Malkin, *The Returns of Odysseus*, p. 50.

of the universally agreed upon system" in the first place.[73] It is not because they must, because no one would dare do otherwise, or because no one who did would be successful. It is because it is useful to do so. The authority of the existing formulation, in other words, is useful to the pursuit of whatever agenda is under construction in a given case. And even if we reframe the conclusion above so that we do not say "a genealogist cannot truly invent a new story or formulation" but "a genealogist cannot do these things and succeed in their ambitions," or "cannot do these things and gain a hearing," an acknowledgement of why this rarely happens better positions us to acknowledge that, nevertheless, sometimes it does. Many people will do things the best and easiest way; others will not.

At any rate, the idea that there are hard and fast rules survives, and—it will not surprise readers who have made it this far—I think this is because the basic premise is continually reinvented in supposedly better and more sophisticated ways. The most common of these involves typically vague references to the idea of "cultural memory" or "social memory." I want to be very clear here; I do not quibble with the *existence* of either quantity. Memory, in any period, is fundamentally social; how other people remember and have remembered the past exerts tremendous influence on how any individual is likely to do it.[74] The stories we hear do have tremendous influence on what stories we think can be told.

At the same time, scholars of ancient traditions in particular have a tendency to define cultural memory in such a way that it is no more than a "substitute" for the linear model of tradition inheritance described in the first chapter.[75] As Ian Douglas Wilson observes, this is especially true of those scholars of ancient traditions who are influenced by Jan Assman's definition of the concept. Generally, Assman "understands 'cultural memory' as transmissive. ... It is 'the handing down of meaning' via significant acts of communication over time."[76] And one can certainly hear in Assman's assertion that "in the world of nonwritten memory transmission the heir to tradition is measured by the amount of this invisible tradition that he is able to embody and present," a direct echo of Milman Parry's argument almost a century earlier that "the good singer wins his fame by his ease and versatility in handling a tradition which he knows more thoroughly than anyone else."[77] This is "cultural memory" reinvented to *mean Naturpoesie*

73. Finkelberg, *Greeks and Pre-Greeks*, p. 28.

74. Eviatar Zerubavel notes the fact that if you ask young Americans who the key figures of American history are, they will tend to name the same ones—"George Washington, Abraham Lincoln, Thomas Jefferson, Benjamin Franklin" (Eviatar Zerubavel, *Time Maps* [Chicago: University of Chicago Press, 2003], p. 3).

75. Pioske, "Retracing a Remembered Past," p. 294.

76. Wilson, *Kingship and Memory in Ancient Judah*, p. 32.

77. Jan Assmann and Rodney Livingstone, *Religion and Cultural Memory: Ten*

and similar, a renaming of the idea that ancient peoples simply handed down the same set of shared traditions *ad infinitum.*

As in the first chapter's discussion of ethnicity, however, things look very different when we revisit the topic of the inheritance of cultural traditions with an understanding of cultural memory that matches how contemporary scholars *of that subject* now understand it. Here, I point once more to Wilson's discussion of the work of Jeffrey Olick, Joyce Robbins, Astrid Erll, and James V. Wertsch. These have revealed that

> there is no such "thing" as social or collective memory. There is no "mystical group mind," as Jeffrey Olick and Joyce Robbins put it; there are instead, "sets of mnemonic practices in various social sites." An individual actually has distinct memories; a society does not.[78]

I draw attention, as well, to Erll's own argument that "societies do not remember literally; but much of what is done to reconstruct a shared past bears some resemblance to the processes of individual memory, such as the selectivity and perspectivity inherent in the creation of versions of the past according to present knowledge and needs."[79] In other words, collective memory is not any less dynamic over time than any other form of tradition inheritance. It changes in the same ways, for the same reasons, and without robbing from individual authors their creativity and personal apprehensions.

Another way to put it is that when we picture individuals working with inherited traditions, we really need to picture *individuals,* who make mistakes, who understand, know, and remember things differently from one another, who can do really surprising things. Even when authors simply repeat, or attempt to repeat, older visions of the past, they may have quite a different sense of what to emphasize in them than the next person. They,

---

Studies (Stanford, CA: Stanford University Press, 2006), p. 83; Parry, *Studies in the Epic Technique of Oral Verse-Making. II*, p. 15. As Miller notes, "Assman marshals no evidence in support of this ... view... but it allows him to conclude that the precise knowledge of oral texts required in oral societies limits cultural literacy to an elite few in a sharper form than in written cultures" (Robert D. Miller, *Oral Tradition in Ancient Israel* (Eugene, OR: Cascade Books, 2011), p. 7 n. 57).

78. Wilson, *Kingship and Memory in Ancient Judah*, p. 24; Jeffrey K. Olick and Joyce Robbins, "Social Memory Studies: From 'Collective Memory' to the Historical Sociology of Mnemonic Practices," *Annual Review of Sociology* 24 (1998), p. 112; James V. Wertsch, "Collective Memory," in *Memory in Mind and Culture* (ed. Pascal Boyer and James V. Wertsch; Cambridge, UK: Cambridge University Press, 2009), pp. 118-24. See Tobolowsky, "The Hebrew Bible as Mythic 'Vocabulary,'" pp. 9-10.

79. Astrid Erll, "Cultural Memory Studies: An Introduction," in *Cultural Memory Studies: An International and Interdisciplinary Handbook* (ed. Astrid Erll and Ansgar Nünning; Berlin: de Gruyter, 2010), p. 5; Wilson, *Kingship and Memory in Ancient Judah*, p. 24.

or anyone, can only "play by the rules," as I have put it elsewhere, "so far as they individually understand them."[80] This means that new games and regional variations can crop up at any time. Nor, even though many of the changes we see in the retelling of familiar stories are either unintentional or the product of these dynamic misapprehensions, should we shy away from the recognition that sometimes someone will tell an old story in a totally different way on purpose to achieve some end, or tell a new story altogether.

Thus, the correct apprehension of the weight of collective memory, or of the authority of an existing tradition, is that it exerts a strong influence but does not prescribe an outcome. It provides a starting point, but not a straitjacket. And this is *especially* true of oral traditions, because of their inherent fluidity. Meanwhile, we have to at least contemplate the difference between how cultural memory can operate in contexts like ours, with universal education, museums, mass dissemination, and mass communication to enforce it, and in an ancient world without.[81] How far does the writ of the familiar tradition run, however popular it may be in the ancient places most visible to us? From Dan to Beersheba? From Athens to the colonies? Perhaps not. And if a very different story can come into existence outside the centers of power, it can presumably occasionally cross the barrier and become the story that is popular in that center, too.

Broadly speaking then, I think it is, once again, the disruptive nature of these recognitions that explains why contemporary "insights from social memory studies" are rarely "incorporated" in biblical studies "in ways that actually affect the work being done."[82] In other words, the continuing hold the idea of an ethnic nation handing down "its" traditions generation to generation in an unbroken line has on the imagination strikes again. Complexity breeds complexity; the ability of one heir of traditions to go rogue, so to speak, multiplies in force over the generations, producing a to-many-unwelcome reality in which the confident recovery of early traditions and their use to reconstruct early realities becomes impossible. And so, cultural memory, rather than a way of describing the influence broadly held and inherited ideas have on the still-individual work of particular authors,

---

80. Andrew Tobolowsky, "The Thor Movies and the 'Available Myth': Mythic Reinvention in Marvel Movies," in *Theology and the Marvel Universe* (Lanham, MD; Boulder, CO: Lexington Books, 2020), p. 177.

81. As K.L. Noll puts it, we often confront the assumption "that the content now preserved in the Bible was known ... over a vastly dispersed population lacking any public system of education, any technology for disseminating complex theological ideas, and any incentive for trying to inculcate as religious norms a set of stories and ideas that offer no practical value in an agrarian society" (Kurt L. Noll, "Was There Doctrinal Dissemination in Early Yahweh Religion," *BibInt* 16.5 [2008], p. 401).

82. Wilson, *Kingship and Memory in Ancient Judah*, p. 32.

becomes another way of justifying an absence of true individual creativity among ancient authors, to an extent that is quite unjustified, and serves mainly to reify the validity of older preoccupations.

Thus, here, in the end, is how I would put it. If someone wishes to make the claim that ancient storytellers simply could not break certain rules in their storytelling, they should make a list of what they cannot do, and then look around to see if anyone has done it. What, precisely, counts as the "system" that cannot be escaped, the "limits" that cannot be altered? And in my view, posing the question this way would indeed very quickly result in the recognition that what we are talking about *is* a tendency and not a rule. After all, might we not—just as easily as we can say that "Odysseus ... must come to Ithaca and nowhere else," in Malkin's phrase—say that "in any story about the Trojan War, Helen must go to Troy?" But we know there were traditions where Helen did not go to Troy, but only a phantom of her as a kind of divine trick. Just as we know that there were stories where Iphigenia was not sacrificed at Aulis but was spirited away by Artemis instead.[83] We might say it would be impossible to write a tradition in which Agamemnon was not killed upon his arrival back at Argos, as in the famous story, and I am indeed not aware of any such story. But for me, at least, it is terribly hard to read the welter of local traditions that appear in the work of a Pausanias or Apollodorus and not think that if I were to encounter one where Agamemnon escaped and came to x place and founded y shrine, I would be entirely unsurprised. How unlikely is it, really, that there is a version of the story where Odysseus never makes it back, and Telemachus becomes king in his place?

In the genealogical case, quantifying and testing what someone could do or would do with inherited traditions is perhaps easier than in most other cases. After all, there are only so many ways a genealogy *can* be changed, and I think it is very hard to come up with a kind of change that genuinely could not happen. Could, for example, ancient genealogists invent a hero whole cloth? Absolutely they could. In addition to transforming geographical and political entities into eponymous figures to incorporate them into genealogical structures, there are outright inventions like Protogeneia, whose name literally means firstborn. She was introduced into the Hellenic genealogy "as a daughter of Hellen, the mother of 'Aethlios.'" This innovation had the immediate rhetorical effect of making the Aetolians of greater stature than the "'Greeks'... themselves," because Protogeneia is, of course, older than her sister Pandora, mother of Graecus.[84] This must

---

83. See Timothy Gantz, *Early Greek Myth* (Baltimore, MD: Johns Hopkins University Press, 1993), II, pp. 574-75; 583-84.

84. Tobolowsky, *The Sons of Jacob and the Sons of Herakles*, p. 179; M.L. West, *The Hesiodic Catalogue of Women: Its Nature, Structure and Origin* (Oxford: Oxford

have happened at some particular moment in the history of tradition before which, of course, it had not happened. Or there were figures like "Achaemenes," a "concocted" son of Perseus, or "Armenus," created to place the Persians and Armenians on the genealogical map.[85]

Could ancient genealogists change seemingly central traditions about who was descended from whom? Certainly they could. We already saw Euripides's swapping of Apollo for Xuthus as the father of Ion. Or what about Dionysius of Halicarnassus, who makes the Romans Greek, of all things, by deriving them from Oenotrians, Pelasgians, Arcadians, and the "Peloponnesians" who invaded the region with Herakles?[86] Could genealogies cross cultural lines in ways that surprise? Absolutely. We know that Odysseus, as Uthuze, was popular in Etruria, along with Achilles and a number of other Greek figures.[87] Indeed, we know that royal dynasties were attaching themselves to Greek and Trojan heroes even into the mediaeval era.[88]

Or how about this: could different authors entertain the possibility of genealogical narratives that embraced biblical and classical figures *together*, and even before the end of the first millennium BCE? They could and did. First Maccabees, a book of the apocrypha likely from the early first century BCE, supposedly reproduces, in its twelfth chapter, a letter from the Spartans claiming shared descent from Abraham. More striking still, Josephus, operating in the first century CE, claims that Greek sources—Cleodemus Malchus and Alexander Polyhistor—describe an incident in which a great-granddaughter of Abraham had *married* Herakles and had a son, Diodorus. In this story, they become the ancestors of a people known as the Sophacians.[89] Both narratives, for all I know, might have been invented by the author who relates them, and I think that is particularly likely in the first case; but that is the point, ancient authors sim-

University Press, 1985), p. 141. West also notes that the fifth-century BCE author Hellanicus tried to add a "Xenopatra" as a kind of all-purpose ancestress of excluded Greek peoples, but this was not widely adopted (West, *The Hesiodic Catalogue*, pp. 47-48).

85. Erich S. Gruen, *Rethinking the Other in Antiquity* (Princeton, NJ: Princeton University Press, 2011), p. 200.

86. Dionysius of Halicarnassus, *Roman Antiquities* 1.89, see Rebecca Futo Kennedy, *Race and Ethnicity in the Classical World: An Anthology of Primary Sources in Translation* (Indianapolis, IN: Hackett Publishing, 2013), p. 23.

87. Helen Nagy, Larissa Bonfante and Jane K. Whitehead, "Searching for Etruscan Identity," *AJA* 112.3 (2008), pp. 413-17; Erika Simon, "Greek Myth in Etruscan Culture," in *The Etruscan World* (London: Routledge, 2013); Malkin, *The Returns of Odysseus*, p. 7.

88. Patterson, *Kinship Myth in Ancient Greece*, pp. 8-9.

89. For both incidents see Tobolowsky, *The Sons of Jacob and the Sons of Herakles*, p. 205; Patterson, *Kinship Myth in Ancient Greece*, pp. 60-63. The latter can be found in Josephus *Ant.* 1.15.

ply could decide, one day, to invent an ethnic connection based on shared descent, and the next day, so to speak, it could be broadly accepted. In a similar vein, Diodorus Siculus claims that there was an Egyptian tradition of the "wanderings of Osiris," who "left behind a son named Macedon" to rule what would become Alexander's kingdom.[90] If this is true, if the Egyptians really told such a story, it shows that even outsiders could participate in the genealogical competition between groups that is such a prominent feature of internal Greek discourses. It also seems as if certain Egyptians were happy to embrace and amplify Greek traditions about figures like Danaus and Cadmus, who were, in the Greek narratives, from Egypt and Phoenicia respectively.[91] They, of course, used these stories to underscore the cultural superiority of the Egyptians.

Ultimately, the fluidity of genealogical traditions, which can indeed overwhelm their "fixity," is not terribly surprising when we consider all the uses genealogies can have. Lee E. Patterson's *Kinship Myth* offers a number of examples of groups that traded on, or even reconfigured, inherited genealogical traditions to attempt to make various bids for alliances, war, peace, or even simple self-promotion. He begins by talking about the people of Magnesia-on-the-Meander, who successfully increased the prestige of a poorly attended festival by, next time around, writing invitations emphasizing the shared descent between these Magnesians and those they were inviting from the Greek hero Aeolus.[92]

Elsewhere, he describes a situation involving the people of Lampsacus, who wrote to Rome "to request an alliance. ... Based on Lampsacus's putative Trojan origins."[93] For us, the importance of these developments lies not only in the recognition that the uses to which genealogies could be put clearly helped reshape them, but the simple fact that it is easy to imagine way leading on to way. If the Lampsacans had multiple origin traditions, as the Romans themselves did, they might have rejuvenated the Trojan claim just for the purpose of making rapprochement with Rome—just as the ascension of Aeneas as Rome's best known founder had much to do with the ascendancy of the family that claimed him as ancestor. And if this bid was successful for Lampsacus—it was not—it is easy to imagine this story gaining cultural ground as a result, and others losing out.[94]

---

90. Gruen, *Rethinking the Other in Antiquity*, p. 201. Gruen points out that this likely originated during the Ptolemaic dynasty and may have been an attempt at a kind of revenge—"Macedonia may have installed an alien dynasty on the Egyptian land. But ... Macedonia itself owed its origin to an Egyptian dynasty."

91. Gruen, *Rethinking the Other in Antiquity*, p. 202.

92. Patterson, *Kinship Myth in Ancient Greece*, pp. 1-2.

93. Patterson, *Kinship Myth in Ancient Greece*, p. 7; Tobolowsky, *The Sons of Jacob and the Sons of Herakles*, p. 185.

94. Tobolowsky, *The Sons of Jacob and the Sons of Herakles*, p. 185.

Ultimately, all of this is yet another reflection of the grappling I have been doing throughout this book with what it would really take to completely move on from inherited models of the stability of traditions over time, and from models in which traditions are essentially memory in early periods, and something else later on. I think the vestiges of these older ideas are doing much more than the evidence itself does, or would do if it were genuinely revisited, to produce supposedly more secure ways of explaining why someone who inherits a tradition cannot alter it tremendously, and that a cascade of alterations over time cannot produce something entirely new. In the prior chapter I mentioned the element of "transformation," the transformative power of a desire to achieve certain scholarly conclusions, and I think the definition of cultural memory in many contemporary studies of ancient traditions has been transformed to serve the purpose of preserving older convictions.

Nevertheless, the diversity of genealogical phenomena we see in ancient Greek traditions is an eloquent testament to what ancient authors were capable of doing. And in the context of this study, the natural question is: did ancient Israel and Judah really host such a range of transformations? It is hard to say; authors in this region may not have had as many uses for genealogical narratives to begin with. But there is some evidence worth considering here. It might be, for example, that Gilead and Machir are described differently in different contexts. In Judges 5, the oldest tribal text in the Bible, there seems no reason not to read the references to Gilead and Machir as references to independent entities, perhaps full tribes. In most other texts, Machir is treated as a son of Manasseh; in Gen. 50.23, he is even "placed ... on Joseph's knees." But in Numbers 32, and probably Deut. 3.15 and Josh. 13.31, Gilead is a region conquered by Machir, while in a number of other texts, Gilead is a son of Machir (Num. 26.29; 27.1; 36.1; Josh. 17.3). This is certainly reminiscent of a number of Greek texts where features of the landscape and political entities are transformed into eponymous individuals, the better to incorporate them into genealogical traditions.[95]

Then there are some of the examples mentioned above: Samuel who became a Levite, after being born an Ephraimite in different texts. David himself may well have begun as a figure with *no* familiar tribal identity, whose ancestry was later redefined to make him a Judahite.[96] Certainly, he is never actually described as a member of one of the twelve tribes in the books of Samuel. And we can ask why the book of Genesis starts with fig-

95. Tobolowsky, *The Sons of Jacob and the Sons of Herakles*, pp. 181-83, 207 n.44.

96. Andrew Tobolowsky, "Othniel, David, Solomon: Additional Evidence of the Late Development of Normative Tribal Concepts in the South," *ZAW* 13.1 (2019), pp. 212-13.

ures like Adam and Noah in the first place, rather than Abraham, or even Jacob. What purposes did the extensive genealogy in Genesis 10, describing much of the region in terms of descent from one or the other of Noah's sons, serve? How did it change as a result? What did it mean that Edom and Israel were, in Genesis, supposedly founded by brothers, Jacob and Esau, while Ammon and Moab were the incestuous offspring of Lot and his daughters, but, nevertheless, Abraham's great-nephews? And were there other traditions that described these relationships in more and less positive terms? I imagine so.

At any rate, as in other chapters, the significance of what we see in ancient Greek traditions has to be at least suggestive for the study of the Hebrew Bible's. We need, in other words, to be prepared to identify genuinely disruptive developments and inventions, even, perhaps, as extreme as a possibility I have broached elsewhere: the idea that Jacob was a fixture of Israelite lore long before he was regarded as the father of the eponymous ancestors of the tribes,[97] long perhaps before all of Israel's tribes had eponymous ancestors at all. Jeremy McInerney comments on the ability of ancient Greek organizations to appear "one minute as descent-based tribes and another as a regional federation, or *koinon*."[98] Could Israel's tribal system shift in this fashion from a paradigm involving eponymous ancestors to one at least partially without? Or we can think of the reforms of Cleisthenes, tyrant of Athens, who is supposed to have abandoned Athens's old four-tribe organization system, named after the sons of Ion, and created a new ten-tribe system, "each named after a different semi-mythical hero, such as Cecrops or Aegeus."[99] Could biblical visions of Israel's tribal past have changed as much? In my view, the answer to both questions must be yes. And in fact, this is the broader significance of this whole discussion of creativity for the study of the Hebrew Bible. Even many scholars who are unusually alive to the fluidity of biblical traditions over time often lack a robust appreciation for just how completely the past can be reinvented and how dramatic innovation can be. Once again, ancient Greek traditions can provide a ready store of examples for what can happen, which facilitates Hebrew Bible scholars proceeding with an appropriately open mind to the question of what *might* have happened.

In the next chapter, I will continue to discuss the scope of ancient creativity with respect to the study of the foundation traditions of both cultures. Here, we have seen that the ability to create genuinely new connections, and totally reinvent ethnic frontiers, is central to the work the genealogical

---

97. Tobolowsky, *The Sons of Jacob and the Sons of Herakles*.
98. McInerney, "Ethnos and Ethnicity in Early Greece," p. 55.
99. Nancy Evans, *Civic Rites: Democracy and Religion in Ancient Athens* (Berkeley: University of California Press, 2010), p. 28.

traditions are supposed to do—by providing charters for different kinds of social and political relationships. There, we will see that this is even more true where the dynamic interplay of traditions about where, how, and by whom various sites and institutions were founded is concerned. And between these discussions we will see ever more clearly how inherited traditions can function as a kind of language *between* groups, and even groups that we are used to thinking of as culturally distinct. This, above all, is why the details of genealogical traditions could indeed be decisively invented or reinvented. They lived at the intersection of many more influences than we sometimes imagine, and many more than are visible at this distance. As in so many other cases in the study of the ancient world, we must try to imagine what we cannot see.

4

Foundation Traditions

Foundation traditions are those traditions that explain, well, lots of things. One story might describe how a city or temple was founded, or even where features of the natural landscape came from. Another might describe the origins of a people or a nation. They are, of course, everywhere in the ancient world, as they are everywhere today. But there, they thronged, a welter of heroes and heroic deeds, divine intercessions, and great tragedies, all crisscrossing in intimate proximity. Read Genesis to find out what altars Abraham established, or why Bethel became a holy site (Gen. 12.7-8; 13.18; 22.9; 26.25, 28; 35.1-7). Read the Homeric Hymns to learn why the Eleusinian Mysteries are celebrated ("To Demeter"), or how Delos and Delphi became Apollo's principal places of worship ("To Apollo"). By the time Pausanias was journeying through the Greek world in the second century CE, we see that there were so many conflicting foundation traditions at so many places that he frequently has to make up his mind which he thinks is true.

So, what is there to say about these all-important traditions? What problems can a comparative approach help us solve? Well, for one thing, we can acknowledge that the study of foundation traditions has, generally speaking, followed the same pattern we see elsewhere in this book, and to a certain extent, as the saying goes, even more so. Precisely because they are stories of legendary foundation, the possibility that they contain kernels of truth about actual foundations has and continues to prove irresistible to any number of scholars. And, here as elsewhere, a kernels-of-truth-based approach is not very useful for two reasons. First, if anything is clear, it is that the relationship between surviving traditions and historical realities, if one exists, is typically so loose that the story tells us nothing. If the *Iliad,* for example, is based on a real conflict of some sort, that conflict still looked completely different from the poems, and there is no evidence it involved any of the characters.

Second, once we move away from the idea of a people faithfully preserving their original traditions generation to generation, and toward the reality that traditions are a medium through which peoples constantly reinvent themselves, we must recognize that any relationship between tradition and reality has no explanatory value for why it survived, and little for why it has its present shape. Stories based on real events, loosely or a great deal, and stories with no such basis were *all* passed down because of some combination of the fact that they were genuinely believed to represent the past as it was, and that they continued to seem useful and relevant enough to someone influential. And they all experienced what stories that are passed down experience, a constant, dynamic reshaping to make them more useful and relevant, happening both consciously and unconsciously, but above all, certainly.

As a result, like all traditions that survive, they may or may not preserve something of experiences that really happened. But they most clearly preserve the record of how people telling that story in a particular context imagined the past, and what they wanted from it. A comparative approach, here as elsewhere, would help make that clear because it expands the range of examples we can use to make points that many are still resistant to embrace. And both disciplines do continue to grapple with the legacy of kernels-of-truth-based approaches in various ways.

At this point in the study, however, I imagine that readers will either accept the need to make the shift I have been advocating for throughout, and agree that its ramifications go much deeper than is often supposed, or not. The question I will deal with here is not, therefore, how the pattern that we saw in other chapters has played out in the history of the study of foundation traditions, too. It is instead, where is the *frontier* where the study of foundation traditions is concerned, and how can a comparative approach help illuminate it? And I will argue something I intimated at the end of the last chapter: that increasingly, scholars are aware that foundations traditions served as a means of establishing connections between groups and that the maintenance and adaptation of those connections changed them in various ways. This is a complex process; there were legendary founders on every level of society, and increasingly it seems that they provided a large cast of characters who could be staged in increasingly complex plays, in ways that authorized new and different visions of identity and the past. But it happened both between groups we are used to thinking of as part of the same ethnic entities—Ionians and Dorians, Judahites and Israelites, and so on—and, at least in the Mediterranean world, between groups that we typically think of as separated by ethnic borders.

This last, especially, is very much a new frontier in the study of Mediterranean interactions, and it deserves attention for that reason alone. But in addition, it is possible that the use of founding traditions as a meeting ground, or, as I will suggest below, a kind of language between groups, has lessons to offer as well, where the study of the processes that produced the familiar biblical visions of the past are concerned. As I have argued throughout, the increasing recognition of the importance of the fact that Israel and Judah were separate places, with separate political systems, and, to some extent, separate experiences raises many questions about where the biblical vision of the history of *all Israel* comes from. If we deem them to be applicable to the Levantine context in which biblical traditions emerged— a difficult question to answer—the lessons of the dynamic interchange between groups that is becoming increasingly clear in the Mediterranean may be useful here.

In what follows, then, I will explore what contemporary classical scholarship suggests about the interplay of foundation traditions between groups, and whether these new ideas are applicable to the question of the relationship between Israel and Judah. I will begin by discussing a general topic: how figures and events can function as a kind of language in the first place. From there, I will discuss a number of recent efforts to show how this language functioned between diverse groups in the ancient Mediterranean, and conclude with a consideration of the ramifications of this discussion for modeling the construction of an all-Israelite vision of history through the combination of Judahite and Israelite founding figures.

Foundation Traditions as Language

Imagine, if you will, strolling through ancient Athens or ancient Jerusalem. Just how many places do you think you would pass that were associated, in some way, with some legendary figure or some legendary event?[1] Even if you were outside of the city, things might not be as different as you would think. In Greece, especially, groves and grottos and caves might all have had their stories. A casual survey of "threshing floors" in the Hebrew Bible, for example, will reveal a number of sites of even this humble sort that had stories attached: the "threshing floor of Atad," where the sons of Jacob mourned their father (Gen. 50.11); or the "threshing floor of Nacon," where Uzzah touched the ark on its way to Jerusalem and died (2 Sam. 6.8). And could local farmers, in this place or that, point visitors to the threshing floor where the judge Gideon had received omens (Judg. 6.37), or where Ruth met Boaz (Ruth 3)? Could people in more than *one* place do it? Were there a number of Gideon's and Ruth's threshing floors? The answer is very likely yes.[2]

---

1. On the Jerusalem side of things, see Pioske, *David's Jerusalem.*
2. Andrew Tobolowsky, "Where Doom Is Spoken: Threshing Floors as Places of Decision and Communication in Biblical Literature," *Journal of Ancient Near Eastern Religions* 16.1 (2016), pp. 95-120.

This is the fundamental fact of founding traditions; they were everywhere. And they were for everyone. Many genealogical traditions might have been "the exercise of an erudite, disregarded by those to whom it is supposed to apply," as Irad Malkin argues.[3] Not everyone had to know the names of Hellen's three sons, or how Aetolus related to Ion. But while no one had to know that *many* founding traditions either, they would still have been a constant presence. They would have been put on stage in the great festivals and described at civic events. They would have been used in political speeches and as justifications for the activity of elite men and women who knew the stories about their noble houses from a very young age. And they would also have been told by a parent to a child on a ramble through the woods or a visit to the city or town to get supplies. There would, presumably, even have been local, regional, and national *versions* of certain stories: what Herakles or David did when they founded kingdoms or built mighty structures, and what they did when they stopped over for the night on their way to see the Hydra, or Goliath.

The interplay of all of these stories, interacting at different levels of society and in surprising ways, is the central concern of this chapter. Rather, what I am interested in is one particular aspect of how these stories functioned as a means of negotiating boundaries between groups, or making connections across them, and how they changed as a result. And, of course, this topic is a variation on a question that has been central throughout: what, precisely *is* the relationship between ancient stories and storytellers? What *could* they do, and what couldn't they do, with the stories they inherited? I have argued for the need for an older, kernels-of-truth-based approach to give way *completely* to one that sees, in the details of surviving traditions, a register of ideology, not historiography, which is to say the constant redescription of identity via the constant redescription of the past. But in foundation traditions especially, there is not only this quality of facilitating the ongoing renegotiation of identity internally but an element of outreach.

I am arguing, then, that not just foundation traditions, but, in fact, the *elements* of foundation traditions—the figures, great events, and great deeds—could serve as a flexible language between groups, which is to say, a means of communicating, especially when they shared the same basic repertoire of figures, events, and deeds, but not only then. And one way of thinking about what it means to say that foundation traditions could serve as a kind of language comes to us from some recent scholarship on the topic of the Homeric poems. The centrality of these poems to so many aspects of this book's discussion is not something I envisioned when I first began to devise this study, but it is a natural consequence of the fact that it

---

3. Malkin, *The Returns of Odysseus*, p. 61.

has served as the epicenter for so many discussions about the relationship between extant texts and older traditions for such a long time. And in this case, it is certainly a context in which scholars have begun to rethink what storytellers draw on when they tell stories.

To put the matter simply, Milman Parry, Albert Lord, and many others had seen Homer, or "Homer," or the Homeric poets, essentially as the best possible storytellers of an already familiar story. Again, as Parry put it, "the good singer wins his fame by his ease and versatility in handling a tradition which he knows more thoroughly than anyone else ... but his poetry remains throughout the sum of longer and shorter passages which he has heard."[4] In more recent years, however, a branch of theorizing has explored the nature of the relationship not between the Homeric poems and other, often hypothetical versions of the same story, but *other early stories*. This approach, as with many other things oral-formulaic, originated with John Miles Foley. Foley, as I mentioned in a previous chapter, is more responsible than anyone for bringing oral-formulaic theory into the twenty-first century.[5]

Foley's idea is what he called "traditional referentiality," essentially the way that the Homeric poems reference what he called "the fecund totality of the entire tradition."[6] What he means here is how the *Iliad* or *Odyssey* nod toward other existing stories about Achilles, or Odysseus, or Hector, or Zeus, or whomever. As Ruth Scodel observes, Odysseus is not actually "much-enduring" or "full of wiles" in the *Iliad,* nor is Achilles so "swift-footed"—in fact, prominent scenes involve him failing to catch Hector or Aeneas.[7] If, however, the audience knows a story where Achilles is swift or Odysseus much-enduring, something like the *Odyssey*, for example, these gestures toward an established character will deepen their portrayal here. And we can imagine that different storytellers will orchestrate their references differently from one another. Thus, while Parry and Lord saw the storyteller as the recipient, in linear fashion, of a *single* established tradition that they make their own, traditional referentiality imagines a storyteller enmeshed within a vibrant universe of traditions that they can draw from dynamically as part of their artistic act.

---

4. Parry, *Studies in the Epic Technique of Oral Verse-Making, II*, p. 15.

5. As Foley puts it, "Traditional referentiality ... entails the invoking of a context that is enormously larger and more echoic than the text or work itself, that brings the lifeblood of generations of poems and performances to the individual performance or text" (Foley, *Immanent Art*, p. 7). See the discussion in Elton T.E. Barker and Joel P. Christensen, *Homer's Thebes: Epic Rivalries and the Appropriation of Mythical Pasts* (Washington, DC: Center for Hellenic Studies, 2020), pp. 21-22.

6. Foley, *Immanent Art*, p. 7. See also Foley and Arft, "The Epic Cycle and Oral Tradition."

7. Scodel, *Listening to Homer*, p. 13.

One point to make, then, is the obvious applicability of this vision of the storyteller drawing from a wider repertoire of figures and events to tell even one story to the project of illuminating the world of foundation traditions. Again, even the average person may well have felt awash in them: stories about who founded the local holy sites, their settlements themselves, and about what great deeds had been done in the vicinity. It would have seemed natural to suppose that all of these inhabited the same world together, so it would have seemed natural to draw connections between them that may not have been there at earlier moments in a tradition's history: more natural, perhaps, than it feels even today. It might have seemed natural to tell a story where a local hero does something reminiscent of Herakles or Samson because of the prestige associated with the deeds of those figures. And this applicability only grows when we consider recent critiques of traditional referentiality as initially conceived.

In a nutshell, Foley's conceptualization of this activity is still based on the idea of a *static* repertoire of traditions that everyone knew. One rather odd effect of this premise is that, even today, many accounts of traditional referentiality begin by imagining a nearly perfect audience for referential art; one, in a sense, that *gets all the references*.[8] As Scodel observes in *Listening to Homer* (2002), however, there is genuinely no justification for imagining ancient audiences were so different from any actually encountered in the wild, and most of what we see in the way of justifications are not justifications, just insistences that it is so. "Everyone knows that audiences within their own culture are never perfect. People fail to understand novels and fall asleep in movies."[9] The idea that it was once so different has no basis. Ancient audiences too had people who were tired, or bored, or hungry, or distracted. And, of course, they had people who knew the story well or knew it poorly, people who were very interested in stories or were just looking to pass an afternoon or evening. Perhaps they were even there on a date.

As a result, referentiality is part of the storyteller's art *whether or not* the audience sees and understands everything that is going on. And again, there is nothing at all surprising in this. Scodel starts her study by describing the experience of watching an episode of the Simpsons with her daughter during a scene which is a parody of *The Great Escape*, a 1963 movie

---

8. There are those who still make this argument. For example, Casey Dué has recently argued that "any audience on any given occasion of performance would already have known the story and the characters. There would have been nothing about the story, the language, the rhythm of the song, or the characters that was new for that audience" (Casey Dué, *Achilles Unbound: Multiformity and Tradition in the Homeric Epics* [Washington, DC: Center for Hellenic Studies, 2019], p. 10). Dué does not offer a justification for this view.

9. Scodel, *Listening to Homer*, p. 7.

that a small child is unlikely to have watched.[10] I myself might refer to a Sesame Street episode I recently watched with my son, which featured a pig architect named I.M. Pig. Her daughter presumably enjoyed her episode, my son his, and nobody had to know any more than they already did. Even for adults, how many of us have had the experience of getting a reference on the second or third time, or when we get a little older, that we didn't get originally? Or, of course, not getting them at all, and perhaps having them explained by someone else? Indeed, one imagines the artist themselves cannot always explain exactly what goes into their art, nor their audience why they are moved by it.

Why this matters goes back to the question of the fundamental nature of the relationship between stories and storytellers. The assumption of perfect audience understanding is also the assumption of the static, broadly shared repertoire of traditions just described, one as familiar to the audience as to the author. In other words, if we do not assume two different people will hear the exact same story even if they listen to the same one, a static repertoire becomes impossible. If the relationship between storyteller and inherited traditions is more individual *and* the relationship between audiences and stories they hear is as well, then the interactions between stories, storytellers, and audiences will be capable of a far greater diversity of expression. Not only what but how a storyteller draws from familiar traditions may be highly individual, and what the audience takes from it too.

Or we might put it this way. The original formulation of traditional referentiality was like Parry's initial belief that Homer's poems were really *all* formula, but with the wider universe of traditions supplementing the repertoire of formulae. The oral poet is, as Rosalind Thomas noted in critique, still essentially a "mechanical too[l] of tradition"; but in addition to combining formulaic expressions to create a new version of an old story, they combine, as well, elements that are nods to other stories the audience knows.[11] But if we imagine a looser fit between story and storyteller, an artist, steeped in tradition, redirecting their special knowledge into new compositions in a *highly individualized process,* not only with respect to what they feel the audience would like to hear but with their own, personal sense of what is important, central, or interesting, we are closer to imagining the ancient world as a real place. And, we are closer to realizing how idiosyncratic, even surprising, the results of these acts of connection-building can be.

In fact, many recent studies have emphasized the idea of a looser fit with, in my view, quite compelling evidence. Graziosi and Haubold, for example,

10. Scodel, *Listening to Homer,* p. vii.
11. Thomas, *Literacy and Orality in Ancient Greece,* p. 30.

have promoted the idea not of traditional referentiality but epic *resonance,* the ability of a story "to evoke a web of associations and implications," without being so overt about it.[12] Rather than requiring full knowledge of the epic repertoire, part of the poetic act, in their view, is "foster[ing] a sense of context and resonance."[13] In other words, referentiality may often have had the goal of simply insisting on the situatedness of a story within a rich universe of heroic action, giving characters depth just as adding lore to more recent narratives is a crucial part of world-building.[14] Similar points are made in Bruno Currie's 2016 study, *Homer's Allusive Art,* which is rich with observations about the too-considerable conservatism in the mode of inheritance envisioned either by Parry and Lord or Foley.[15]

Indeed, even the idea that inherited epic traditions form a kind of language which the poet draws from and redeploys dynamically in much the way somebody might from the elements of their native language is not new. It actually appears in a recent study by Elton T.E. Barker and Joel Christensen: *Homer's Thebes* (2020). They begin with introducing what I consider to be the crucial idea that opens the door to the claims I am making: that referentiality can operate in the context of "agonistics," essentially competitive storytelling.[16] In this particular instance, they argue specifically that the Homeric poems repeatedly gesture toward the Theban Cycle—Oedipus, Antigone and so on—which is where their title comes from. And they suggest that these references are not merely meant to con-

---

12. Barbara Graziosi and Johannes Haubold, *Homer: The Resonance of Epic* (London: A. & C. Black, 2013), p. 8. "We must assume that in the Archaic period, just as today, different listeners had different levels of familiarity with the wider epic tradition. Some members of the audience will have known many different epics by Homer, Hesiod and other poets. Other listeners will have been less knowledgeable and yet will have enjoyed listening to the poems. In the course of the performance, they will have started to work out an overall picture of what went on before and after the main story. The point, then, is not that one needs to have full command of a whole poetic tradition in order to appreciate the Iliad and the Odyssey; but rather that these two poems deliberately and carefully present themselves as part of a larger narrative" (Graziosi and Haubold, *Homer*, 40).

13. Graziosi and Haubold, *Homer*, p. 41.

14. Graziosi and Haubold, *Homer*, p. 61.

15. Currie points out, for example, that "the detection of allusion even in fully literate traditions is never a scientific matter; one interpreter may, quite legitimately, see an allusion where another, equally legitimately, may not" (Bruno Currie, *Homer's Allusive Art* [Oxford: Oxford University Press, 2016], pp. 5-6). He also takes more seriously than others the fact that the poems exist today as written compositions, not as oral ones, and that they show some signs of making use of techniques we tend to associate with written compositions, such as allusions backwards to particular passages.

16. Barker and Christensen, *Homer's Thebes*, p. 10.

jure this cycle for their audience for dramatic effect but to signal the superiority of this story to that in the process of telling it.

More broadly, Barker and Christensen argue that the Homeric poems draw on "a long established repertoire of phrases, scenes and stories," while "playing off it for particular effect."[17] They refer to the "familiar language, motifs, and themes" the poems rework "for sometimes very different ends."[18] And in the more explicitly relevant aspects of their study, they suggest that how a particular "instance" of a poem plays with inherited materials is echoic with the way human "communication" *generally* "relies on shared inheritances with particular offshoots."[19] They go beyond Foley's own account of oral poetry as "like a language, only more so" to the idea that the activity of composition-in-performance "emerges from the same structures and dynamics that condition 'natural language.'"[20] They note current work, by Cristobal Cánovas and Mihailo Antović, that explores the idea that "oral formulaic theory is functionally equivalent to usage-based cognitive grammar."[21] In short, an epic poet draws from everything they know about the heroic past *in the same way* the rest of us draw from the vocabulary of the language we speak—organizing and dynamically combining diverse particles into a communication act—but often idiosyncratically.

This is *not* how Parry and Lord understood Homer, and it is not, I think, how Foley did. In fact, one recent study of *biblical* traditions, which, in my opinion, is overly rooted in older understandings of Homer, suggests specifically that Homeric poetry is "not a 'natural' language ... in the Chomskyan sense," which means that it is not "generative" enough to be the basis of a spoken language, in part because "it consists of a finite set of formulae" only.[22] But a more dynamic model of how the poet uses what the poet inherits will inevitably convey a greater sense of flexibility than the first blush of oral-formulaic theory, and it is quite appropriate, in my view,

17. Barker and Christensen, *Homer's Thebes*, p. 10. "Over the past decade the study of epic poetry has been revitalized by a focus on the ways in which meaning is generated in each oral performance both by drawing on a long established repertoire of phrases, scenes and stories ('traditional referentiality') and by playing off it for particular effect ('agonistics')."

18. Barker and Christensen, *Homer's Thebes*, p. 13.

19. Barker and Christensen, *Homer's Thebes*, pp. 23-24.

20. John Miles Foley, *How to Read an Oral Poem* (Urbana: University of Illinois Press, 2002), p. 127; Barker and Christensen, *Homer's Thebes*, p. 24.

21. Barker and Christensen, *Homer's Thebes*, p. 25; Mihailo Antovic and Cristóbal Pagán Cánovas, *Oral Poetics and Cognitive Science* (linguae&litterae; Berlin: de Gruyter, 2016), p. 56.

22. Robert S. Kawashima, *The Archaeology of Ancient Israelite Knowledge* (Bloomington: Indiana University Press, 2022), pp. 169-70. This is to oppose it to biblical traditions, which are, Kawashima argues, composed from a real language, Hebrew.

to think of the elements of inherited traditions more like a natural than an unnatural language, a repertoire, a shared inheritance, etc., but capable of an extraordinary flexibility of expression. In addition, agonistics is not the only relevant context in which the development of new variants of traditions occurs. There is also what we might call a "dialogics." Certainly, far from all attempts to retell stories toward new ends occurs in the context of competitions. They could occur instead as precursors, attempted or achieved, of cooperation as well, and they could serve as a means of building connections that otherwise would not exist. Indeed, in some cases, the creation of a connection was the precursor to competition, now that there was a common language to compete through.

If we were to apply this framework to the study of foundation traditions, we would find it very useful. These, too, form a kind of language, because the elements that will be used to make meaning already exist in the form of the traditions of a given place, the same way the vocabulary of a language does. Then, the foundation traditions of a city, region, or holy site were constantly being redeployed for effect in the context of various ceremonies, political movements, and diplomatic and military endeavors. Agonistics and dialogics have a role to play here as the reshaping of these stories was constantly effected in order to make a claim or connection. And as with epic poetry, new versions of older stories were open to influence from other traditions in a wide variety of ways and could respond to them in a variety of ways. The result is not a stable repertoire of stories but, instead, an ongoing conversation.

Unlike epic poetry, however, there is nothing about foundation traditions that resembles a circumscribed corpus. As I have said, they existed on every level of society, on local, regional, and supraregional levels. There were potential inputs all around, a wide variety of uses and requirements, and always the possibility of local innovations trickling up and more popular details trickling down. Thus, describing the interchange of foundation stories and its effects is if anything even more complicated than describing how epic traditions relate to other stories in whatever context. Yet if we say that the elements not just of foundation traditions but of many traditions served as a flexible repertoire of figures, events, and episodes, to be deployed in the context of agonistics or dialogics that are at once a reflection of the cultural context in which the story is told *and* the individual sensibilities and intentions of the author, we get, I think, close to the real situation.

Thus, what I would suggest here, in search of a more flexible description of the operation of this language than either referentiality and allusion can afford, is focusing less on how the elements in question are used than on what the elements are—a sort of supply-side approach to foundation economics. I would describe these elements as a traditionary "vocabulary," a term I have used before in an article where I advanced the concept of a "mythic vocabulary." I have avoided the term "myth" in this chapter and in this book overall both because of the tendency to refer to Greek traditions as Greek "myths" in a way that contradistinguishes them from biblical "traditions" and because I did not want the complexities of the term to be a distraction.

Still, in this prior discussion, my point was that a flexible metaphor like a "vocabulary" could serve specifically as an antidote to the shortcomings in still-common "structuralist" approaches to myth. This is true both in the original form associated with the work of Claude Lévi-Strauss, and more recent attempts to describe myth as "taxonomic," familiar from the work of J.Z. Smith, Bruce Lincoln, and, recently, Debra Ballentine.[23] These are, in essence, models of how storytellers make meaning by rearranging and redefining the relationships between elements in inherited stories: their structure, as it were. And I think this is often precisely what happens, but I also think that it misses a wide variety of mythographic phenomena. In a nutshell, and like traditional referentiality, structuralism treats the whole story as the basic unit of sense. But in fact, these "units" can show up separately in new stories, too. Herakles can perform his labors in different ways and different places, but he can also briefly travel on the Argo and so on.

Thus, the distinction I am making, in describing how foundation traditions actually work against older models of a stable repertoire of familiar tales, is indeed like the difference between a "natural language" and an artificial one. But that is a complex topic, and my focus is specifically on the extent to which I am insisting on the individual creativity of storytellers in using the *whole world of traditions* they knew in new ways. That is what we see in foundation traditions as they actually were, a tremendous openness to bringing in figures from other traditions, linking figures to significant events, and changing any number of details for ideological reasons. That, therefore, is what we need to describe. And in allowing storytellers, in our imagination of the ancient past, to be creative in *familiar* ways, which is to say, familiar to those of us who live in the real world of individuals, and not in the unfamiliar, circumscribed way dictated by variants of the Great Divide, we can come closer to the reality. Classical scholarship has started to move in this direction; biblical scholarship can follow.

---

23. Claude Lévi-Strauss, "The Structural Study of Myth," *Journal of American Folklore* 68.270 (1955), pp. 428-44; Jonathan Z. Smith, "In Comparison a Magic Still Dwells," in *Imagining Religion: From Babylon to Jonestown* (Chicago: University of Chicago Press, 1982), pp. 19-35; Jonathan Z. Smith, "A Matter of Class: Taxonomies of Religion," *HTR* 89.4 (1996), pp. 387-403; Lincoln, *Discourse and the Construction of Society*; Bruce Lincoln, *Theorizing Myth: Narrative, Ideology and Scholarship* (Chicago: University of Chicago Press, 1999); Debra Scoggins Ballentine, *The Conflict Myth and the Biblical Tradition* (Oxford: Oxford University Press, 2015).

Founding Vocabularies

What I am describing in this chapter is something like what was described by Arjun Appadurai in a 1981 essay called "The Past as a Scarce Resource." We might assume, he says, though it is worth noting how unusually resistant many scholars of *ancient* tradition have been to assume anything of the sort, that "the past is a limitless and plastic symbolic resource infinitely susceptible to the whims of contemporary interest and the distortions of contemporary ideology."[24] Instead, the requirements of what a tradition is intended to do in a society—and here we can think of both higher-level activities such as justifying war and colonization, and very much lower level indeed—mean they are constrained by the need to channel "authority ... continuity ... depth ... interdependence."[25] In language terms, we might say that they are limited by the need to be mutually intelligible. Rather, as I mentioned in the last chapter, storytellers are not *barred* from genuinely inventing new traditions in the way some suppose. But selecting from a pre-existing set of traditions and tradition elements that already have meaning in a community is a shortcut to intelligibility, and any given story can accommodate enough messages that the constraint of using a shared language of story is not much of a constraint at all. Just so, a broadly shared set of founding traditions is constantly finding new life in the context of new needs, although, in this case, also often expanded and reorganized.

In another way, however, I am simply trying to help move the conversation from a focus on a Romantic fantasy, no matter how subsequently moderated, to the real world where new and interesting foundation traditions appear all the time, involving odd combinations of figures and events. What I was looking for, when I develop the concept of a "mythic vocabulary" was precisely this: a flexible metaphor that could accommodate the fact that repertoires of traditional stories and figures exist, that there are narratives and legendary figures that are much better known than others, but that not just these stories but their individual elements could be used more flexibly and more widely than is often supposed. I landed on a vocabulary because in the context of a language, too, there are a circumscribed number of nouns, verbs, adjectives, adverbs, and so forth. All of them have a pre-existing meaning that to some extent shapes how they can be used. There are even common phrases and stereotypical usages, combinations of words, that appear frequently, with a collective meaning. And yet, and yet. We all know how many different ways the same words can be put together, with how many different meanings, and we know that beyond common

---

24. Arjun Appadurai, "The Past as a Scarce Resource," *Man* 16.2 (1981), p. 201.
25. Appadurai, "The Past as a Scarce Resource," p. 203.

phrases, there are surprising combinations available to anyone who wishes to try them.

When we combine this idea of the discrete elements of founding traditions as an available vocabulary for expressing ideas, justifications, and ambitions with agonistics, we arrive at what I believe to be true about foundation traditions. Their use is governed less by the retelling of familiar accounts than by the reuse of their elements as flexible ingredients in the perpetual renegotiation of boundaries between groups. Whatever meaning was granted these elements by the earlier stories that served as their context functioned as the starting point for the next step. So, it is the *fact* that Odysseus was known as a traveler that made him an obvious choice for colonists who wanted to connect their foundation to an illustrious figure, making Odysseus what Malkin calls a "protocolonial hero."[26] The fact that Herakles was both traveler and monster slayer made him a "postcolonial hero," conceptually opening up places like Libya for colonization by defeating Antaios there, for example.[27] What the original stories were, however, did not *prescribe* how they would be used. It just made it likelier that in an instance where a proto- or postcolonial hero was needed, these would be the ones to appear.

Then, as time went on, the "dialogics" that produced developments in these traditions met an "agonistics" that directed them. More practically, we might say that not just the character but the tracks laid by prior stories through actual contexts in earlier periods made them available for later adaptations. As Greek colonies spread west, for example, Herakles's labors, which once had taken him into largely mythic geographies, were discovered in real places:

> Aristotle called the path Heracles followed when chasing the Kerynian hind, the "Heraclean road," which ... was a route that offered protection to travelers on their way to Iberia. Another labor brought Heracles to Tartessos, where Herodotus places the first meeting of Phokaians and Iberians, to capture the cattle of Geryon. The incorporation of the western Mediterranean into the myths of the Greeks is one of the ways in which encounters with other ethnic groups altered Greek culture.[28]

As a result, Herakles gradually became the centerpiece of more and more traditions that incorporated distant regions into Greek understandings of the world, and repeatedly served as the means through which diverse groups negotiated their relationship to each other. In other words, as Denise

---

26. Malkin, *The Returns of Odysseus*, p. 15.
27. Malkin, *The Returns of Odysseus*, p. 4.
28. Denise Demetriou, *Negotiating Identity in the Ancient Mediterranean: The Archaic and Classical Greek Multiethnic Emporia* (Cambridge, UK: Cambridge University Press, 2012), p. 25.

Demetriou puts it, "the myths surrounding the person of Heracles ... were enriched by these additional stories that ultimately connected the Greeks with the westernmost coasts. ... Interactions among Mediterranean populations ... were conducive to the production of new identities for both mythical heroes and ethnic groups."[29]

This is what I mean when I say that if we think about storytellers interacting with foundation traditions the way many Homerists think about traditional poets interacting with epic poetry, we will think wrongly.[30] Indeed, we have to recall that figures such as Achilles, Hector, Herakles, Moses, and David were not really understood, first and foremost, as figures in stories at *all,* which is to say not as *literary* figures like an Ebenezer Scrooge or a Stephen Dedalus, whom we know *as* the protagonists of books. Instead, many ancient people thought of them as *real people,* some of whose exploits were captured in this or that tale, but surely not all.[31] This, of course, by its very nature, means that no existing repertoire of stories could be imagined as entirely complete.

In our own time, we might think of something like the increasingly frequent phenomenon of the cinematic universe.[32] Most often, an individual movie—or, say, a trilogy—will tell a single story involving certain characters. We know Neo, for example, as the protagonist of the Matrix movies. The function of a cinematic universe—Marvel's for example—is, however, precisely to give the suggestion of depth that is the simulacrum of a real world. In other words, the universe introduces characters, and both a geographical and chronological structure in which they interact, but simultaneously makes us feel as if we are receiving glimpses only of a reality that goes on beyond and around the episodes that appear on the screen. As a result, new installments positively beg the question of what familiar figures who are not accounted for were up to during the events described within, and we are never surprised to see a familiar face from another story show up. They are always conceptually out there, available, even expected.

29. Demetriou, *Negotiating Identity in the Ancient Mediterranean*, p. 25.
30. Patterson adds that "local myths can provide a glimpse into a given community's sense of its own identity, which is far more likely to be the identity it projects internationally. ... The surprising result ... [is] the extent to which communities found ways to bridge their local myths through some Panhellenic stemma (usually one of the sons of Hellen) and even reconciled these accounts despite variations in the respective local traditions" (Patterson, *Kinship Myth in Ancient Greece*, p. 20).
31. Graziosi and Haubold get at this when they note that Homer himself was not in fact understood in antiquity as the author of two poems but as the author of "a vast number of poems ... all epic texts relating" to the Trojan War, "just about everything that was heroic epic in Archaic Greece" (Graziosi and Haubold, *Homer*, p. 24).
32. See the discussion in Tobolowsky, "The Thor Movies and the 'Available Myth.'"

Thus, in one story, we might learn how the supervillain Thanos destroyed half the life in the universe; in another, how the Avengers managed to reverse what he achieved, five years later. But in a third installment, we might learn about the consequences of the fact that some of the students at Spiderman's high school went through puberty five years before their classmates, or that Antman was in the Quantum Realm the whole time. There are any number of episodes or ramifications that might be expanded in subsequent stories and a large, already extant cast of characters to use to staff them. And, within the swirl of interlocking, but independent stories, surprising things can happen—way can lead on to way.

We might call this the "universal" paradigm of storytelling—stories emanating out of an existing universe of figures and events, conjured by stories but existing outside of them, at least in the imagination. In the ancient world, the universe was typically an ostensibly real "heroic age," organized into discrete eras, and it meant that audiences did not encounter heroic figures only in the amphitheater or at the festival, but all around. The actual world they lived in was, as I have already said, crisscrossed, even layered over, with the traces *left* by these great heroes and events. The ancients "perceived ... reality ... through screens woven of both experience and myths," as Irad Malkin put it—referring to one of the most popular and prevalent forms of foundation tradition in ancient Greece, the Nostoi traditions, which narrated the journeys home of diverse Trojan War heroes, and what they encountered and accomplished along the way.[33] These could serve as a simple explanation for the founding of a settlement or a shrine, but they also formed a dynamic vocabulary for describing "new lands, articulating landscapes ... providing cultural and ethnic mediation with non-Greeks," and so on.[34] Just as it is never truly surprising, when watching a Marvel movie, for Thor or Captain Marvel to turn up, it was never surprising, in antiquity, to learn that Odysseus or Herakles had had yet another stop along the way.

Thus, one point to make is that we ought to be able to read in the details of foundation traditions the history of interactions between parties, histories of encounter and negotiation. But another, central to this chapter, is that this history of encounters produced in storytellers the ability to draw from multiple corpora at once, from multiple levels of society, to perform the agonistics and dialogics described above. This introduced a porousness to the proceedings, an openness of story to story. And it is this set of facts that explains the interesting frontier I am attempting to explore in this chapter: the ability of foundation traditions to serve as a medium through which encounters between different groups could be mediated, new rela-

---

33. Malkin, *The Returns of Odysseus*, p. 1.
34. Malkin, *The Returns of Odysseus*, p. 1.

tionships established, and old ones renegotiated. Crucially, this was true even between groups we are used to thinking of as culturally distinct.

Practically, what this means is that we do not want to think only of how a particular storyteller made a new set of claims through a new account of events, in isolation, but as part of a series of efforts to build and negotiate connections between peoples: a dialogics, as above. And here, we work our way back up from vocabulary to language. The repertoires in question could form a *common* language between groups, anyone who felt as if they shared a past, because they could pick and choose from a diverse set of figures and events to advance claims. Internally to cultural groups, broadly construed, this means that shared stories provided a touchstone through which different participants in shared systems could make and modulate relationships, which is to say, a way to talk to each other and explain themselves. Thus, one phenomenon associated with the use of founding traditions to create identity articulations and explain the origins of cities, kingdoms, and peoples is the building of narrative *systems* that many people could connect to in many different ways.[35]

An example that I have discussed before comes from the tradition known as the "Return of the Herakleidae."[36] Basically, this is the story of how a certain group of descendants from Herakles first fled the Peloponnese upon his death, out of fear of his lifelong enemy Eurystheus, then returned generations later at the head of an army of Dorians to recapture their patrimony.[37] This was, from the beginning, a foundation tradition embracing at least a dynasty at Argos, the Temenids, and perhaps Sparta and Messene as well. Before long, however, the cities and colonies that either claimed some part of the Return legacy or described foundations that were the result of related dislocations grew tremendously, including at least Corinth, Elis, Macedon, Epidaurus, Amyklai, Sikyon, Crete, and Rhodes.[38]

---

35. This is what Malkin refers to as the ability of traditions like the *Nostoi* myths to be "particularized" in a way that expressed the specific character of different cultural groups (Malkin, *The Returns of Odysseus*, p. 3).

36. Tobolowsky, *The Sons of Jacob and the Sons of Herakles*.

37. The tradition is first mentioned in the work of the seventh-century CE Spartan poet Tyrtaeus, but Euripides has at least two plays embracing it—his *Herakleidai* and *Cresphontes*—and we can see it referenced in Pindar's *Pythian* 1.60, Plato's *Laws* 3.683d, Isocrates's *Speeches* 6.17-27, Thucydides's *History* 1.9.1-3, 1.12, Herodotus 9.26.1–9.27.2 and elsewhere. In the later sources, see Pausanias (2.4.3–2.4.4; 2.18.6–2.19.2; 2.28.1-7; 3.1.3-9; 4.3.1–4.3.8; 5.3.7–5.4.3), Diodorus Siculus (4.57-58), and Apollodorus (2.8). See Tobolowsky, *The Sons of Jacob and the Sons of Herakles*, pp. 189-90.

38. For example, Ephorus describes how Temenus's grandsons fell out with each other, so Althaemenes went to Crete and then to Rhodes (Brill's New Jacoby 70 f 18c), for which see Koiv, *Ancient Tradition and Early Greek History*, pp. 37-38. "Amyklai

Naturally, the study of this tradition was long dominated by the search for "kernels of truth," in this case of the so-called Dorian invasion, which was purported to explain the arrival of Doric speaking peoples in the region.[39] Indeed, early scholarship largely blamed this mythical invasion for the actual downfall of Mycenae at the end of the Late Bronze Age, based on little more than this story.[40] Again, my opinion is that this form of analysis is essentially useless, not only in the likely event that there are very few such kernels but even if we could somehow prove that there were plenty. What we can say for certain is that whatever the tradition is based on, its actual form is so different from anything that *might* have happened that it cannot shed any light on real developments. Nor, for the same reason, do any real developments explain anything important about what happened to the story in later periods.[41]

was supposedly given to Philomenes, an Achaian who betrayed his people to help the Herakleidai. ... Temenos' sons become embroiled in a conflict because Temenos favored his son-in-law Deiphontes, to whom he leaves Argos over them, but Kissos, one of Temenos' sons, is victorious, leaving Deiphontes to found Epidauros. ... Sikyon is founded by Temenos' son Phalkes. ... Strabo (8.8.5) tells us ... [of] the founding of Achaia by Tisamenos, son of Orestes, after being evicted by the Herakleids" (Tobolowsky, *The Sons of Jacob and the Sons of Herakles*, pp. 191-92).

39. "Historical traditions, too, such as the Return of the Heraclids, were useful, since they could be interpreted as the myth-historical memory of actual population movements that had resulted in the fusing of the Greek tribes" (McInerney, "Ethnos and Ethnicity in Early Greece," pp. 52-53). Hall describes how a "particular configuration of the archaeological evidence" which produced early confidence in "the romantic vision" of a Dorian invasion included these destructions, the arrival of a new form of pottery, certain new customs, and certain new technologies (Hall, *Ethnic Identity in Greek Antiquity*, pp. 114-17). Subsequent investigations, however, showed that the Mycenaean sites were destroyed at different times from each other, the supposedly distinctive pottery has been found elsewhere, and so on and so forth (Hall, *Ethnic Identity in Greek Antiquity*, p. 118). Today, "the only certain evidence for hostile action is constituted by the appearance of arrowheads associated with the last of no fewer than six destructions of ... Tiryns" and "little (if any) break in cultural continuity" at Lakonia (Hall, *Ethnic Identity in Greek Antiquity*, pp. 118-19). Likewise, like the collared rim jar, the so-called "Barbarian Ware" associated with the Dorians has now been found at Mycenae and Tiryns prior to their destructions, and it cannot therefore be considered evidence of invading Dorians (Hall, *Ethnic Identity in Greek Antiquity*, p. 220). See an earlier critique in James T. Hooker, "New Reflexions on the Dorian Invasion," *Klio* 61.1-2 (1979), pp. 353-60.

40. Hall, *Ethnic Identity in Greek Antiquity*, p. 114. As Hall observes, Christos Tsountas, whose early synthesis of Mycenaean finds was discussed in an earlier chapter, was one of those who believed the Mycenaean civilization was brought down by this invasion.

41. As Sofia Voutsaki notes in a review of somewhat recent effort to revive the idea of a Dorian Invasion by Birgitte Eder, "This is a brave attempt to shed some light on the Dark Ages, but the evidence still refuses to fit a neat explanation. The linguistic change from Mycenaean Greek to Doric is indisputable, but the archaeological evidence shows

After all, take another apposite example, the story of the exodus. What, at this point, would it even matter if, as one scholar recently claimed, "some of the parallels between the second-millennium B.C.E. culture of the Levant and the cultural background portrayed in the Patriarchal stories … are too close to be ignored," including "private names, place-names, and the status of a Semitic prince in the Egyptian court?"[42] To say that the familiar story, which was shaped almost entirely by the work of later storytellers with their own intentions, might nevertheless preserve a handful of real elements offers essentially no advantage where either understanding the story or reconstructing the event is concerned.

At any rate, in this case, "the linguistic change from Mycenaean Greek to Doric is indisputable" in the region, and there must be some explanation for it.[43] But there simply is no evidence of a genuine conquest. Nor do our theoretical assumptions permit us to imagine any longer that a story would continue to be told, and take so many different forms, merely because it represents the memory of a real event. Thus, in recent years, the more typical tack has been to focus on the fact that familiar versions of the tradition represent "a cumulative aggregation of accounts, rather than a dim reflection of genuine population movements."[44] In other words, scholars today are indeed often more interested in the *fact* that the tradition grew in the telling than that it may vaguely reflect something historical.

Thus, some have explored the diverse uses to which it was put over time, and even in a single place, like Sparta. Malkin notes that his own inquiry covered its deployment "at one point in terms of its continuous validation of the Spartan royal houses, at another in terms of its impact on and use for legitimating the attempts of the Spartan Dorieus to settle in western Sicily … at a third point in terms of its relationship to the religious festival of the Karneia, and at a fourth in relation to the Dorian invasion."[45] Similarly, Herakleid descent at Macedon, which seems to

---

the changes to be much more diffuse, gradual, and spatially uneven than they are made out to be in this study" (Sofia Voutsaki, "The Dorian Invasion," *Classical Review* 50.1 [2000], p. 233).

42. Amihai Mazar, "The Patriarchs, Exodus, and Conquest Narratives in Light of Archaeology," in *The Quest for the Historical Israel: Debating Archaeology and the History of Israel* (ed. Brian B. Schmidt; Atlanta, GA: Society of Biblical Literature, 2007), p. 59.

43. Voutsaki, "The Dorian Invasion," p. 50. We are, at the very least, speaking of "miscellaneous population movements … by no means all of them associated with the Dorians proper" (Margalit Finkelberg, "Dorians," in *The Homer Encyclopedia* (Chichester, West Sussex: John Wiley & Sons, 2011).

44. Hall, *Ethnic Identity in Greek Antiquity*, p. 57.

45. Malkin, *The Returns of Odysseus*, p. 22. "The representation remains 'collective' but its function and appearances are multivalent and multiform." Here he is also referring back to Malkin, *Myth and Territory in the Spartan Mediterranean*.

have developed some time in the early fifth century BCE, clearly had a number of uses at well: at one instance to punch Alexander I's ticket to the Olympics; at another to aid in Philip's rise to power; at a third to serve as the basis of "kinship diplomacy" throughout Alexander the Great's conquests.[46] That is, his purported descent from Herakles helped Philip become "hegemonial commander" of the Thessalians, and Alexander, arguably the most famous self-identifying Herakleid in history, would use his supposed ancestry in many different ways.[47] I consider these arguments, and others like them, valuable, and not dissimilar to approaches I have advocated for in other chapters of this study.

In this chapter, however, what is interesting about this story is that as it grew and grew, it repeatedly swept up figures of local tradition and transformed them. Aletes, who would be the Herakleid conqueror of Corinth, likely began life as a non-Herakleid figure of local Corinthian legend. He gained these new family connections only in "an attempt ... to incorporate [the Corinthians'] own myths of origin within the general pedigree of the Herakleidai and Dorians of the Peloponnese."[48] The same may well be true at Sparta itself, despite the fact that the earliest reference to the tradition comes from the work of the seventh-century BCE Spartan poet Tyrtaeus, and that Sparta may have been the place where the Return had the most enduring importance. Argos, where myths about Herakles are probably the oldest, was, nevertheless, actually a democracy from early times, while the dynasty claiming descent from Aletes is supposed to have been expelled in the seventh century BCE.[49] Sparta, meanwhile, was led by kings claiming descent from Herakles into the second century BCE—in fact, two kings, from two royal houses, both claiming descent from the Herakleid conqueror.

However, just as at Corinth the royal house does not bear the name of Aletes but Bacchis, who was king a few generations later, at Sparta the

46. The earliest reference to Herakleid descent in Macedon comes from a story told in Herodotus where Alexander I, who ruled in the first half of the fifth century BCE, petitioned the Olympic committee to let him compete on the basis of his Greek ancestry (Herodotus 5.22.2) (Patterson, *Kinship Myth in Ancient Greece*, p. 171).

47. Philip used it to justify his elevation among the Thessalians because "he was their kin as a descendant of the legendary Heracles and therefore perfectly qualified for the post" (Thomas R. Martin, *Ancient Greece from Prehistoric to Hellenistic Times* [New Haven, CT: Yale University Press, 1996], p. 189). Meanwhile "the tradition of the Argeads' Heraclid descent could potentially serve him [Alexander] in the cases of Aspendus, Soli, and Mallus in Asia Minor. It also gave Alexander an opportunity to cite kinship with the Thessalians, in particular the ruling Aleuadae, who likely looked back to Aleuas the Red, son of Thessalus son of Herakles" (Patterson, *Kinship Myth in Ancient Greece*, p. 159).

48. Hall, *Ethnic Identity in Greek Antiquity*, p. 59.

49. Jonathan M. Hall, "How Argive Was the 'Argive' Heraion? The Political and Cultic Geography of the Argive Plain, 900–400 B.C.," *AJA* 99.4 (1995), p. 581.

two royal houses were named neither for Aristodemus the Herakleid conqueror nor his sons Procles and Eurysthenes. Instead, they are named after *their* sons, Agis and Eurypon: the Agiads and the Eurypontids.[50] Thus, in both places, a reasonable explanation is that the traditions concerning the founding of the royal houses predated the assumption of Herakleid myth and that a certain amount of grafting has occurred to create a coequivalence between these city-states of mainland Greece. In other words, Agis, Eurypon, and Bacchis probably predated the expansion of the Herakleid framework to these regions and were made Herakleids by the expansion of existing genealogical traditions.

Meanwhile, at Messene, something even more interesting happened, something that reveals the *ongoing* character of the redeployment of tradition vocabularies. We can note first that the early version of the Messenian tradition might be shaped around a partial justification for the basic fact of early Messenian history, which was its domination by Sparta. In it, the Herakleid conqueror of Messene, Cresphontes, is murdered shortly thereafter and his son, also named Cresphontes, is placed on the throne, but only with Spartan help. This appears to be the subject of a lost play by Euripides, his *Cresphontes*. In later versions of the myth, however, the son of Cresphontes is now named *Aepytus,* a development that likely only occurred after the battle of Leuctra, in 371 BCE, which broke Spartan power and freed Messene from its grasp. Aepytus, like Aletes, appears to have been a figure of local myth before ever he was a Herakleid, and is mentioned already even in the *Iliad* (2.604). In this case, however, he was not a *Messenian* figure at all, but an Arcadian one.

Thus, what seems to have happened here is that, first, Messenian authors wanted to rhetorically free their nation from the version of the tradition that had been used to justify their subjugation, but, in a way that continued to assert their coequal prestige with other regional powers. So, they kept the Herakleid story but changed the Herakleid in question to someone more congenial. Second, however, they seem to have done so in a way that was also meant to emphasize "the close ties between Arkadia and Messene after Leuktra."[51] Such was the openness of tradition to tradition that when creat-

---

50. For all of this, see the discussion in Tobolowsky, *The Sons of Jacob and the Sons of Herakles,* pp. 195-97. See also Patterson, *Kinship Myth in Ancient Greece,* pp. 31, 36.

51. This idea is discussed in Patterson, *Kinship Myth in Ancient Greece,* p. 36. The quoted words, however, are mine, and, as I further note, Funke "expands this discussion with reference to the post-Leuktra relationships between Thebes, Messene, and Arkadia, as well as to other forms of inter-city appropriation like the recovery of the shield of Aristomenes, a Messenian hero, by the Thebans and the bones of Arkas by the Mantineans" (Tobolowsky, *The Sons of Jacob and the Sons of Herakles,* pp. 196, 196 n. 27; Peter Funke, "Between Mantinea and Leuctra," in *Politics of Ethnicity and the*

ing a new link to the Return system, the Messenians could actually draw on *someone else's* tradition vocabulary in order, one might say, to kill two birds with one stone.

And, in fact, this is a reality also represented in a more literal fashion by the interesting ancient Greek practice of appropriating the supposed *remains* of ancient heroes. One would think that a city-state might primarily be interested in the founding figures relevant to its own institutions, but, in practice, this was often not the case. The annals of this form of activity include the transfer of the bones of Hippodameia, wife of Pelops, to Olympia, of Arkas to Mantinea, and many others.[52] McCauley describes quite an interesting episode, in which the Sicyonian Cleisthenes wanted to get rid of the bones of Adrastus, "whom he considered an Argive traitor"; but after being refused by Delphi, he "decided to import Adrastus' greatest enemy, the Theban hero Melanippus, and transfer all of Adrastus' former honors to him."[53] The decision, here, to make Adrastus coexist with Melanippus, since Adrastus was apparently unmovable, but make the latter the real hero of the story renders physical what in other contexts is literary, the essential fungibility of existing heroes.

Meanwhile, from the inside, the porousness of the borders of the Return, the extent to which it was not experienced as a single story or set of stories but a flexible part of a wider universe, is the best explanation for the career of a figure like Dorieus, a Spartan nobleman and the older brother of the famous Leonidas. In a previous study, I discussed his ill-fated attempt to conquer Sicily.[54] Sicily had not been conquered by the Herakleids who feature in various versions of the Return tradition—nor did they even attempt to conquer it. In other words, Dorieus's claim could not be premised on the story of the Return itself. However, there are many stories about Herakles, and in one of them he slew a king named Eryx there, and so, according to Herodotus, had "won all the region of Eryx" (Herodotus, *Histories* 5.43).[55]

Crisis of the Peloponnesian League (ed. Peter Funke and Nino Luraghi; Washington, DC: Center for Hellenic Studies, 2009), p. 2.

52. Barbara McCauley, "The Transfer of Hippodameia's Bones: A Historical Context," *Classical Journal* 93.3 (1998), pp. 225-39; Funke, "Between Mantinea and Leuctra." McCauley mentions "the transfer of the bones of Tisamenus from Helice to Sparta … of Aristomenes' bones from Rhodes to Messene," "of the shoulder blade of Pelops … of the bones of Orestes from Tegea to Sparta," and others (McCauley, "The Transfer of Hippodameia's Bones," pp. 228-29).

53. McCauley, "The Transfer of Hippodameia's Bones," p. 229.

54. Tobolowsky, *The Sons of Jacob and the Sons of Herakles*, pp. 192-93; Malkin, *Myth and Territory in the Spartan Mediterranean*, pp. 61-72, 90-111, 190-218; Malkin, *The Returns of Odysseus*, pp. 20-22.

55. Malkin, *Myth and Territory in the Spartan Mediterranean*, pp. 61-72, 90-111, 190-218; Malkin, *The Returns of Odysseus*, pp. 20-22, 218-32.

Thus, operating from within the universe, Dorieus saw what looks to us like two different bodies of tradition as, of course, essentially one.[56]

What we see here, in this example, is, first of all, the basic fact that foundation traditions did not exist in isolation either from other traditions in a particular region or from *other* foundation traditions; we see the illusion of depth I discussed above. Next, we see how, once established, the nature of connections forged by foundation traditions grew and changed through agonistics and dialogics in the constant redefinition of self and other that is fundamental to the articulation of identity itself. At bottom, many foundation traditions had the purpose of communicating the prestige and importance of a place, temple, priesthood, or settlement. So, changing registers of prestige and changing conversation partners change these stories, too. In other words, an adjunct of Appadurai's view that narratives are constrained by the need to channel "authority … continuity … depth … interdependence" is that what is authoritative changes over time and interdependence is evolvingly complex.[57]

Thus, the ability not only to change the story but to connect it to figures who were not originally part of it, or to events that did not originally feature in it, conveys a flexibility to the question of what can be communicated or claimed through foundation traditions that is hard to fathom. The result is that these traditions served not only as register of the agendas pursued through them and with them but a palimpsest of registers, as adaptation led on to adaptation and connection provided the starting point for new connections. Alexander I may have only wanted to compete in the Olympics, or, more likely, to be regarded as part of the Greek watershed more closely than previous Macedonian kings had been, but Philip and Alexander the Great could build out from there and make new claims along the same now-established lines. The Messenians may not have employed a Return foundation tradition in early periods had it been up to them, but once it became so central to Peloponnesian identity in later periods it made sense to simply jettison what they did not like, claim what they did, and make a bid for another regional connection at the same time. As a common language, the Return tradition served as a means through which multiple participants could make broadly intelligible claims about themselves, for themselves, and for their relationship to others.

As in other chapters, how useful this framework is for illuminating under-appreciated aspects of the Hebrew Bible's various foundation traditions depends to some extent on how we conceptualize the difference between the groups involved to begin with. There is some evidence of intertribal competition, especially between Judah and Benjamin: for example, there are three

---

56. Tobolowsky, *The Sons of Jacob and the Sons of Herakles*, pp. 192-93.
57. Appadurai, "The Past as a Scarce Resource," p. 203.

stories of the conquest of Jerusalem. The most famous is no doubt the tradition of David's conquest of the Jebusite citadel, recounted in 2 Samuel 5; but there is also an account, in Judg. 1.8, of the Judahites conquering it already centuries before David. And lest we think that we can definitively say which one of these two is older, there is actually a scene in 1 Sam. 17.54 where David takes the grisly trophies of his defeat of Goliath to store them in the city *before* he is supposed to conquer it, revealing a version of the David story aligned with the earlier conquest of the city. And in addition, also in Judges 1, we see the claim that it was the Benjaminites who conquered it (Judg. 1.21), and we may see a reflection of that story in 1 Chronicles 8, which describes a number of important leaders among the Benjaminites who lived in Jerusalem (1 Chron. 8.28, 32).[58] So, we see both a competition between groups *and* an effort to associate an important figure with the conquest all as examples of how foundation traditions changed over time.

As for figures crossing boundaries, it has, as I mentioned in the last chapter, long been supposed that the patriarchal traditions might have had separate origins: Jacob is more often associated with Israelite places, and Abraham Judahite. So, making one the grandfather of the other might indeed be just the kind of dynamic redeployment of an available vocabulary of figures and events that I described above. More prosaically, in 1 Kings 11–12, the figure of Jeroboam, first king of divided Israel, is likely portrayed through a combination of Israelite and Judahite sources; he is simultaneously the king chosen by God because of the perfidy of the Davidic line and the man whose great sins will ultimately doom Israel.[59] And, as for the account in this text of the foundation of the Bethel and Dan temples, we can note that Jeroboam's erection of golden calves at each location, with the declaration "Here are your gods, O Israel, who brought you up out of the land of Egypt" (1 Kgs 12.28) is an almost exact echo of what Aaron says in Exod. 32.4, in the more famous golden calf episode.

Overall, however, it is much harder to answer the question of how differences between Israel and Judah were negotiated without knowing how different they understood themselves to be in the first place, since the biblical conceit is that these two different kingdoms always understood themselves as part of all Israel. And again, there are other differences

---

58. In particular, 1 Chron. 8.28, which describes "the heads of ancestral houses" among the Benjaminites living in Jerusalem.

59. See, among others, the discussion in Steven L. McKenzie, "The Source for Jeroboam's Role at Shechem (1 Kgs 11:43–12:3, 12:20)," *JBL* 106 (1987), pp. 297-300; Mark Leuchter, "Jeroboam the Ephratite," *JBL* 125 (2006), pp. 51-72; Kristin Weingart, "Jeroboam and Benjamin: Pragmatics and Date of 1 Kings 11:26-40; 12:1-20," in *Saul, Benjamin, and the Emergence of Monarchy in Israel: Biblical and Archaeological Perspectives* (ed. Joachim J. Krause, Omer Sergi, and Kristin Weingart; Atlanta, GA: Society of Biblical Literature, 2020), pp. 133-60.

between the wide world of ancient Greece, which colonized the Mediterranean and existed as a series of settlements strung out across thousands of miles, and the rather insular world of ancient Israel and Judah, which did not. But this is where the interesting new frontier in the study of ancient foundation traditions—that the openness of foundation tradition to foundation tradition also exists, to some extent, across cultural boundaries—can offer intriguing suggestions about how the relationship between Israel and Judah might have been negotiated. And, it raises the possibility, which might be very useful indeed, that Israelites and Judahites could share stories and figures even in periods where they did *not* consider themselves part of all Israel together.

A Mediterranean Exchange

In the course of his discussion of Nostoi traditions, Malkin refers to David Ridgway's suggestion that "what the Greeks had to offer the peoples of the west" was "myth."[60] In other words, he, or at least Ridgway, explains the apparent willingness of non-Greeks to adopt and adapt Nostoi traditions as their own foundation traditions by suggesting that it offered a framework that was "sufficiently flexible to articulate and accommodate local genealogical and group identities" in a way that was sufficiently prestigious.[61] Recent scholarship, however, suggests that this is not quite true, that the Greeks did not simply offer their well-known traditions to other peoples who were going without but may have been equal partners in an exchange of foundation traditions that went both ways. In other words, "myth" might be what different Mediterranean groups had to offer *each other.*

Not all the recent studies making this point deal with foundation traditions directly. But they do all show that the openness of tradition to tradition I have described—the ability of the figures and events in one story to intrude on or influence another—could indeed operate between *different* cultural groups. Thus, for example, Denise Demetriou's study of identity in "multiethnic emporia" shows many things, but among them the ease with which "foreign" gods entered the pantheons of other people over the course of sustained interaction. She mentions "the Athenian state's adoption of Thracian Bendis or the Roman introduction of the Phrygian Magna Mater," but also substantial evidence that self-identifying foreigners could use or patronize Greek temples: "Etruscans and Carthaginians used the temples at Pyrgi," and ancient notables from Croesus to Amasis patronized Delphi.[62] In other

60. Malkin, *The Returns of Odysseus*, p. 6; David Ridgway, *The First Western Greeks* (Cambridge, UK: Cambridge University Press, 1992), p. 138.
61. Malkin, *The Returns of Odysseus*, p. 6.
62. Demetriou, *Negotiating Identity in the Ancient Mediterranean*, p. 7.

cases, "Greeks adopted Carthaginian coin iconography while adapting it so that it made sense to a Greek audience, and Iberians saw Dionysius scenes on Greek vases as carrying funeral meanings and ... used them in funerary contexts."[63] Meanwhile, she observes, "the appearance of Egyptian objects with Egyptian divinities" was not unusual in certain Greek temples; "the temple of Hera on Samos has yielded several important Egyptian figures, including one that features Bes and another with the goddess Neith."[64] Bes it seems would go on to be "adopted" by the Greeks "as a male kouro-trophic deity."[65] In short, foreign peoples visiting Greek holy sites could believe that their own deities were also present there, especially if the god or goddess was equivalent in some way, and worship them as they *knew* them back home, which, in turn, could result in their assumption into local tradition as well.

Once again, however, the crucial recognition is not so much the existence of cultural interchange as the evidence of developments that are clearly the product of sustained interactions over time. As Demetriou puts it, "empha-sizing Mediterranean connectivity highlights that with the creation of new communities founded upon common Mediterranean political, religious, and maritime perspectives, new collective identities are also articulated."[66] This was even true for the Greeks themselves. At Naukratis in Egypt, one of the best-known emporia in the ancient world, the Greeks who lived there responded to the Egyptian elision of the distinctions between their cul-tural groups. That is, it was the Egyptians who did not see the difference between a Greek from the Ionian islands and a Greek from somewhere else, and the Greeks responded by developing a sense of shared identity for *themselves* that was expressed in the construction of the "Hellenion," a shared temple.[67] In other words, Demetriou argues, "it was the strength of the Egyptian collective identity and the Egyptian perception of the Greeks as a single collective identity that led the Greeks to recognize their com-monalities and express their Hellenic identity."[68]

This, interestingly, is one of the earliest cases where a Greek collective identity, a kind of local Panhellenism, was clearly expressed in the first

---

63. Demetriou, *Negotiating Identity in the Ancient Mediterranean*, p. 62.
64. Demetriou, *Negotiating Identity in the Ancient Mediterranean*, p. 89.
65. Demetriou, *Negotiating Identity in the Ancient Mediterranean*, p. 89.
66. Demetriou, *Negotiating Identity in the Ancient Mediterranean*, p. 14.
67. "Naukratis necessarily involved interactions between Greeks and Egyptians, which in turn produced a Greek response unlike any other. Faced with a bureaucratic kingdom and a strong Egyptian identity, the Greeks of Naukratis founded a common temple in 570 BC and called it 'Hellenion,' a unique name in the archaic period and symbolic of one of the earliest expressions of a Hellenic identity in the Greek world" (Demetriou, *Negotiating Identity in the Ancient Mediterranean*, p. 109).
68. Demetriou, *Negotiating Identity in the Ancient Mediterranean*, p. 151.

place. Demetriou notes that it "represents the one and only case in the whole of the *Histories*"—meaning Herodotus's *Histories*—"in which the Ionians, Dorians, and Aeolians are said to undertake any common endeavor."[69] It matters, however, that the Egyptians are part of this picture, too; that, in fact, the Egyptian sense of who the Greeks were and how they worshiped seems to have seeped in and reshaped the Greeks' own sense of these things. Demetriou suggests that this was common in emporia, which were border-lands by their very nature. When different groups had to work together in contexts like emporia, they seem generally to have made strides toward a collective identity in a way that was premised on the discovery of simi-larities, especially in terms of gods and heroes, whether that collective was forged from different Greek groups *or* Greek and non-Greek.[70] Certainly, in addition to borrowing and exchanging gods there were often "new hybrid divinities ... syncretism ... hybridization."[71]

Similar conclusions have also been advanced in a recent study by Robert Parker on a well-known topic: so-called *interpretatio graeca* and *romana*. In other words, it is typical of Greek and Roman sources to call the gods and goddesses of other people by the names of the gods in their own pan-theons. As I put it in another book, "Herodotus, reporting from Egypt, refers to the Egyptian oracles of Apollo, Athena, Artemis, Ares, Zeus, and Leto ... (Hdt. II.83)." Julius Caesar characterized the Gauls as especially devoted to the worship of Mercury, followed by Apollo, Mars, Jupiter, and Minerva (Caes. Gal. VI. 17).[72] Obviously, neither was true, and in the early days of contacts, Egyptians and Gauls could hardly even have heard of these figures. But this is the verbal form of the physical reality described above, where not just Greeks and Romans but other Mediterranean peoples seem to have tended to see other people's gods as, in reality, their own gods with different names. But despite how widely recognized this phenomenon is, it has often escaped significant scholarly attention *as* a phenomenon, except to the extent that it has generally been regarded as a species of cul-tural imperialism performed by the Greeks and Romans on non-Greek and Roman subjects.

As Parker points out in his thorough study, however, the evidence at least strongly suggests that the latter could often be willing participants in this

69. Demetriou, *Negotiating Identity in the Ancient Mediterranean*, p. 147.
70. "The Greeks of Naukratis had extra impetus to see themselves as Hellenes, because this is how the Egyptians viewed them. ... On the other hand, the formation of a collective identity, even a Hellenic one, was characteristic of multicultural emporia, where Greeks acknowledged their similarities in their recognition of all their deities as something they had in common" (Demetriou, *Negotiating Identity in the Ancient Mediterranean*, p. 151).
71. Demetriou, *Negotiating Identity in the Ancient Mediterranean*, pp. 6-7.
72. Tobolowsky, *The Myth of the Twelve Tribes of Israel*, pp. 112-13.

process, and even its initiators.[73] "Not all external *interpretationes* were accepted or persisted ... but many were attempted and accepted."[74] So, for example, bilingual tablets in which the name of the relevant gods are rendered according to the pantheon that corresponds to *each* language; an Etruscan bilingual inscription dedicated at Pyrgi that calls the goddess "Uni in the Etruscan version and Astarte in the Phoenico-Punic," say, are a relatively common phenomenon in the ancient Mediterranean. A Nabataean on Cos dedicated something "to Aphrodite (in Greek) and Astarte (in Nabataean)."[75] "A silver vase of Greek manufacture (early fourth century) which depicts the judgment of Paris bears inscriptions in Lycian. ... Athena is here identified for the Lycian viewer as Maliya, a Lycian goddess."[76] And in at least some of these cases, what is going on is not just calling a known god by a different, supposedly equivalent, name, but an organic kind of syncretism. That is, references to gods such as Zeus Ammon are not just attempts to redefine the Egyptian Ammon for Greek audiences but the creation of a figure with attributes of both. In the same vein, Parker refers to "Antiochus I of Commagene's ambitious though unsuccessful attempt to synthesize Greek cult with Persian in the first century B.C. through composite figures such as Zeus Oromasdes, Apollo Mithras, and so on."[77] Meanwhile, "on Delos, the Syrian goddess Atargatis becomes consistently for her Athenian worshipers Aphrodite Hagne, 'Reverend Aphrodite'; on the same island, a single instance of Herakles Halios 'of the sea,' may be a Greek rendering of Melqart."[78]

Of course, while these are examples of Mediterranean exchange, they do not concern foundation traditions per se. Rather, they concern traditions about gods and religious practices. Indeed, Demetriou, for one, highlights the importance of polytheism in particular in creating "flexible systems, which could be easily adapted depending on the social circumstances and used for mediation."[79] She argues that it was specifically "the translatability of pantheons among Mediterranean cultures" that "allowed Greeks and whichever local populations they encountered to recognize similarities between their respective gods, who acted as mediators between groups, facilitating their coexistence."[80] That is the aspect of mediation and facilitation I am interested in here.

---

73. "*Interpretatio* is always potentially a two-way process" (Parker, *Greek Gods Abroad*, p. 40).

74. Parker, *Greek Gods Abroad*, p. 39.

75. Parker, *Greek Gods Abroad*, p. 40.

76. Parker, *Greek Gods Abroad*, p. 40.

77. Parker, *Greek Gods Abroad*, p. 43.

78. Parker, *Greek Gods Abroad*, p. 44.

79. Demetriou, *Negotiating Identity in the Ancient Mediterranean*, p. 104.

80. Demetriou, *Negotiating Identity in the Ancient Mediterranean*, p. 233. She further suggests that "religion was a way for different ethnic groups to liaise with

Yet even if we only think of the few foundation traditions discussed in depth above—Nostoi traditions or Return traditions—we will see immediately that the crucial element in facilitating exchange is not the flexibility of *polytheistic* traditions specifically but simply the flexibility of traditions period, which is to say, the existence of a large cast of characters and events that can be used, flexibly, to encompass many different kinds of phenomena. And this is clearly revealed in a recent study of foundation traditions, Erich Gruen's *Rethinking the Other in Antiquity*. Indeed, the title itself nods at the purpose of this section: that enmeshed in a web of *shared* traditions, because they could cross boundaries, the differences between groups in the ancient Mediterranean and Levant could at least blur. As Gruen puts it,

> Communities and peoples, rather than considering themselves as hermetically sealed entities, regularly proclaimed ties to other societies, even inserting themselves into their history and traditions. By setting their patriarchs and legendary heroes into the folklore of other folks, they could attach themselves to the other peoples' experience and take credit for their qualities and achievements.[81]

Gruen's vision of this process may be a little too conscious and opportunistic for my liking; most often, it probably happened more organically and without so much explicit intent to steal and take credit as this particular gloss suggests.[82] But his basic point is what I have been arguing all along, that the elements of foundation traditions were not exchanged merely as part of whole stories but as individual figures, events, and developments, and they were exchanged between groups that are typically regarded as distinct with some frequency. Then, one set of interchanges could become the basis for a tightening web thereof, creating new stories and even new identities.

We do, it must be said, have a certain problem of evidence here. That is, the evidence we have tends to be from Greek sources not only for Greek instances of flexible interchange but for other groups as well. It is, for example, Hecataeus of Abdera who suggested that the Egyptians were quite as invested in the idea that an Egyptian, Danaos, had founded Argos in Greece as the Thebans were, and in Cadmus as well: "Nevermind that Cadmus normally counted as Phoenician. Egyptians were happy to claim

one another" (Demetriou, *Negotiating Identity in the Ancient Mediterranean*, p. 234). Parker, likewise, describes a world in which it may be "a mistake to speak of ancient polytheisms in the plural at all. From an actor's perspective the world was divided between different countries and tribes and political systems, but it was not divided between different gods" (Parker, *Greek Gods Abroad*, p. 78).

81. Gruen, *Rethinking the Other in Antiquity*, p. 233.

82. Malkin is probably closer when he observes that "as far as we know, Greeks regarded 'Foreign' gods much as they did Greek ones, albeit with different names, rites, and representations" (Malkin, *A Small Greek World*, p. 8).

him as their own."[83] In fact, Hecataeus states that the "Egyptians claimed Moses too," who was, in their traditions, given a mission by the Egyptians "to settle Egyptians elsewhere."[84] Many other such stories appear in Herodotus and Thucydides. But if we accept the testimony of these sources even in a limited way, we indeed have evidence of a vibrant, two-way interchange of figures and narratives that could lead to surprising new syncretisms and syncretistic accounts.

In addition, there is the example that is so well-known it is almost invisible. The *Aeneid,* of course, is built on an act of cultural appropriation. More specifically, it is based on the appropriation, at Rome, of a Nostoi founding myth centered on an existing Trojan War hero, Aeneas. Indeed, even the tradition that originally sent Aeneas to Italy was not Roman in origin but Greek.[85] At the same time, crucially, this is not to say that the *Aeneid* is on some level a Greek story. A great many of its features, and presumably those of the older Roman traditions that it channels, are perfectly Roman, and it comes out of what Gruen calls an ongoing "swirl of stories" in the region that also embraces Odysseus.[86] "Hesiod already included Italy among the wanderings of Odysseus. ... Some traditions [of Roman foundation] traced links to Odysseus or his sons, to descendants of Herakles, to the Arcadian Evander, or to a fictive Trojan captive named Rhome who gave her name to the city. The diverse threads overlapped, entangled themselves, and formed no coherent picture."[87]

Then, "once Aeneas was added to the mix, the entanglements multiplied." The local figure Evander has a notable role to play in the *Aeneid* as the father of the tragic Pallas; and anyway, the Romans of course had their own "indigenous traditions ... of the twins Romulus and Remus."[88] The *Aeneid* explicitly describes Romulus and Remus as the descendants of Aeneas (6.756-800), and so brings these tradition elements together. Thus, "Greek authors converted the sagas of Troy to bring Romans within the matrix of Hellenic traditions. And Romans in turn spun these stories to their own taste."[89] The result was certainly a rich pallet to paint with. We might think of the portion in the text that concerns the emissary the Latins

83. Gruen, *Rethinking the Other in Antiquity*, p. 226.
84. Gruen, *Rethinking the Other in Antiquity*, p. 226. Gruen also mentions a story reported in Diodorus Siculus in which "Osiris was head of a great military force that roamed the entire earth and brought civilization" and the story "adds Herakles to its narrative, only now he is a subordinate of Osiris. The god set up Herakles as general over all the realm" (Gruen, *Rethinking the Other in Antiquity*, pp. 266-67).
85. Gruen, *Rethinking the Other in Antiquity*, p. 243.
86. Gruen, *Rethinking the Other in Antiquity*, p. 243.
87. Gruen, *Rethinking the Other in Antiquity*, pp. 243-44.
88. Gruen, *Rethinking the Other in Antiquity*, pp. 243-44.
89. Gruen, *Rethinking the Other in Antiquity*, p. 247.

send to Diomedes, now settled in Italy, and his reply that Aeneas, now in his guise as Roman founder, was too mighty for the Latins to defeat (*Aeneid* 11.375-390). And this version of the story is different, in interesting ways, from the same hero's reply to the same entreaty in Ovid's *Metamorphoses*, where he pleads only lack of manpower because of a curse turning his men into birds (also mentioned in the *Aeneid* 14.445-82). But for us the significance of the *Aeneid* is that this is a genuinely clear example in which one instance of cross-cultural interchange evolved dynamically over time in such a way that an originally foreign figure was deeply interwoven into the fabric of an indigenous tradition system, so much so that he became a founding figure, enmeshed in local geography and genealogy.

I think we have to imagine stories like this all across the Mediterranean rim, where the famous tales of globe-trotting heroes were attached to local realities or local genealogies. We see other notable examples in the *Aeneid* itself, for example, in Aeneas's embassy to Evander. In this part of the narrative, the Latin king describes local rites due to Hercules for his defeat of Cacus in a nearby cavern, while bringing the cattle of Geryon to Eursytheus (8.255-370). How many caves might there have been that had similar stories told about them? And Herakles, or Hercules, was of course a figure who provided many connections to other groups of unknowable real-world importance. These included even his supposed connection to the Celts, whom Diodorus Siculus describes as his offspring through a son named Galates (Diodorus Siculus 5.24.3). While in that region fighting Geryon, he is also supposed to have founded the city of Alesia (5.24.1).[90] And so on.

Overall, then, what the evidentiary record increasingly shows is that, for many ancient Mediterranean peoples, from Egypt to Spain, the stories they lived among indeed formed a flexible vocabulary that they used in surprising and dynamic ways, *including* to talk to one another. Each of the examples discussed above suggests that there was genuinely more of a *koine* between what we are used to thinking of as distinct cultural groups, and that the interchange of foundation traditions and deities was part of what we would now call an international system with many participants. Widespread polytheism indeed seems to have played an important role. Yet it was certainly not only religion and gods that groups could exchange with one another toward the end of developing a kind of common tongue. Heroes and great events could be exchanged too. Herakles and Odysseus crossed boundaries at least as easily as Aphrodite and Zeus.

In addition, events like the Trojan War served as the setting for foundation traditions long after the first millennium BCE. Sometimes new heroes were invented for the explicit purpose of making connections. Gruen describes how the "invention of fictive founders" was a "common feature" across the

---

90. Tobolowsky, *The Sons of Jacob and the Sons of Herakles*, p. 193.

Mediterranean and notes the "frequency with which such legends associated nations with foreign founders."[91] Other times, existing characters simply took on new roles and had new adventures, sometimes with each other. The cumulative result of centuries of boundary crossing was "a plethora of associations" that "reinforc[ed] the theme of constructed connections that crossed ethnic boundaries," or even what we are used to *thinking of* as ethnic boundaries which turn out to be almost dissolvable under the right circumstances.[92] And each new story could serve as the basis for more, intensifying the web of connections that made the interchange of heroic figures and heroic settings a common feature of borderlands.

Again, just how much this Mediterranean exchange, or something like it, is applicable to the study of the Hebrew Bible is a difficult question to answer. Certainly, we see something of the same translatability of deities throughout the Levantine and Near Eastern region, a topic covered extensively by Mark S. Smith in his 2010 study *God in Translation*. As he notes, an older view represented by Jan Assman among others suggested that a resistance to "translatability" was one of the many contrasts *between* biblical religion and Near Eastern.[93] However, Smith gestures at various passages—Genesis 31, for example, where Jacob and Laban apparently solemnize a compact by referencing their respective deities—that show that the Assman view is not universally applicable.[94] Another, similar instance may appear in Gen. 14.17-24, where Melchizedek of Salem blesses Abraham by El Elyon, shares bread and wine with him, and receives a tithe, long before it makes sense to think that other people besides Abraham could be Yahwists.

It also seems as if figures from external traditions could make their way into biblical texts. Many have long believed, for example, that Ezek. 28.3, "you are wiser than Danel (or Daniel)," is a reference to a prominent figure by that name in the Aqhat epic from Ugarit.[95] And indeed, in the previous chapter I mentioned examples from the postbiblical period, in 1 Maccabees 12 and in Josephus, which would have fit in perfectly with what we see elsewhere in the Mediterranean—in the first case, a supposed letter from the Spartans claiming shared descent from Abraham; in the second, a story describing the union of the lines of Abraham and Herakles.

91. Gruen, *Rethinking the Other in Antiquity*, p. 355.
92. Gruen, *Rethinking the Other in Antiquity*, p. 356.
93. "While translatability was a common feature of the ancient Near East, Israel introduced what Assmann calls 'the Mosaic distinction,' namely a rejection of translatability for Israel's God with other deities" (Mark S. Smith, *God in Translation: Deities in Cross-Cultural Discourse* (Grand Rapids, MI: Eerdmans, 2010), p. 91).
94. Smith, *God in Translation: Deities in Cross-Cultural Discourse*, pp. 104-107.
95. For example John Day, "The Daniel of Ugarit and Ezekiel and the Hero of the Book of Daniel," *VT* 30.2 (1980), pp. 174-84.

What I wonder, however, is whether the idea of foundation traditions as a language that can exist *between groups* as much as within them might not be a good framework for rethinking the use of Israelite traditions in the—Judahite—Hebrew Bible. In other words, acknowledging first and foremost the inevitability of the conclusion that the Hebrew Bible's visions of the Israelite past and its heroes are Judahite productions, it is still difficult to say what precisely that means. And it is possible that exposure to a wider range of instances in which traditions crossed cultural boundaries of various sorts can offer some insights here. Specifically, I think these Mediterranean comparisons, if they are valid, need to change the extent to which we imagine that a biblical tradition or tradition element *is* Israelite, in its current context, if we can determine that it originated in Israel, because of how clear it is in other contexts that those who appropriate tradition elements can genuinely make them their own. But, at any rate, the utility of these recent debates about the exchange of foundation traditions and their creative redeployment in the context of ongoing agonistics and dialogics for the whole problem of the relationship between the distinct ancient places of Israel and Judah deserves attention.

An Israelite Language

When it comes to foundation traditions, what the Mediterranean evidence clearly shows is, well, that a lot more can happen to them than we once suspected. Traditions do not only change over time in their own cultures; they can easily cross boundaries and play crucial roles in cultural interchange. A hero from one region—think Aeneas—can enter fully into the traditions of another and take on new life. A famous event can suddenly have new participants who, in the process, manage to do some new inaugurating *thing*. Unrelated figures can become family, or one can take credit for the deeds of another, or they can work together, or come to seem almost the same in syncretic acts. And once a connection is established, however tenuous, it can, as we saw over and over again, become the basis for the next generation of stories, knitting two narrative systems closer and closer. Founding traditions can operate like a language through which one author or one group stakes a claim or attempts to establish a relationship, and they can be the language through which another group responds, sometimes establishing shared dialects, and reshaping tradition *universes* over and over again.

These are facts that can have extraordinary ramifications, or at least potential ramifications, for the study of the Hebrew Bible's visions of Israelite history as soon as we acknowledge what that very history so insistently tries to deny: that Israel and Judah themselves were *actually* different places. They may or may not have been populated by people who *once* operated as a unified ethnic nation—I doubt it—but it hardly matters. We might think that Israel and Judah were no more different than Athens and Sparta, or Sparta and Messene, even after Panhellenism. We might think they were as different as Greece and Macedon, Greece and Rome, or for that matter Israel and Edom, whether originally, or simply typically. Either way, different they remain, a consequence of the very border that explains why they have separate names in the first place. As a result, they would not have had one set of traditions but two, some perhaps about the same figures, and some about quite different ones. And so, it may be fruitful to imagine the Hebrew Bible's vision of all Israelite history as a Judahite attempt to meld Judahite and Israelite tradition vocabularies into a new, Panisraelite whole, especially through combining foundation traditions about figures such as Abraham, Jacob, Moses, Joshua, and David.

Establishing the ramifications of this possibility for the study of biblical traditions is a complicated matter, especially since the recognition that the narrative that appears in Genesis through Kings *features* a combination of originally Israelite and Judahite traditions is actually quite old in scholarship. It has, however, taken on different forms over time. In earlier periods, scholars of the Alt–Noth school, and Gunkel before them, had a lot of theories about how small tradition units were combined to form the pentateuchal narrative at least, but typically imagined that this process had been completed very early in Israel's history. [96] In addition, since more or less the beginning of historical-critical scholarship, there has been a pronounced tendency to see many texts in the Hebrew Bible, first and foremost, *as* whatever they originally were. In other words, if we discover evidence that a story was originally an eighth-century BCE Israelite composition, we treat it as an eighth-century BCE Israelite composition even now. Indeed, many scholarly accounts of the history of the Hebrew Bible, today, still begin with the effort to identify pre-existing parts and treat descriptions of the process through which they were combined to create a whole as a complete history of the Hebrew Bible's own narratives. [97]

In other words, one way or another, quite a lot of scholars have viewed the Pentateuch in particular, and to some extent Genesis–Kings, as essen-

---

96. For example, Noth's account of an "East Jordan Jacob"—a Jacob figure whose deeds were limited to that region and whose traditions were only later "arranged into a massive coherent narrative, the 'Jacob-Esau-Laban saga cycle'" (Noth, *History of the Pentateuchal Traditions*, pp. 85-86).

97. To cite just one example—without intending to comment on its overall worth or detract from its many fine qualities—we can consider Konrad Schmid's recent *The Old Testament: A Literary History,* which offers an eight-part discussion of that history. The middle six are periodized—"The Literature of the Assyrian Period," "The Literature of the Babylonian Period," and so on, with subsections that detail which biblical texts were written in which era. See Konrad Schmid, *The Old Testament: A Literary History* (trans. Linda M. Maloney; Minneapolis, MN: Fortress Press, 2012).

tially a straightforward product of the combination of pre-existing parts, in a way that preserves the basic character of those parts: what Frank Moore Cross called the "great conflate amalgam of many ages."[98] In this model the Pentateuch itself, and indeed much of the Hebrew Bible, is imagined perpetually to be "somewhere out there," somewhere available, slowly gathering elements like a snowball rolling downhill.[99] An eighth-century BCE text is written; it becomes part of the whole which grows by the addition; and, in the end, the whole is simply a product of a history of combination.

Another way to put it is that much previous tradition-historical scholarship might be accused, at least to some extent, of what Marc Bloch once called confusing "ancestry with explanation," the idea that an explanation of where stories originally came from and how they were put together is also an explanation of what they are in their present condition.[100] Scholars of this bent do not imagine that the final product can distance its constituent elements a great deal from where they began either by shifting their semantic meaning or by physically adapting them in ways that cannot be reversed with historical-critical effort. Nor is there often a great deal of sensitivity to the possibility that just because a text reflects a ninth-century BCE discourse, it does not mean it necessarily gives us a good window into the whole *picture* of ninth-century BCE discourses; later editors could have chosen something they liked and left the rest behind.

On the one hand, there is, perhaps, some justification for all this that does not exist in the Mediterranean context. Briefly, the Pentateuch in particular might well have been composed in a fashion that has no equivalent anywhere in the world: through the *literal* combination of pre-existing compositions in a way that often did not smooth out the differences between them, and sometimes does the opposite.[101] As a result, this ninth-century BCE Israelite composition indeed still looks much more like, or perhaps is even physically identical to, its original form in a way that is not true of an early Greek tradition preserved in a later work, such

98. Cross, *From Epic to Canon*, p. 52.

99. Albert de Pury, "The Jacob Story and the Beginning of the Formation of the Pentateuch," in *A Farewell to the Yahwist? The Composition of the Pentateuch in Recent European Interpretation* (ed. Thomas B. Dozeman and Konrad Schmid; Society of Biblical Literature Symposium Series, 34; Atlanta, GA: Society of Biblical Literature, 2006), p. 52.

100. Marc Bloch, *The Historian's Craft* (trans. Peter Putnam; New York: Vintage Books, 1964), p. 33.

101. On the uniqueness of this process, see Seth Sanders, "What If There Aren't Any Empirical Models for Pentateuchal Criticism?," in *Contextualizing Israel's Sacred Writing: Ancient Literacy, Orality, and Literary Production* (ed. Brian Schmidt; Atlanta, GA: Society of Biblical Literature, 2014), pp. 281-304.

as Pausanias or Apollodorus, but still rewritten by Pausanias and Apollodorus. It is easy to see why the prevailing view remains that one can simply extract the ninth-century text and so study ninth-century foundation traditions.

At the same time, I have, in the past, argued against this approach on both narrative and practical grounds. In the first case, I've argued that we habitually underrate the extent to which combining traditions, sequencing them in new ways and editing them even lightly, distances how we understand them from how we would have understood them in their original context.[102] In other words, even if an eighth-century BCE Israelite poem appears in the Hebrew Bible with exactly the same words in the same order as it had at the beginning, our understanding of it is transformed, to some extent, by its new context within an overarching narrative; we still read it through the lens of texts that were not always its neighbors. Just as, say, the *Star Wars* prequels and sequels might change how we understand the original trilogy, without actually altering that trilogy in any way—when we learn, for example, that the Luke, Leia, and Han-led rebellion ultimately failed— so combining any narrative with others will affect how we understand it.

More practically, I think scholars often underestimate how little in the way of edits can be required to genuinely transform how we understand a narrative. An example I have discussed before is the valiant effort by David Carr to establish "ground rules" for identifying Northern and Southern traditions in the Hebrew Bible.[103] Carr suggests three identifying features of the former; they will have a

> preponderance of references in a given biblical text to Northern place-names and/or figures primarily associated with the north ... evidence in a biblical text of a Judean adaptation of a precursor text with Northern elements. ... And ... reference to a potential Northern text in the book of Hosea.[104]

Hosea, interestingly enough, is the only prophet in the entirety of the prophetic books who seems to be from the kingdom of Israel, which is why the fact that he knows about a tradition is indeed telling. The Jacob tradition, which, in Genesis, provides the foundation tradition of Israel itself, is perhaps the best possible example of the phenomenon described here. Hosea 12 not only mentions Jacob but clearly refers to a number of the episodes that appear in Genesis's account of his life: Jacob's struggles in the womb with his twin, his physical combat with God, his vision at Bethel, his sojourn in

102. Tobolowsky, "The Primary History as Museum Exhibit."

103. Tobolowsky, *The Sons of Jacob and the Sons of Herakles*, p. 99. See also the discussion in Tobolowsky, "The Problem of Reubenite Primacy," pp. 38-39.

104. David M. Carr, *The Formation of the Hebrew Bible: A New Reconstruction* (New York: Oxford University Press, 2011), p. 473.

Aram-Naharaim, his marriage there, and his service as a shepherd. Thus, it seems clear that Hosea is indeed aware of an Israelite, or Northern, version of the Jacob tradition that approximates what actually survives in some ways, which, for many scholars would mean that the Genesis version of the story, even in its present form, *is* an Israelite tradition still.[105]

There are, however, certain internal reasons to think this is not a very good description of what is going on—internal in the sense that biblical evidence already suggests this by itself, without going into more conceptual questions. I noted, and I am not the only one, that Hosea 12 is surprisingly light on details.[106] It does refer to all of these narratives, but it does not tell us *who* Jacob's twin is; it does not mention marriage to more than one woman; it does not refer to any of his children.[107] Therefore, the question of how "Israelite" or "Judahite" the final story in Genesis may be depends a great deal on just how many different stories we think could or would be told around the same sequence of episodes, and how many additional details that do not appear in Hosea might be entirely Judahite in origin.

Thus, even on the level of the actual text, I think the idea that we can tell with confidence when something is really an almost pristine version of an early Israelite or Judahite tradition actually depends a lot more on the older idea that the transmission of traditions over time is more stable than we now know it to be, and on the idea, as well, that minor changes must have minor effects than many acknowledge. The composition-by-compilation aspect of the Pentateuch in particular exacerbates this tendency to minimize the creativity of tradition inheritance in various ways. Specifically, I think that an older vision of how an original set of traditions fares over time has been sustained, here, by clear evidence that certain discourses in the Hebrew Bible *are* considerably older than the Hebrew Bible itself, and equally clear evidence that certain traditions, and even texts, have disparate origins from each other. But this vision still depends on the idea that the only way to reinvent a tradition is to physically rewrite it to a degree that is not borne out when we have a wider range of tradition phenomena to study and draw conclusions from. And, often, it depends on the idea that the same

---

105. The section is titled "texts that may originate from the early northern monarchy." He acknowledges that "the Hebrew Bible is, in the final analysis, a Judean corpus" and that "any Northern texts preserved in it were transmitted and preserved … in Judean contexts" but suggests the above guidelines as a means of identifying "early Northern documents" (Carr, *The Formation of the Hebrew Bible*, pp. 472-73). The question, even if we can identify a pristine Israelite text, is whether we can really read it as we would have before it was so transmitted and preserved.

106. Tobolowsky, *The Sons of Jacob and the Sons of Herakles*, pp. 98-99.

107. See Tobolowsky, *The Sons of Jacob and the Sons of Herakles*, pp. 99-100; Tobolowsky, "The Problem of Reubenite Primacy," pp. 37-43; Na'aman, "The Jacob Story and the Formation of Biblical Israel."

story *structure* implies that we are in the presence of essentially the same story when we know that is not true.

What the Mediterranean world can offer to scholars attempting to reconstruct the processes through which the overall narrative Genesis through Kings came to be, and on some level, what it is, is both a source of insights into what *can* happen when traditions are combined together and diverse models for what *might* have happened. This is particularly true if, as I believe we should, we can begin by imagining that the very different way the Pentateuch and Genesis through Kings were physically created, compared to the other examples discussed above, is, nevertheless, simply another method of performing the same work. In other words, let us suppose that there is not a great deal of difference between an author using, remixing, connecting in new ways, and redescribing actual, physical, pre-existing compositions and an author drawing dynamically from the less-well-defined swirl of stories and story elements in the ways that I have discussed at length above. Let us allow that someone combining actual, physical compositions is capable of as much creative reinvention in the process as someone combining pre-existing traditions in new narratives, the same way that we can acknowledge that an artist creating a collage can be as creative as an artist painting a landscape. Let us imagine that, just as an epic poet, a biblical author has access to a "natural language" of tradition elements as well.

Consider, as quite a useful example, the case of Jacob discussed above. As I mentioned already, the basic elements of the *Aeneid,* Rome's founding myth, actually appear in earlier Greek traditions, including even the idea of his surviving to found a Latin kingdom. If we did what scholars often do with Hosea and argued that the *Aeneid* itself is "really" a Greek story, because so many of the episodes in Virgil's work have antecedents somewhere or another, how wrong would we be? Or, consider Hellen, in many respects the Greek Jacob. We can absolutely prove that he is an early figure of Greek myth, and many aspects of his traditional biography remained the same through succeeding centuries. But in early traditions he is a much more marginal figure, and Panhellenism itself did not yet exist. So, if we took the evidence that he was already a fixture of early narratives and imagined that he was already also the centerpiece of the genealogical web that charters Panhellenic identity, we would once again be wrong.

In the same vein, it seems perfectly reasonable to say that Jacob indeed is a figure of early Israelite tradition, or that Abraham, who spends most of his time in a southern geography, was likely originally a figure of Judahite tradition alone, or even a more local context.[108] But we should not take for

---

108. A rather extreme, though not necessarily inaccurate, version of the latter argument can be seen in an article by E.A. Knauf, who argues that "Israel and Judah were

granted that Jacob had the same descendants, who had the same roles vis-à-vis the Israelite people in Hosea's understanding of the tradition, where no such details appear, as he would have later on. We should not imagine that the Abraham who appears, however encased in a Judahite geography, is the one much earlier generations of Judahites would have known. We should not imagine that the surviving account of the lives of these figures in Genesis is *still* early and Israelite, or still early and Judahite, any more than we should imagine that the Panhellenic vision of Hellen as *Urvater* is Thessalian.

As a result, many different possibilities suggest themselves even if we acknowledge the early, Israelite origins of the basic vision of Jacob's life and deeds. We could imagine that, originally, he was only the ancestor of the Israelite tribes and not the Judahite, or even an ancestor who was not the father of eponymous tribal figures at all.[109] But we also see, in the Mediterranean example, that Jacob's Israelite origins might tell us little because we can see how easily groups who both did and did not share various cultural touchstones could take figures and deities from each other and make them their own. In this case, if the Judahites could take Jacob and recast him in Judahite terms, the way the Romans did Aeneas, or the Messenians Aepytus, or the Persians Perses, or the Etruscans Odysseus, then we should understand what the new story is in a fundamentally different way than we would when we assume a linear model of development over time. We might describe Jacob as an originally Israelite figure who now takes his place as the starring character in a Judahite drama *as* a Judahite figure, just like Aeneas was a Roman one. All of these possibilities are suggested by phenomena we see in the use and development of founding traditions in the Mediterranean, which offer useful counterpoints to typical ways that biblical scholars reconstruct the same histories.

As for the broader picture—how a Judahite vision of all Israelite identity, sweeping up founding traditions of both, developed in the first place—we can once again see how useful Mediterranean comparisons can be as a source of potential models.[110] And this is especially the case when we acknowledge the likelihood that the Judahites did not originally, or did not always, identify as Israelites, either in general, or first and foremost. The former seems likely, at this point; some have pointed out how obvious

---

… cantonized with regard to local traditions" into late periods. "It is conceivable that the name Abraham was unheard of in Jerusalem prior to 597 BCE, if even by that time" (Knauf, "Bethel," pp. 291-92).

109. I discuss these possibilities in Tobolowsky, *The Sons of Jacob and the Sons of Herakles*.

110. I discuss the process to some extent in Tobolowsky, *The Myth of the Twelve Tribes of Israel*, pp. 22-65.

it is that when sixth-century BCE prophets like Jeremiah and Ezekiel say "Israel" they mean Israel and Judah, and how much less obvious that is earlier.[111] And, of course, many have noted the absence of the tribe of Judah, or Simeon, or Levi from Judges 5, the earliest picture of tribal Israel that we have. But in addition, given the fluidity of ethnic identity over time, I think it is very likely that sometimes the Judahites felt more Israelite than others. Perhaps we might imagine something like what happened between Macedon and the Greeks of the Peloponnese, where Macedon's marginal status on the periphery of Greek identity was, for a time, mediated by the development of Macedonian connections to other Greeks through foundation traditions like the Return, but overall came and went in different periods.[112]

In that case, the examples above might, perhaps, help illustrate the contours of a scenario in which, throughout their separate histories, Judahites and Israelites participated in a form of exchange now familiar from the above discussions of the ancient Greek world. Basically, their close proximity and frequent interactions could have led to an interchange of stories and figures that, in turn, could be used to knit ties that bind, or, from time to time, cut them apart. In that case, we might not need a binary model at all, in which the Israelites and Judahites either did or did not think of themselves as absolutely the same, or absolutely other, in early periods. Instead, it may well have been the case in early periods that they thought of

111. "Scholars agree that 'Israel' in Amos and Hosea primarily refers to the Northern Kingdom and includes both the people of Israel and Judah only in exceptional cases or in redactional passages, as it usually does in Micah" (Reinhard G. Kratz, "Israel in the Book of Isaiah," *JSOT* 31.1 [2006], p. 115). Daniel Fleming and Philip Davies have also discerned differences between the treatment of Israel in what many scholars take to be the original parts of the book of Isaiah, and in later parts, the so-called Deutero- and Trito-Isaiah (Fleming, *The Legacy of Israel in Judah's Bible*, pp. 49-51; Philip R. Davies, "The Origin of Biblical Israel," in *Essays on Ancient Israel in its Near Eastern Context: A Tribute to Nadav Na'aman* [ed. Yairah Amit *et al.*; Winona Lake, IN: Eisenbrauns, 2006], p. 146). At the very least, as I previously observed, "the accessibility of Panisraelite sentiment in later texts demonstrates how reasonable it is to expect that it *would* have been unambiguously visible earlier had it existed earlier" (Tobolowsky, *The Sons of Jacob and the Sons of Herakles*, pp. 37-38).

112. On the other hand, Hall is quite right to note that the idea that Macedon was "peripheral" in early periods and more central later is to some extent based on a primordialist view of identity itself—and Macedon could be treated as peripheral *or* central by various Greek groups in any period. However, the Greekness of the Macedonians did rise to "salience" in the mid-fourth century BCE between Philip and Alexander (Jonathan M. Hall, "Contested Ethnicities: Perceptions of Macedonia within Evolving Definitions of Greek Identity," in *Ancient Perceptions of Greek Ethnicity* [ed. Irad Malkin; Cambridge, MA: Harvard University Press, 2001], pp. 159-60). Hall further observes that while Herodotus had granted "the Hellenic pedigree of both the Macedonian rulers and their subjects" others in the fifth century BCE did not feel that way—including Hecataeus of Miletus, who thought of them as barbarians.

each other as no more alike, or different, than either was to the Moabites, Edomites, or Ammonites. And there could have been times when either felt more alike to a different group than to each other.

Indeed, for all we know, the tradition that makes Jacob and Esau not only brothers but twins is a vestige of this era. Esau is described as the ancestor of Edom, so if either Israel or Judah *could* have had closer ties with Edom than with each other at one point or another, this is the tradition that could have offered the justification for that relationship. Likewise, it is too often neglected that the Assyrian conquest of Israel may have been precipitated by an alliance between Israel and Aram *against* Judah (2 Kgs 16), and that various regional kingdoms besides Israel and Judah were also supposed to be part of the United Monarchy (2 Sam. 8). I call attention to the episode in 2 Kings 3, where Israel, Judah, *and Edom* ally together against Moab, and to the fact that segmented genealogical frameworks, which include Genesis's accounts of Abraham's family, are habitually used to renegotiate identity constructions between different groups embraced within them.

Yet even if we imagine that Israel and Judah always had a closer relationship than we see in those eras when Macedon and Greece were farthest apart, there are useful Greek models. We seem to know that the worship of YHWH was important in both regions early on, and that the people of the two kingdoms spoke a very similar language. We might, then, imagine a process of gradually tightening links like the one Demetriou describes between different Greek groups that were especially devoted to the worship of the same god, whenever emporia brought them together.

> In Emporion, for instance, the Phokaian-Massaliote Greeks venerated the goddess Artemis, who they had borrowed from the Ephesian Greeks. In Pistiros, the Thasian and Apollonian Greeks who lived there, as well as the citizens of Pistiros, had the worship of Dionysus in common. Aphrodite mediated among different Greek groups residing in Gravisca. Having been brought together in one settlement, Greeks who came from different poleis acknowledged that they had in common the worship of this goddess.[113]

Over time, "all the Phokaian colonies in the west" came to worship "Ephesian Artemis," and in the East, too, she "had become a symbol of a regional Ionian identity, because she had saved not only Ephesos and Phokaia, but also Magnesia and Teos." "On the North Aegean coast," a shared affinity for Dionysus helped facilitate a development "of a regional identity" that could also include the Thracians.[114] The shared worship of YHWH, which is quite secure as a data point, is often used as proof that Israel and Judah always identified with each other, but that was not true for different Apollo

113. Demetriou, *Negotiating Identity in the Ancient Mediterranean*, p. 234.
114. Demetriou, *Negotiating Identity in the Ancient Mediterranean*, p. 238.

worshipers in different places of the Greek world.[115] Might shared worship of Yhwh have provided the foundation for an organic project of conceptual ethnic-nation-building here as well? And might this have happened gradually, starting from an era where Yhwh worship in each region was conceptually separate?

Or perhaps we might think of a process like the one Irad Malkin describes in a recent book, *A Small Greek World*. The title nods to a concept in Network Theory, the "small world," because it is meant to explain the kind of phenomena that might make someone say, "What a small world!" In other words, it is a model that explains, among other things, why we encounter people who know other people that we know, or went to our college, or come from our city, or have the same doctor seemingly randomly. This is not, however, a random phenomenon; it is a result of the fact that *the more people you know,* the more likely you are to know someone who knows someone else you know.[116] More technically, the more nodes there are in a network—people can be nodes, or cities in the ancient or modern world—the more the distance between nodes *shrinks.*[117] A colony in Egypt might have no connections with one in Spain, but both might have them with one in Italy, for example. As a result, over time, a "small world" may develop including all three.

Malkin uses this theory to argue that as Greek colonies spread out into the Mediterranean, they actually became more closely connected rather than less because they increased the total number of connections. In the latter part of this study he explores a specific phenomenon, the process through which certain Greek colonies abandoned the reverence of historical founders—Myskellos of Rhypai, for example, who had founded

---

115. It is secure, among other reasons, because there are so many names preserved in both regions that include theophoric elements referring to Yhwh.

116. Malkin cites Mark Granovetter's work on the "strength of weak ties" to observe that since your acquaintances, as opposed to your friends, have their own friend groups, it is surprisingly likely that one of them "may be precisely the eye doctor you happen to need" (Malkin, *A Small Greek World*, p. 27; Mark Granovetter, "The Strength of Weak Ties," *American Journal of Sociology* 78 [1973], pp. 1360-80). See also D.J. Watts and Steven H. Strogatz, "Collective Dynamics of Small-World Networks," *Nature* 393 (1998), pp. 440-42.

117. Or, in network terms, "the addition of a small number of random links drastically reduces the longest direct path between any two 'vertices'" (Malkin, *A Small Greek World*, p. 27). So, he imagines "a colonist who ended up in Megara Hyblaia in Sicily" who "was miserably trying out a few Sicilian sites until finally receiving an invitation from King Hyblon to settle in an unprotected plain (around 728 BCE) ... would then have been busy building, tilling the land, participating in the new social order, and so on. It is unclear how aware he could have been that he was also participating in the creation of a Megarian network that eventually involved cities such as Chalkedon and Byzantion at the Bosporus and even Selinous" (Malkin, *A Small Greek World*, p. 31).

Kroton—for the heroes of ancient tradition, especially Herakles.[118] "Greek cities in the western Mediterranean of Classical times began to appropriate mythic origins in response to the challenge of their national youthfulness."[119] Soon, in an expression of the kind of arbitrariness in the nature of tradition adaptation I have tried to draw attention to throughout, the "cities of 'old Greece'" would follow their lead, "telling themselves similar stories, with mythical founders who were more venerable than the obscure historical founders of the Archaic period."[120] The result was, of course, the possibility for new connections as two different places could suddenly come to have the same founders. In other words, all of a sudden, historically unrelated colonies and metropoleis might all believe themselves to have been founded by Herakles or Odysseus or whomever, which could start the process of building ties between them. And, as Malkin put it, eventually a back and forth developed: "the more ancient cities adopted the colonial foundations frameworks but with heroes as founders, which were in turn adopted by colonies."[121]

Thus, "in network terms 'founders' could function as 'ties' by connecting a variety of 'actors' or 'nodes.'"[122] I noted above that one of the interesting things about the Return of the Herakleidae tradition is that Herakleid ancestors appear grafted on to the genealogies of the Spartan royal houses—the Agiads and the Eurypontids—and the Corinthian royal house, the Bacchiadae. And this is what Malkin means, that Agis, Eurypon, and Bacchis did not have the cultural cache of a figure like Herakles, however more deeply rooted in their soils, so those roots were grafted onto a stemma of greater international repute in a more international age. Then, of course, the fact that all of these places were drawing from a shared repertoire, or vocabulary, of founding heroes means that they had additional means of making connections between them. Malkin argues that this process offered significant grist for the mills of a developing Panhellenic identity, which were just then beginning to turn. In other words, an increasingly rich network created a context where developments in what stories were told in one region affected how they were told in another until each region was telling stories that shared a context with the others. But practically what that means can be seen at Messene, where an older version of the story that justified, to some extent, their subjugation by Sparta was maintained, but with the substitution of different figures that not only made the new version more Messenian but provided the means of connecting Messene

118. Malkin, *A Small Greek World*, p. 120.
119. Malkin, *A Small Greek World*, p. 121.
120. Malkin, *A Small Greek World*, p. 121.
121. Malkin, *A Small Greek World*, p. 121.
122. Malkin, *A Small Greek World*, p. 121.

to potential new, post-Leuctra allies. The network the original story had brought them into was still a useful one, and, by existing, gave storytellers the means of negotiating a new position.

In Israel and Judah, of course, geographical proximity meant that some level of connectedness was an inevitability. I wonder whether a useful model for how Judah became Israel, and vice versa, might indeed come from certain "small world" dynamics, a pattern of increasing connection that drew them resolutely into the same basic world of traditions. Or, we could just as easily suppose that a kind of agonistics, discussed above, made jockeying for position with each other *through* a shared language of figures and events desirable. I mentioned Arjun Appadurai's idea of "the past as a scarce resource," that in order to make mutually intelligible claims, it sometimes behooves groups to use the same basic past as a medium for pursuing them. It might be, say, that Jacob developed into the Panisraelite ancestor precisely because his existing status as Israelite ancestor made him useful to Judahites who wanted to assert their claims to identity with, and perhaps hegemony over, the people of Israel.

More generally, we could imagine that external pressures, like encroaching empires or imperial rule itself, could then have fostered a kind of dialogics that turned this growing repertoire of shared touchstones toward the articulation of a shared identity. Then, as we have seen throughout this chapter, the integration of tradition systems would only have picked up steam as it became more and more useful to employ prior efforts at connection building as the basis for additional rhetorical and ideological moves. Jacob, a central figure in Israel's foundation traditions, becomes a figure binding Israel and Judah together. Once he is, traditions about him become the medium for ideological battles between the two, or, when necessary, for appeals for aid. The result of *both,* strangely enough, could plausibly be an ever more substantial sense of connection, which provided the next generation with the language it would use to make its own set of bids and visions. The founder of one place becomes the founder of another, or the brother or sister of another founder, or the enemy of another founder, and way leads on to way.

Yet here, once again, we return to the point I started with. This process of connection building, of the development of a Panisraelite identity where once there was no such thing, was surely mutual, in the sense that both "sides" participated. But that does not mean that they agreed, or that the final narrative, the founding tradition of biblical Israel, is a mutual product, or a collective production, in the term I have used more often. It remains a Judahite attempt to use a vocabulary developed through centuries of dialogics and agonistics at a particular time, for particular reasons, even if the elements of that vocabulary are more like extended narrative units than disassociated figures and events. And this is not just an issue to keep in mind when we consider how the narrative is formed, but what elements of it give us its apparently most fundamental significances.

So, for example, I think it is of basic significance for understanding the particulars of the Primary History's vision of the Israelite past that one of its most notable features is how, over the course of the narrative, it gradually but repeatedly narrows the size of the *surviving* group to whom Israel's history and legacy can apply. As is now well known, 2 Kings 17, the Primary History's account, claims, falsely, that all of the Israelites who lived in Israel were taken away into Assyrian exile, never to return. 2 Kings 24 and 25, which describe the Babylonian conquest of Judah, are not as explicit but are still among the texts that construct what has been called, however fairly, "The Myth of the Empty Land," the false idea that every Judahite of any distinction whatsoever was taken into Babylonian exile.[123] Other texts strongly suggest that every exiled Judahite returned from exile at around the same time, and in around the same way.[124] This isn't true either; the returns seem to have been piecemeal, over a long period of time, and far from complete, which is to say, many remained behind or moved to different parts of the Persian Empire. Many never left Judah at all.

Nevertheless, the cumulative effect of these exclusions is that by the end of the story—though the Chronicles history tells things a bit differently, and so do other parts of the Hebrew Bible's collection—the community of Judahite returnees is positioned as *the only group of Israelites remaining in the region.* In other words, an overall reading of this biblical account of the history of all Israel produces the impression that at the end of that history, its entire legacy rests in the hands of one visible community, the representative of all that once was.[125]

Broadly then, we are perhaps best off separating the two parts of the discussion in the latter part of this section. On the one hand, we have the question of how the founding traditions of Israel and Judah were knit

123. Hans M. Barstad, *The Myth of the Empty Land: A Study in the History and Archaeology of Judah during the "Exilic" Period* (Symbolae Osloenses Fasciculus Suppletorius, 28; Oslo: Scandinavian University Press, 1996); Oded Lipschits and Joseph Blenkinsopp, "After the 'Myth of the Empty Land': Major Challenges in the Study of Neo-Babylonian Judah," in *Judah and the Judeans in the Neo-Babylonian Period* (Winona Lake, IN: Eisenbrauns, 2003), pp. 3-20; Jill A. Middlemas, "Going Beyond the Myth of the Empty Land: A Reassessment of the Early Persian Period," in *Exile and Restoration Revisited: Essays on the Babylonian and Persian Periods in Memory of Peter R. Ackroyd* (ed. Gary N. Knoppers, Lester L. Grabbe, and Dierdre N. Fulton; London: T. & T. Clark, 2009), pp. 174-94.

124. Bob Becking, "'We All Returned as One!' Critical Notes on the Myth of the Mass Return," in *Judah and the Judeans in the Persian Period* (ed. Oded Lipschits and Manfred Oeming; Winona Lake, IN: Eisenbrauns, 2006), pp. 3-18.

125. Tobolowsky, *The Myth of the Twelve Tribes of Israel*, p. 234.

together. I think the evidence strongly suggests that this happened at a different end of the history of the period of biblical composition than scholars once believed, but also that phenomena from the wider Mediterranean can provide useful suggestions for how it might have occurred. There is the possibility that an "all-Israel" identity developed slowly over time around a steadily growing repertoire of figures and events, as in Malkin's "small world" model, or around the worship of YHWH, as in Demetriou's. But the crucial thing here is this: the actual porousness of cultural boundaries in the context of Mediterranean exchange means that the relationship between Israel and Judah may have taken many different shapes over time and may have started out quite a bit more separate than we usually think. In other words, Israelites and Judahites may really have thought of themselves as fundamentally distinct at one point, or no more similar than the other nations, even despite their shared worship of YHWH. They may have adopted each other's traditions, first, agonistically, and only later as part of a developing dialogics. The enlargement of the foundation traditions of one to include the other could have had many significances, and, indeed, many interpretations before reaching its familiar form. And so on.

At the same time, we seem to have a clear line here on the particular agonistics that give shape to how the final narrative treats its inherited elements, in the particular *instance* of telling a familiar enough story that the Primary History represents. We know what mediates the interaction between the story and the vocabulary it deploys: the effort by a particular set of Judahite authors and editors, in a particular context, to position their community as the only remaining heir to *all Israel*. Thus, this program is what must be visible as we consider what the story does with what it is made from. There is value in continuing to ask what the current version of the Abraham story, or Joseph story, the current accounts of the conquest of Jerusalem, the current vision of the founding of the Temple descend from. But if we wish to understand the Primary History's visions of history not as an inert distillation of all these histories but an active attempt to make something through them, asking what role the finished products play in the effort that presents them to us today is, once again, the central question.

In short, the unique way that Genesis through Kings was created indeed gives us more to work with in reconstructing previous levels of discourse, and tracing the history of traditions, than most, a compensation of sorts for the fact that this is the only textual composition of any length that survives from ancient Israel and Judah at all. But what we are learning about, in my view, is still what produced the vocabulary, not what gives it its meaning in context. We should *not* confuse ancestry with explanation. When we see just how creative the use and reuse of inherited vocabularies of foundation tradition elements can be in other parts of the Mediterranean, we should at least be willing to wonder if we might see that same creativity here, too.

And if "all Israel" was a long time building, gradually woven around the shared touchstones of God and heroes, on a loom that turned on the rush of events, that does not make the biblical one *the* all-Israel story; it makes it the version told by these authors, at this time, for their reasons. It makes it a Judahite product of, probably, the immediate postexilic period.

Or we might put it this way. There might have been many reasons that Israelites and Judahites began speaking about each other in the dynamic language of inherited tradition elements. There might have been many reasons they began to speak *to* each other in this same language, starting the process of entangling their traditions. Subsequent developments, like trade arrangements and external pressures that affected one or both, may have changed the tenor of the ongoing conversation in any number of ways. The version of diverse foundation traditions we find in the Hebrew Bible are snippets of this conversation as it had evolved by the time the final narrative was taking shape, but also, in some respects at least, profoundly individual. As with the Homeric poems, it was still up to the authors who rendered an inherited vocabulary into intelligible speech to determine what to say with it—shaped both by the needs of the wider context in which this process took place *and* the individual creativity, apprehensions, and intentions of those authors.

Aftermaths

This is another chapter that deals with aftermaths. From the late eighteenth century on, a great deal of scholarship converged on the point that we should imagine a certain kind of storyteller as what Rosalind Thomas calls "mechanical tools of traditions."[126] That is, they were seen as little more than lightly differentiated vessels through which traditions passed. In that model, stories might change over time by misadventure, but rarely on purpose; and if on purpose, the nature of these changes was close enough to something that might be called corruption that they were hardly of interest. The job of the scholar was to excise the imperfection and recover the original purity of the narrative that was once, long ago, the distilled memory of the tribe. There are still scholars working in this tradition, and scholars who endlessly find new reasons to preserve it, scholars who claim that contemporary ways of thinking about oral traditions, or memory, or cultural memory, or the ways that ancient contexts differ from modern, let them reach old conclusions safely. It is not true. So what comes next?

I have proposed in this chapter and in many ways throughout this book that traditions are not only far better understood as a dynamic medium through which inheriting generations speak than the fossilized imagina-

---

126. Thomas, *Literacy and Orality in Ancient Greece*, p. 30.

tion of the earliest ones, but far more interesting in that paradigm. It is not really, for the most part, my own proposal, even if the application to biblical traditions is unusual. Except for the terminology, however, my conclusions strike me as a natural evolution of a good deal of recent work I tried to synopsize above and map on to the context of foundation traditions where so many different things are going on at so many different levels of society. What I have suggested is that the world of foundation traditions, rather than existing in the ancient imagination as discrete *narratives,* entire stories known and repeated, instead supplied a ready repertoire of figures, events, and episodes that created a narrative universe. Storytellers, drawing from that universe, or repertoire, construct new visions of the past and stage familiar figures in new dramas. These modifications took many forms: connecting a well-known event to a local place, adding a local hero to a more embracing tradition, changing the details of a familiar story, and much more. But they were achieved by the dynamic redeployment of local, regional, and supraregional repertoires, which redeployments in turn served as the basis for the next round of negotiations. I have called these repertoires tradition *vocabularies.*

In the study of ancient Greek traditions, the recognition of how much was possible within the ongoing swirl of story on story has already opened new frontiers. Most of all, we are increasingly aware that other Mediterranean peoples were not just *subjects* of *interpretatio graeca* or of efforts to give Greek ethnographies to the rest of their world. These acts of boundary-crossing were something other groups participated in, in an active way, certainly by occasionally embracing Greek traditions of origin and by identifying their gods and goddesses with Greek gods in multiethnic emporia. And if Greek sources are to be believed, these non-Greeks could do more—telling their own versions of stories about Danaos, Cadmus, Herakles, and others, including their own heroes, in order to position themselves advantageously within a kind of *koine* formed by Mediterranean interconnections. These actions incurred counter-reactions, a dynamic two-way process that shaped and reshaped the map of foundational events: sending Aeneas, for one, to Rome, where he became very Roman indeed, and then, the ancestor of the Julio-Claudian dynasty.

Finally, I wondered what lessons this increasingly visible interchange might have for understanding the foundation traditions of the Hebrew Bible, which are certainly formed from both Israelite and Judahite tradition vocabularies. It is always possible that there aren't any, that the context in which Israelites and Judahites interacted is too different from the multisided processes that created what we see in the wider Mediterranean. But I suggested there were two lessons at least. First, that the creation of connections between two groups can be the starting point for ever tightening links between them that produce a new and embracing vision of identity. Second, that each subsequent attempt to redescribe that identity still belongs to the person doing the describing—that they are not as constrained by the weight of tradition as we once believed. Thus, one level of analysis can follow how the link between Israel and Judah was forged through shared figures, or figures who became shared, like Abraham and Jacob, and another, the evolution of the general shape of that relationship over time. But neither level of analysis actually explains the finished text as we have it, which is more than merely the neutral result of histories of development. The fact that Greek tradition made Aeneas into an Italian king, and Roman tradition advanced along this line, linking him to Rome and the Julii, explains where Virgil was coming from. It could not foresee that, in the fullness of time, an adopted son of the Julii would become emperor of Rome, and it did not write Virgil's poem.

Thus, Mediterranean phenomena might indeed offer useful examples of how two different groups came to identify as one group, whether they started out, like the Ionians and the Dorians, sharing a great deal, or were once considerably more different than we used to think. But they more certainly offer a kind of antidote to the anonymity of biblical narrative, which, in my view, is one of the strongest forces preserving an outdated approach to what these narratives represent. In other words, I think it is very hard to escape the fact that the Hebrew Bible's charter traditions *look* like the *beau idéal* of the Romantic imagination, an anonymous set of narratives that present themselves as *the* traditions of the Israelites. But not even Homer was simply a vessel through which an older tradition passed; in fact, it increasingly seems, far from it. Neither was the author of *this* version of the lives of Abraham, Isaac, and Jacob, the founding of the temples at Jerusalem, Bethel, and Dan, the rebuilding of Jericho, and much else besides, a vessel.

Instead, whether in ancient Israel or Greece, we have to imagine each instance of storytelling in a *real-world* context, alive with traditions that did not always seem to storytellers to be confined within discrete stories that they could either repeat or not repeat. A narrative universe. People like Dorieus could simply decide that their Herakleid descent meant they had a claim to Sicily, too. And there were many hanging threads of old traditions to grab on to, for those who wanted. Why not? The *Iliad* does not present itself as the complete story of every aspect of even the year of the war it presents, neither do the Nostoi tales explain how every single soldier came home. That the heroes of this text, or even figures not mentioned by it, should have more adventures, or that it should touch on more developments in other places, would never come as a surprise, however newly invented. That these new stories should build, refashion, or break connections between groups is only natural, too. Thus did old stories become what I have called not a register of agendas but a palimpsest of registers, while still, in each instance, being shaped toward one end.

Most of all, we have to imagine the storytellers themselves, real individuals with their own sense of what was important, what was useful, and what was necessary to do, their own apprehensions about who mattered or what might have happened. These individuals are creative, they have intentions, they have ideas, and these come across in their stories. They are speaking a language that is passed down, but it is as *flexible* as a language, as capable of a wide variety of expression as a language, as able to produce neologisms, new combinations, and even to grow a little along the way. It is, as it always is, what the speaker makes of it; and that makes the world anew, again and again. And then the word, once spoken, could be used by someone else for something new, as part of a new sentence. In this way, between the dynamic swirl of what they inherited, the needs of the moment, their own sense of what they could do, and what they had to do, new authors could tell new stories that were always in the process of rhetorically reorienting peoples to new realities, new requirements, new registers of prestige, and new desires. And when a new story posed a new connection, journey, event, or possibility, it was opening a door, intended or not, for someone else to walk through, too.

CONCLUSION

"The Circus Animals' Desertion," by William Butler Yeats, is a melancholy poem. It is one of his last, and resonant with an awareness of that fact. The circus animals themselves represent Yeats's own poetic imagination, the sparks of creativity that let him, so to speak, put on a show. But it contains one of the most beautiful descriptions there is of where imagination *comes from*: "Those masterful images because complete / Grew in pure mind but out of what began? A mound of refuse, or the sweepings of a street, / Old Kettles, old bottles, and a broken can, / Old iron, old bones, old rags." "Now that my ladder's gone," he says, "I must lie down where all the ladders start / In the foul rag and bone shop of the heart."

I think it is in the business of conclusions to consider what passed between shop and street—where the ladder began, and what actually climbed out into the light. And this, I confess, is a book that wandered, in some ways, from what I had in mind. Not in its overall plan, not in its purpose. I had always intended to use how scholars in two disciplines concerned with the study of ancient traditions approach similar questions and problems differently from each other to explore what approaches make the most sense today. And I hope that those who make it this far will feel that I have done that. Where, however, I had imagined focusing almost exclusively on surveying the scene and reporting back, I kept encountering the same obstacles on the way. In many cases, the question was not what shifts in our understanding demand, which virtually all converge on the point that inheritances of all sorts are fluid, not static. It was why so many of the necessary changes had not been made *already*.

After all, I hope and think there are new ideas and new proposals here. But many of the recognitions that require them, in my opinion, are not themselves new, and I am far from the first to offer something *like* the responses I have offered. So, I felt that in fact I could not simply survey and state what I thought needed to happen. I had to think very carefully about what might make my conclusions *stick* when similar ones, however insightful and convincing, had not, or, at least, had not succeeded in diverting the majority of scholarship from its familiar course. I didn't think this was something I could achieve by force of rhetoric, as if no one else had written well enough to deserve to bring about a more general paradigm shift. But I did think there were things I could do, structurally, that might make both the seriousness of the *need* for such a shift and some of the reasons it has not occurred more visible than they have sometimes been.

Thus, this book, in addition to its primary concern, was also occupied for much of its length in establishing the *relationship* between certain aspects of contemporary approaches and assumptions, many of them Romantic, that would be widely rejected if they still had to be articulated explicitly. And some of it was devoted to the effort to draw attention to a consistent pattern in the history of ideas where the study of ancient traditions is concerned. This is a truly titanic tendency, in every sense of the adjective, namely hitting the same icebergs, to find a way to use new evidence first, foremost, and perhaps ever after to reassert the validity of familiar approaches. And with this tendency comes others, including a willingness to conflate offering more modest versions of the exact same conclusions with a responsible skepticism when the very basics of the approach that produced the original are in question. Often, this is coupled with a further willingness to let really minor critiques, almost any potential problem at all, derail attempts to bring about systemic change.

In other words, it was, it is, and it perhaps may be very common for a scholarly argument to display what I came to think of, while writing, as a "push–pull dynamic." This, as dances go, is a rhetorical two-step. The scholar acknowledges the justice of some aspect of a new critique—the push forward—then finds some justification for minimizing the scope of its impact on familiar approaches—the pull back toward the older approach. In the process, the older model loses something of its robustness but gains new fortifications and survives, and even seems the more justified because the new argument appears the more responsibly formed *through* its handling of the too-robust argument. But in each case, essentially the same argument is made, and it is the argument that was desired all along, transforming the evidence into something it is not.[1] The evidence of archaeology or epigraphy becomes, from the right perspective, just the thing to put solid ground under the feet of Romantic fantasy. A particular way of characterizing oral-formulaic theory makes it indistinguishable from the argument that an ethnic nation holds its traditions in common and passes them down through the generations. A distorted construction of cultural memory makes it functionally equivalent to the argument that the past cannot be refashioned to any significant degree by those who inherit it. And so on and so on.

I know that, as a result, the book just completed is characterized nearly as much by *insistences,* more frequent and extensive than I had anticipated feeling necessary, as by the topics of its varied discussions. Above all, I

---

1. I discuss the role of desire in transforming evidence in the context of mid-century parallelomanias in Tobolowsky, "On Comparison with Ancient Greek Traditions," p. 2.

wanted to insist on an absolute *end to exceptions*, to efforts to find reasons or models that made ancient traditions *exceptional*, in the sense of not having to play by the rules that all other kinds now seem to play by, where change over time is concerned. This is not because there are no differences between antiquity and the present; there are any number of them. But the ability to create collectively and preserve continually is not among them, no matter how the Great Divide is redevised. Then, there is no special kind of story—an epic, or a legend, or a myth—that can exempt itself from the ongoing creativity of generations of storytellers such that we can say most forms of narrative are fluid over time but *not these.* The depth and intensity of my attempts to describe this problem reflect the depth of my desire to make an effective critique with an awareness of the history of accurate and ineffective critiques in mind. If it seems that I returned to certain points too often, it is, likewise, a reflection of my sense that many of my critiques would no longer be necessary *already* if a more elegant approach could have carried the day, at least as far as it actually needs to go.

Thus, I chose to thread a sketch of the history of certain ideas through the first two chapters' discussions of the ramifications of a constructivist model of ethnic identity for the study of what ancient texts preserve and reflect, and of what any correspondences between traditions and extraliterary evidence can prove and mean. I wanted to show how the largely Romantic roots of the idea that the original tradition is the collective memory of the ethnic nation, if it could only be recovered, first helped give shape to historical-critical approaches, or at least shaped apprehensions of why they were important and what they could achieve or explain. Then, I wanted to be explicit about the fact that the idea that extraliterary evidence could prove that a given tradition really *was* essentially memory after all—if only there were enough correspondences between the literary and material record, or if new, conservative models of oral composition and transmission were valid, or if one selectively employed the results of folkloric or sociological research—constituted a reinvention of the older preoccupation on apparently modern terms that did not, in fact, make those preoccupations more plausible. Only more plausible *seeming.*

With those discussions as a foundation, it was easier in subsequent chapters to simply gesture at what I think is true and move on, so to speak, to the main course. The compulsion, of a sort, to insist that a tradition is really earlier than we might think, or more accurate than we might think, or more stable over time than we might think, because of various reinventions of the Great Divide, is a reflection of two inherited ideas. First, that an early tradition is better and more revealing than a later. Second, again, that if there are enough genuine memories in a text, it can still prove that it is really a fundamentally different *kind* of tradition after all, something like *Naturpoesie,* the collective, unaffected, memory of the ethnic group. These are the ideas that have been constantly reinvented, given new terminology, and new justifications, in my view because they helped give shape to what it meant to study an ancient text, in the days when the disciplines themselves were taking shape. And they are the essence of the sixth-sense problem; they are ideas that don't know they are dead.

Without them, we will still sometimes find early traditions and accurate memories though I think it will turn out that we find them substantially less often *when we do not want them to be there so badly*—which is why I spent so much time in this study discussing why, historically, scholars *have* wanted to find them there. But we will not find that a single tradition served in one era as the collective expression of what the ethnic nation understood and believed, and ever afterwards remained the single, stable vision of the past, held in common. Early traditions reflect early discourses as later traditions reflect later discourses, and early elements in later traditions have a role to play that is at least as interesting as where they came from. Therefore, we move from linear models and qualitative frameworks to active processes where what texts and traditions that survive, in their current form, primarily reflect is the past constantly remade and used to build a new world.

The question remains why there *is* so much resistance to genuinely moving on from the idea that ancient traditions are first and foremost the memory of real events, however distorted. And, the related question, which I first broached in the introduction, also remains: why does there seem to be a more serious version of the problem in the study of the Hebrew Bible than of ancient Greek traditions? I stress as emphatically as someone can, bound by print and page, that this is not because the study of the former is a paragon where assimilating the lessons of contemporary recognitions is concerned. As I noted throughout, it also might be little more than the natural outcome of certain natural advantages in the study of the former: no recent history of regarding the texts as scripture, and a great deal more to work with where studying the processes of tradition inheritance are concerned. Finally, I want to be very clear about this: what I have in mind strictly concerns questions of memory, tradition, and tradition inheritance. New frontiers—all-important topics like race, gender, and sexuality—are ones where both fields have considerable work to do. And in each, there are wonderful scholars doing that work and pushing them ahead in ways they need to go.

Yet here I return to another idea I broached in the very beginning, one largely unrecognized and perhaps even unnerving: that the study of the Hebrew Bible's traditions would simply have considerably further to travel if it was really to meet the demands of contemporary recognitions about the fluidity of traditions over time, *through no fault of its own*. Instead, the

Hebrew Bible may simply be *much more different* from what it appears to be than the bulk of ancient Greek traditions are, requiring a more substantial reassessment in order to be properly understood.

What do I mean? For one thing, it just so happens that inquiries into Homer could hardly help being inherently more plausible than many of the corresponding arguments in biblical studies. Certainly, early arguments in both disciplines were equally as poorly formed, based on the same inaccurate assumptions, and suffering from many of the same flaws. They encountered, and often dealt with as poorly for a while, the same challenges from shifting assumptions. But the simple fact that the Homeric poems still seem likely to be eighth-century BCE compositions that, if they have any relationship to history, refer back to events of perhaps the mid-thirteenth century means that traditions, or the memory of events, would have to survive the passage of perhaps five hundred years. This is a tall order, no doubt, but not in comparison to what would have to be true for the patriarchal traditions of Genesis, say, to be based on real events. This is a text from, perhaps the fifth century BCE that describes events that likely would have had to have taken place in the early second millennium BCE, which means that, to reach the same conclusions about the history behind the text, we would have to believe that memories of a sort survived *more than twice as long.*

In addition, the idea that the Homeric poems, which are essentially about one great event and its aftermath, survived as two among many stories about early Greece is considerably more plausible, on an inherent level, than the idea that a single tradition of national origin remained at the center of how the Israelites *and* their distant ancestors understood themselves and their past for that entire time. And while many Greeks lived around, among, and even within the physical remains of the Mycenaean world that the poems purport to reflect, what remains could there even have been of Abraham, Isaac, and Jacob in monarchical Israel and Judah to aide in memory or inspire stories? Meanwhile, subsequent investigations have at least turned up hints of some form of conflict between Hittites and a people known as Ahhiyawa—presumably the Achaeans of the *Iliad*—while even the possibility that an Amorite migration in the early second millennium BCE could have central relevance for an Israelite people that emerged more than half a millennium later has faded into remoteness.[2] Finally, while it

---

2. I refer here to the handful of Hittite letters that might allude to a conflict between Ahhiyawa—presumably the Achaeans—and Troy (Wilusa), for which see Beckman, Bryce, and Cline, *The Ahhiyawa Texts.* As for the other claim in this sentence, what I mean is that new visions of ethnic identity would cast doubt on the possibility that even the early Israelites were very attached to any long ago Amorite ancestry they may have had.

was widely assumed from the beginning of the modern disciplines that both the pentateuchal and Homeric narratives reflected important early traditions, *because it was supposed that traditions of that sort always did,* there simply is a good deal of evidence testifying to the central importance of Homer well prior to the age of classical Greece. Meanwhile, nothing of any significance suggests the same about the Pentateuch in the first half of the first millennium BCE.

As a result, the exact same conclusions about the antiquity, reliability, and historical importance of one set of traditions were indeed much more likely to come closer to the truth than the other, even though both were perfectly normal conclusions to arrive at, about any important traditions, for quite some time in the history of scholarship, and without any significant difference in the sophistication of the relevant arguments. It was *a priori* less likely that the traditions concerning the patriarch—and the exodus— reflected real events to any significant degree than at least the *Iliad.* It was less likely that they reflected important early traditions than either the *Iliad* or the *Odyssey.* And so, the same assumptions and the same approaches yielded worse results in one case to begin with. And to the extent that both disciplines live equally in the aftermath of those formative efforts, this early imbalance continues to place one discipline, in at least a few ways, in a worse position than the other.

Finally, there is simply no Greek analogy to what we might call the problem of Judah: the Judahite origins of the biblical vision of Israel. It may not be precisely like discovering that Homer was really a Roman, or thinking, until some new discovery, that Virgil was really a Greek. At the same time, future analysis must indeed, in my view, start with the recognition that the idea that Judah and Israel were, first and foremost, two parts of "all Israel" in a totally uncomplicated away is a biblical premise that *could not* have been a consistent, real-world premise. In other words, I do not think that, knowing as we do the relationship between identity and political formations, it is even possible that two separate political entities with different kings and courts, different neighbors, different experiences, and even different conquests could consistently regard each other simply *as* members of a single ethnic nation. And that is even if they both thought of themselves as Israelites in very early periods, or later ones. A consciousness, in Judah, that Judahite Israelites were *also* Judahites would certainly have existed, too, and would have found its way into the Judahite vision of Israel and its past that is presented in the biblical accounts of Israelite history.

In short, there are certainly still different ways of thinking about the actual nature of the relationship between Judah and Israel, and no absolute clarity will be forthcoming. But there is no remaining way to deny the Judahite origins of what Wilson calls the "discursive formation" of these narratives.[3] It is not just, as Daniel Fleming put it, that the inheritance of materials that produced the Hebrew Bible is "literally Judahite," by virtue of taking place in Judah, but that the processes that shaped these into a comprehensive account of Israelite history were, too. And indeed, the final product is the work of a particular group of Judahites, in a particular context, with particular intentions. And now that we have to imagine the heirs of any tradition not just adapting, in a linear fashion, a single old story, but choosing which ones to tell, and how—and likely writing some of their own—we have to imagine all of the traditions in this Judahite book not only as "literally" Judahite but *actively* Judahite.

The scope of this problem is what I find daunting. There is no way to overstate the extent to which the idea of the Hebrew Bible as *Israel's* traditions has sunk into our collective psyche. The libraries and bookstores are full of studies of the history of ancient Israel, the religion of ancient Israel, the laws of ancient Israel. But they almost always start with this Judahite *vision* of Israel, mediated, for us, by the story these Judahite authors and editors wanted to tell. This means that even when we feel we have identified an early Israelite tradition, we still have to ask whether the Judahite authors and editors involved chose this Israelite tradition out of a host of others that would have given us a different impression. We have to ask how framing what they chose with other traditions that they *also* chose reshapes how we understand them.[4]

In addition, and perhaps most disruptively of all, we should recognize that the field's central interest in the study of ancient Israel *came out* of an interest in biblical Israel. I quite agree that there is value in studying the history and traditions of Israel qua Israel the same way there is value in studying any aspect of the past. But the fact that *biblical Israel was really Judah,* or perhaps created in Judah, should change the questions we *prioritize* all the same. There has been a tendency in recent years to respond to the growing recognition that what we have is essentially a Judahite version of the Israelite past by refocusing on the familiar question of what, therefore, we *really* know about Israel qua Israel, the topic we are used to studying.[5] But I wonder if this too is not, to some extent, another effort to rescue traditional preoccupations and priorities that do not really need to be rescued.[6] In other words, if *biblical Israel* is *Judah's Israel,* we should prioritize the

---

3. Wilson, *Kingship and Memory in Ancient Judah*, p. 6.

4. See, in particular, Tobolowsky, "The Primary History as Museum Exhibit."

5. This is, by and large, the project of Fleming's book and of others such as Finkelstein, *The Forgotten Kingdom*.

6. See the discussion in Andrew Tobolowsky, "Redescribing, but Really, Finally Moving On from Israelite Origins," *Method and Theory in the Study of Religion* 5.35 (2023), pp. 434-44.

study of Judah's Israel over the study of ancient Israel, no matter what past preoccupations inspired. Anyway, this is what a great many of the developments discussed in this book suggest about all traditions: they are mainly registers of what their authors believed or wanted from the past, even when they preserve authentic reminiscences of an actual past.

This is a recognition that points the way toward two concluding thoughts, as this book finishes its own journey upwards into the light of day. First, precisely because of the time I spent here exploring the endurance of patterns that ought not to endure, and wondering why, and investigating how, I feel tremendously aware that I am writing into a long tradition of scholarship that has always been dismissed, often enough with invective, as *needlessly skeptical.* In some cases, the tone of the dismissal often suggests that the dismisser, so to speak, is offended by the dismissee, as if the only reason to be skeptical of the traditional image of the Hebrew Bible and its traditions is to be deliberately provocative, perhaps for some kind of notoriety. Albright, who once said that "only hypercritical pseudo-rationalism" could lead someone to reject the "essential historicity" of the Moses tradition, was a master of this genre.[7] So was Frank Moore Cross. But it's still around, too.[8] And I would—hopefully more politely—simply turn those critiques around.

After all, it is worth asking where the resistance to the idea of later and less reliable texts comes from in the first place. Is the early or the more reliable tradition a natural scholarly preoccupation, or does it rely, as I have argued throughout, on certain assumptions about traditions and nations that are *neither* natural nor inevitable? If we did not, for example, take a

---

7. Albright, *Archaeology and the Religion of Israel,* p. 96.

8. We can note, e.g., a not-so-distant account by Lawrence E. Stager of those who would dare doubt the historicity of King David and King Solomon—that they *start* their inquiries with believing that "the period of the United Monarchy is a complete fiction" and so dispose, *a priori,* of such supposedly overwhelming evidence "as the list of Solomonic officials and the provinces of his kingdom, a document that every great biblical scholars has considered, in part or in full, authentic." In the process they "expose themselves as nothing more than ideologues," who sometimes "retreat to the last resort of the scoundrel," in this case by "declaring the Tel Dan Stela to be a forgery and a hoax" (Lawrence E. Stager, "The Patrimonial Kingdom of Solomon," in *Symbiosis, Symbolism, and the Power of the Past: Canaan, Ancient Israel, and their Neighbors from the Late Bronze Age through Roman Palaestina* [ed. William G. Dever and Seymour Gitin; Winona Lake, IN: Eisenbrauns, 2003], p. 64). Personally, I *don't* think the Tel Dan Stele is a forgery; I do think it's likely, at least, that a King David existed. But to treat all critics of the historicity of the Davidic narrative, which has virtually no archaeological evidence supporting it, as if they were all unscrupulous "scoundrels" who made up their mind beforehand, and to essentially define a "great" biblical scholar, in a circular fashion, as one who agrees with others on the subject of 1 Kgs 4, speaks to the general tenor of these critiques.

traditionally historicist approach to texts, prioritizing the question of how well they can serve as sources for scholarly histories, would we still mind discovering that they are not very good at that? If we did not think, even on some instinctive level, that there *must* be a kind of tradition that really was collective memory, so that enough correspondences between text and reality could reveal its presence, amid a mass of invention, would so many scholars continue to insist that the skeptics are out of line? If we did not continually rehearse some version of the view, however qualified, that the historical development of traditions is fundamentally linear, and that there are somehow laws for what someone who inherits a tradition can do with it? Would it be as difficult for scholars to acknowledge the likelihood that even when we can identify early elements in what survives, we might not know that much about them? Or that the explanation for what was done with them does not *lie* in a history of the elements themselves?

This is where we arrive at the polite, return-serve of the question "why be needlessly skeptical?" It is, why should it bother anyone if ancient traditions do not preserve early elements or early realities very well?[9] And maybe the question has a good, twenty-first century answer, something that will stand on its own two feet. But if it does, it is still worth actually trying to answer; we should, after all, learn to be specific about what we think we will lose *after* the original tradition has lost its superlative value and historicist concerns have lost their urgency. And until we do, it may not matter how many ways the case for a more dynamic vision of tradition histories is made, just as it has not mattered enough so far. After all, no study or series of studies, no argument or series of arguments, can, by themselves, alter the popularity of an approach that *already* is not upheld by contemporary understandings, but by something more like the desire for an outcome. And between the continued treatment of skepticism about the antiquity and reliability of traditions and of their stability over time as something like mischief-making and such a strong tendency to discount a disruptive argument if it makes any apparent missteps, it may well be that conservative approaches to what surviving traditions preserve and reflect will survive and thrive.

All the same, I offer these final conclusions as clearly and explicitly as I can. I do believe that the most basic ramifications of the recognition of the fluidity of identity and memory over time include the fact that the traditions of an era are fundamentally the product of that era, whatever earlier traditions they draw on, and especially if they are the kinds of traditions that provide a charter *for* inherently fluid identities. I believe that the most basic

---

9. There *are* answers where more contemporary traditions are concerned that include the importance of respect for traditions reflecting memory in establishing the rights of different groups.

ramification of the downfall of the idea of a primitive group mind is that every text is truly particular to its author and its context to some considerable degree. As a result, even when we successfully extract an early tradition or tradition element from what survives, we have much more surely recovered one of the tools the final artist used in their craft than anything that represents what earlier generations believed or understood or practiced in some general way. And I do think a host of other recognitions converge on these points, especially those that underscore the absence of a meaningful distinction between ancient and modern storytelling or oral and written traditions. Not in an absolute sense—they are, of course, different in some ways—but in the sense that their differences offer a way to *really* preserve older models of analysis from new recognitions.

Indeed, I think one of the most important observations that I cited in this study was Rosalind Thomas's that most of the ways of idealizing oral traditions are not *caused* by anything we observe about them but an *effect* of how they present themselves: "a shallow, unchanging past can be the effect of the oral tradition, not a fundamental characteristic of oral societies."[10] In other words, since we do not have earlier oral traditions to check the later against, it is much easier for someone to believe the oral poet's claim that here is a story handed down from long, long ago, which, no doubt, the oral poet also believes. When we can investigate, however, we more or less always find, not surprisingly, even more rapid change and greater fluidity than we see in other kinds of traditions, and far less reason to believe in the historical accuracy of the surviving narrative. Bernard Knox cites James Notopolous's investigations into oral poetry on the island of Crete in the early 1950s, where he found, for example, that the account of the capture of a German general by British soldiers on the island a scant nine years before had already emerged as a tradition with a Cretan hero and at best peripheral British characters.[11]

In addition, I think the idea that there is a way of defining "cultural memory" or "collective memory" that reinvents and defends the basic stability of traditions over time is an expression of the same impulse to find *some* way of achieving this task because it allows scholars to investigate the questions we have historically privileged much as before.[12] The recognition, discussed in Chapter 3, that here, too, there is no collective groupmind,

---

10. Thomas, *Literacy and Orality in Ancient Greece*, p. 7.

11. As Knox put it, "the British protagonists have been reduced to one nameless general whose part in the operation is secondary," and the Cretan tradition "promoted to the leadership of the heroic enterprise a purely fictional character of a different nationality" (Knox, "Introduction," p. xii).

12. See the extensive discussion in Ian Douglas Wilson, "History and the Hebrew Bible: Culture, Narrative, and Memory," *Brill Research Perspectives in Biblical Interpretation* 3.2 (2018), pp. 1-69.

only the vagaries of a social remembering that is like *individual* remembering—that forgets, that reconsiders, that invents, or changes emphases and interpretations—is a crucial step toward a more realistic kind of investigation, not only in terms of what we can find, but what we should be interested in finding. This, however, will take wanting to look for what *can* be found and being glad enough to find it.

Thus, the hope that I have articulated throughout and that I articulate once again here is that what I have called a "combined approach" can be useful for many reasons. Two corpora can be more useful than one where rethinking assumptions is concerned, two bodies of traditions from roughly the same period, in roughly the same region, looking back on an era of legendary endeavor that was, in the imagination at least, roughly the same amount earlier. Two sets of texts that ask us: What was remembered and what was not? What role did real events play in giving shape to stories, and what role can they ever play? What can someone who inherits a tradition do with it, and are there things they truly will not do, after all? How do storytellers speak through their versions of the stories they know, and how can we learn to hear what they meant to say? What role does what they meant to say play in shaping the text, compared to some essential meaning located in the story itself, inalienable in anything that has to do with Odysseus, or Jacob, or Achilles, or Ruth?

I have suggested my own answers to many of these questions throughout this book, and, generally, put my thumb on the side of the scale marked redescription or reinvention. But *having more to answer our questions* with— questions that are so difficult to answer precisely because the ancient evidence is so sparse—is a wonderful place to start, either way. And the value of comparing scholarly approaches rather than ancient texts is that scholars can read and consider scholarly ideas whether or not they can parse the intricacies of a complex verb in yet another ancient language. They can test what they apprehend of an outside argument on inside data without feeling that similarity must necessarily bleed into identity. They can navigate around some of the pitfalls of not being as familiar with the size and shape of a different corpus by simply trafficking in ideas and models. There is no particular reason why two ancient civilizations without too many contacts in early periods should both hit upon the same rules for "epics," say. But two compositions that *look* like epics from two different places will raise the same questions about their relationship to real events, how they were passed down over time, how their authors infused them with ideology, and so on. Two scholars working on different aspects of such a tradition will have things to say to each other regardless of how similar they really are.

Above all, however, I hope that a combined approach can be useful for this: cutting ourselves truly free from a past that has knotted itself around our oars. The circularity of any discipline can be a prison, forcing ideas back into a shape that resembles an existing consensus.[13] I would even go so far as to say that if either field is ever to completely exorcise the ghosts who don't know they are dead, a less insular approach might well be a *prerequisite*. Insularity protects ideas generally, in both disciplines, for obvious reasons. What seems normal at conferences, in journals, to peer reviewers, and so on, seems normal, even if an outside observer might immediately raise concerns. Comparison, therefore, can be the key that unlocks the door. And the instinct to think about an audience larger than scholars of one set of texts might be very helpful in reshaping assumptions, even if the new audience is only scholars of *two* different sets of texts.

Of course, comparison is no panacea, no matter what form it takes. The history of both disciplines has shown that the comparativist is no less likely to fall prey to motivated reasoning in the form of parallelomanias than any other scholar.[14] And it is easy to perform comparisons too superficially to be of use, or without taking the necessary pains. I have often noticed a tendency in comparison to assume that the big ideas in another discipline have weathered reassessments better than any in our own. In the introduction, I noted the tendency of biblical scholars to imagine that classicists universally subscribe to oral-formulaic theory just as it was formulated by Milman Parry, without acknowledgment of nearly a century's worth of qualifications and critiques, or to related, older ideas about the fundamental difference between oral and written traditions that have not, in fact, survived the test of time. In the other direction, we can consider the fact that M.L. West, the great scholar of Greek genealogies, when comparing these to the genealogies of Genesis, could refer, in a 1985 book, to the dates of biblical texts as laid out by Otto Eissfeldt in *The Old Testament: An Introduction*, which was first published (in German), in 1934, or that Hall, referring to the twelve tribes of Israel as an example of an ethnic group tracing its descent "back to an eponymous ancestor," cited only West himself.[15] One's own field is familiar territory; others always start out as other, and it can be difficult to know how to prepare for the journey.

---

13. See, on this topic, Lester L. Grabbe, "The Case of the Corrupting Consensus," in *Between Evidence and Ideology: Essays on the History of Ancient Israel Read at the Joint Meeting of the Society for Old Testament Study and the Oudtestamentisch Werkgezelschap, Lincoln, July 2009* (ed. Bob Becking and Lester L. Grabbe; OTS, 59; Leiden: E.J. Brill, 2011), pp. 83-92.

14. Tobolowsky, "On Comparison with Ancient Greek Traditions."

15. West, *The Hesiodic Catalogue*, p. 13; Hall, *Hellenicity*, p. 34. Eissfeldt's study *Einleitung in das Alte Testament* did achieve a third edition in 1964, which the English version of 1965 was based on, but even so this was more than twenty years before West's was published.

Thus, it is true that, just as reassessing ancient traditions requires us to acknowledge, first and foremost, that ancient people were *people* like us, not deprived of individual creativity, not removed from individual agency, apprehension, or misapprehension, understanding the debates and conclusions in another field seems to me to require recognizing that it is a *field*, full of countless scholars doing innumerable kinds of work year after year, generation after generation. It does not stand still, no more than our own; it does not speak with one voice; and its apparent consensuses, from the outside, can also be an old world failing to give way, even with its supports knocked from under it. To compare intellectual approaches successfully, we certainly have to invest as heavily in reading in each other's disciplines, where the topics that we are interested in are concerned, as we do when studying those topics in our home disciplines, and assume the same dimensions of multivocality and change over time.

Yet I still think it is, or should be, much easier to *responsibly* compare how scholars in different disciplines think about what the traditions they study preserve, reflect, and reveal—how they might have changed over time, and what they might have been used to do—than to actually master the *primary sources* of another discipline in the way that is required of scholars in that discipline. I think that what is fraught about this kind of comparison is more easily dispelled by effort and intellectual humility than when comparing traditions to traditions, where similarity and difference can rest so heavily on the subjectivity of the eye of the beholder. And I think what is useful about it—as a source of suggestions *that may not prove applicable,* as a way of building a larger scholarly community to work with, and a larger data set than we would otherwise have—is very much worth having, even with the attendant risks. What I have tried to do here is simply to provide a starting point for this kind of investigation where a handful of crucial topics are concerned. It is my fond hope that it will inspire others to do more and better. The ancient world is a distant shore, hidden from us by the swirling fog of years, but a real world all the same—whole, entire, and deeply connected, not dissected by the scalpel of scholarly disciplines. It is a world, like our own, where stories and ideas did not stay where they were put, but sailed like ships across storm-tossed seas, rushed like wind over towering peaks, and poured like rivers through rolling hills. We will draw closer to it the more we pull together—the more lanterns we lift to dispel the mist and see what lies beyond.

BIBLIOGRAPHY

Abrahams, Roger D., "Phantoms of Romantic Nationalism in Folkloristics," *The Journal of American Folklore* 106.419 (1993), pp. 3-37.

Albright, William F., *Archaeology and the Religion of Israel* (Louisville, KY: Westminster John Knox Press, 2006).

—*From the Stone Age to Christianity: Monotheism and the Historical Process* (Baltimore, MD: Johns Hopkins University Press, 1946).

—*From the Stone Age to Christianity: Monotheism and the Historical Process* (Eugene, OR: Wipf & Stock Publishers, 2003).

—"Introduction," in Hermann Gunkel, *The Legends of Genesis* (New York: Schocken Books, 1964), pp. vii-xii.

Alt, Albrecht, *Die Landnahme der Israeliten in Palästina: Territorialgeschichtliche Studien* (Leipzig: Druckerei der Werkgemeinschaft, 1925).

—*Die Staatenbildung der Israeliten in Palästina: Verfassungeschichtliche Studien* (Leipzig: Edelmann, 1930).

Anderson, Bernhard W., "Introduction," in Martin Noth, *A History of the Pentateuchal Traditions* (trans. Bernhard W. Anderson; Chico, CA: Scholars Press, 1981), pp. xiii-xxxii.

Antović, Mihailo, and Cristóbal Pagán Cánovas, *Oral Poetics and Cognitive Science* (linguae&litterae, 56; Berlin: de Gruyter, 2016).

Appadurai, Arjun, "The Past as a Scarce Resource," *Man* 16.2 (1981), pp. 201-19.

Assmann, Jan, and Rodney Livingstone, *Religion and Cultural Memory: Ten Studies* (Stanford, CA: Stanford University Press, 2006).

Baier, Christian, "Homer's Cultural Children," *History and Memory* 29.2 (2017), pp. 35-62.

Ballentine, Debra Scoggins, *The Conflict Myth & the Biblical Tradition* (Oxford: Oxford University Press, 2015).

Barker, Elton T.E., and Joel P. Christensen, *Homer's Thebes: Epic Rivalries and the Appropriation of Mythical Pasts* (Washington, DC: Center for Hellenic Studies, 2020).

Barstad, Hans M., *History and the Hebrew Bible: Studies in Ancient Israelite and Ancient Near Eastern Historiography* (Tübingen: Mohr Siebeck, 2008).

—*The Myth of the Empty Land: A Study in the History and Archaeology of Judah during the "Exilic" Period* (Symbolae Osloenses Fasciculus Suppletorius, 28; Oslo: Scandinavian University Press, 1996).

Barth, Fredrik, "Introduction," *Ethnic Groups and Boundaries* (Prospect Heights, IL: Waveland, 2nd edn, 1998).

Bartlett, F.C., "Some Experiments on the Reproduction of Folk Stories," *Folklore* 31 (1920), pp. 30-47.

Barton, John, "Historical-Critical Approaches," in *The Cambridge Companion to Bib-*

lical Interpretation (ed. John Barton; Cambridge, UK: Cambridge University Press, 1998), pp. 9-20.

Bayart, Jean-François, *The Illusion of Cultural Identity* (trans. Steven Rendall; Chicago: University of Chicago Press, 2005).

Becking, Bob, "'We All Returned as One!' Critical Notes on the Myth of the Mass Return," in *Judah and the Judeans in the Persian Period* (ed. Oded Lipschits and Manfred Oeming; Winona Lake, IN: Eisenbrauns, 2006), pp. 3-18.

Beckman, Gary, Trevor Bryce, and Eric H. Cline, *The Ahhiyawa Texts* (Leiden: E.J. Brill, 2012).

Ben Zvi, Ehud, "On Social Memory and Identity Formation in Late Persian Yehud: A Historian's Viewpoint with a Focus on Prophetic Literature, Chronicles, and the Deuteronomistic Historical Collection," in *Texts, Contexts and Readings in Postexilic Literature: Explorations into Historiography and Identity Negotiation in Hebrew Bible and Related Texts* (ed. Louis Jonker; Tübingen: Mohr Siebeck, 2011), pp. 95-148.

—"The Memory of Abraham in the Late Persian/ Early Hellenistic Yehud/Judah," in *The Reception and Remembrance of Abraham* (ed. P. Carstens and N.P. Lemche; Piscataway, NJ: Gorgias, 2011), pp. 13-60.

Bérard, Jean, "De la légende grecque à la Bible. Phaéton et les sept vaches maigres," *RHR* 151.2 (1957), pp. 221-30.

—*La colonisation grecque de l'Italie méridionale et de la Sicile dans l'antiquité: l'histoire et la légende* (Bibliothèque des Ecoles françaises d'Athènes et de Rome; Paris: Ed. de Boccard, 1941).

Bérard, Victor, *Les Phéniciens et l'Odyssée* (Paris: Armand Colin, 1902).

Biran, Avraham, and Joseph Naveh, "The Tel Dan Inscription: A New Fragment," *IEJ* 45.1 (1995), pp. 1-18.

Blenkinsopp, Joseph, *The Pentateuch* (New York: Doubleday, 1992).

Bloch, Marc, *The Historian's Craft* (trans. Peter Putnam; New York: Vintage Books, 1964).

Bloch-Smith, Elizabeth, "Israelite Ethnicity in Iron I: Archaeology Preserves What Is Remembered and What Is Forgotten in Israel's History," *JBL* 122.3 (2003), pp. 401-25.

Boeckel, Peter Benjamin, "Exploring Narrative Forms and Trajectories: Form Criticism and the Noahic Covenant," in *Partners with God,* vol. 2 of *Theological and Critical Readings of the Bible in Honor of Marvin A. Sweeney* (ed. Shelley L. Birdsong and Serge Frolov; Claremont, CA: Claremont Press, 2017), pp. 27-40.

Brubaker, Rogers, *Ethnicity without Groups* (Cambridge, MA: Harvard University Press, 2004).

—*Nationalist Politics and Everyday Ethnicity in a Transylvanian Town* (Princeton, NJ: Princeton University Press, 2006).

Burkert, Walter, *Structure and History in Greek Mythology* (Berkeley: University of California Press, 1979).

Calder III, William M., "How Did Ulrich Von Wilamowitz-Moellendorff Read a Text?" *The Classical Journal* 86.4 (1991), pp. 344-52.

Carr, David M., *The Formation of the Hebrew Bible: A New Reconstruction* (New York: Oxford University Press, 2011).

Choi, John H., *Traditions at Odds: The Reception of the Pentateuch and Second Temple Period Literature* (London: T. & T. Clark, 2010).

Conroy, Charles, "Hebrew Epic: Historical Notes and Critical Reflections," *Bib* 61.1 (1980), pp. 1-30.

Crielaard, J.P., "Past or Present? Epic Poetry, Aristocratic Self-Representation, and the Concept of Time in the Eighth and Seventh Centuries BC," in *Omero Tremila Anni Dopo* (ed. Franco Montanari and Paola Ascheri; Rome: Edizioni Di Storia E Letteratura, 2002), pp. 239-96.

—"The Ionians in the Archaic Period: Shifting Identities in a Changing World," in *Ethnic Constructs in Antiquity: The Role of Power and Tradition* (ed. Ton Derks and Nico Royman; Amsterdam Archaeological Studies, 13; Amsterdam: Amsterdam University Press, 2009), pp. 37-84.

Cross, Frank Moore, *Canaanite Myth and Hebrew Epic: Essays in the History of the Religion of Israel* (Cambridge, MA: Harvard University Press, 9th edn, 1997).

—*From Epic to Canon: History and Literature in Ancient Israel* (Baltimore, MD: Johns Hopkins University Press, 1998).

—"The Epic Traditions of Early Israel," in *The Poet and the Historian* (ed. Richard E. Friedman; Chico, CA: Scholars Press, 1983).

Crouch, Carly L., *The Making of Israel: Cultural Diversity in the Southern Levant and the Formation of Ethnic Identity in Deuteronomy* (Leiden: E.J. Brill, 2014).

Crüsemann, Frank, *Der Widerstand gegen das Königtum: Die antiköniglichen Texte des Alten Testamentes und der Kampf um den frühen israelitischen Staat* (Neukirchen-Vluyn: Neukirchener Verlag, 1978).

Currie, Bruno, *Homer's Allusive Art* (Oxford: Oxford University Press, 2016).

Darshan, Guy, "The Biblical Account of the Post-Diluvian Generation (Gen 9:20–10:32) in the Light of Greek Genealogical Literature," *VT* 63.4 (2013), pp. 515-35.

—"The Story of the Sons of God and the Daughters of Men (Gen 6:1-4) and the Hesiodic Catalogue of Women," *Shnaton, an Annual for Biblical and Ancient Near Eastern Studies* 23 (2014), pp. 155-78.

Davies, Philip R. *In Search of 'Ancient Israel': A Study in Biblical Origins* (JSOTSup, 148; Sheffield: JSOT Press, 1992).

—*In Search of 'Ancient Israel': A Study in Biblical Origins* (Edinburgh: T. & T. Clark, 2nd edn, 2004).

—"The Origin of Biblical Israel," in *Essays on Ancient Israel in its Near Eastern Context: A Tribute to Nadav Na'aman* (ed. Yairah Amit, Ehud Ben Zvi, Israel Finkelstein, and Oded Lipschits; Winona Lake, IN: Eisenbrauns, 2006), pp. 141-48.

Dawisha, Adeed, "Nation and Nationalism: Historical Antecedents to Contemporary Debates," *International Studies Review* 4.1 (2002), pp. 3-22.

Day, John, "The Daniel of Ugarit and Ezekiel and the Hero of the Book of Daniel," *VT* 30.2 (1980), pp. 174-84.

Day, Peggy L., "Dies Diem Docet: The Decipherment of Ugaritic," *Studi Epigrafici e Linguistici* 19 (2002), pp. 37-57.

De Geus, C.H.J., *The Tribes of Israel* (Studia Semitica Neerlandica, 18; Assen: Van Gorcum, 1976).

De Pury, Albert, "The Jacob Story and the Beginning of the Formation of the Pentateuch," in *A Farewell to the Yahwist? The Composition of the Pentateuch in Recent European Interpretation* (ed. Thomas B. Dozeman and Konrad Schmid; Society of Biblical Literature Symposium Series, 34; Atlanta, GA: Society of Biblical Literature, 2006), pp. 51-72.

Demetriou, Denise, *Negotiating Identity in the Ancient Mediterranean: The Archaic and Classical Greek Multiethnic Emporia* (Cambridge, UK: Cambridge University Press, 2012).

Dickey, Eleanor, *Ancient Greek Scholarship: A Guide to Finding, Reading, and*

Understanding Scholia, Commentaries, Lexica, and Grammatical Treatises, from their Beginnings to the Byzantine Period (Oxford: Oxford University Press, 2007).

Doniger, Wendy, *The Implied Spider: Politics and Theology in Myth* (New York: Columbia University Press, 2011).

Dué, Casey, *Achilles Unbound: Multiformity and Tradition in the Homeric Epics* (Washington, DC: Center for Hellenic Studies, 2019).

Dupré, Louis, "What Was and What Is Romanticism?" in *The Quest of the Absolute*: *Birth and Decline of European Romanticism* (Notre Dame, IN: University of Notre Dame Press, 2013), pp. 1-20.

Eichhorn, Johann Gottfried, *Introduction to the Study of the Old Testament* (trans. George Tilly Gollop; London: Spottiswood, 1888).

Engelstein, Stefani, *Sibling Action: The Genealogical Structure of Modernity* (New York: Columbia University Press, 2017).

Erll, Astrid, "Cultural Memory Studies: An Introduction," *Cultural Memory Studies: An International and Interdisciplinary Handbook* (ed. Astrid Erll and Ansgar Nünning; Berlin: de Gruyter, 2010).

Evans, Nancy, *Civic Rites: Democracy and Religion in Ancient Athens* (Berkeley: University of California Press, 2010).

Evans, Paul S., "Creating a New 'Great Divide': The Exoticization of Ancient Culture in Some Recent Applications of Orality Studies to the Bible," *JBL* 136 (2017), pp. 749-64.

Evans-Pritchard, E., *The Nuer* (Oxford: Clarendon Press, 1940).

Faust, Avraham, *Israel's Ethnogenesis: Settlement, Interaction, Expansion and Resistance* (London: Equinox, 2006).

Finkelberg, Margalit, "Dorians," in *The Homer Encyclopedia* (Chichester: John Wiley & Sons, 2011).

—*Greeks and Pre-Greeks: Aegean Prehistory and Greek Heroic Tradition* (Cambridge, UK: Cambridge University Press, 2005).

—"The Cypria, the Iliad and the Problem of Multiformity in Oral and Written Tradition," *Classical Philology* 95.1 (2000), pp. 1-11.

Finkelstein, Israel, *The Forgotten Kingdom* (Ancient Near East Monographs, 5; Atlanta, GA: Society of Biblical Literature, 2013).

Finkelstein, Jacob J., "The Genealogy of the Hammurapi Dynasty," *Journal of Cuneiform Studies* 20.3/4 (1966), pp. 95-118.

Finley, Moses, *The World of Odysseus* (New York: New York Review of Books, 2002).

Finnegan, Ruth, *Oral Literature in Africa* (Oxford: Clarendon Press, 1970).

Fleming, Daniel, *The Legacy of Israel in Judah's Bible* (New York: Cambridge University Press, 2012).

Fletcher, K.F.B., "Systematic Genealogies in Apollodorus' Bibliotheca and the Exclusion of Rome from Greek Myth," *Classical Antiquity* 27.1 (2008), pp. 59-91.

Foley, John M., and Margalit Finkelberg, "Meta-Cyclic Epic and Homeric Poetry," in *The Greek Epic Cycle and its Ancient Reception* (ed. Marco Fantuzzi and Christos Tsagalis; Cambridge, UK: Cambridge University Press, 2015), pp. 126-38.

Foley, John Miles, *How to Read an Oral Poem* (Urbana: University of Illinois Press, 2002).

—*Immanent Art: From Structure to Meaning in Traditional Oral Epic* (Bloomington: Indiana University Press, 1991).

—*Oral-Formulaic Theory and Research: An Introduction and Annotated Bibliography* (New York: Garland Pub., 1985).

—*The Theory of Oral Composition: History and Methodology* (Bloomington: Indiana University Press, 1988).

Foley, John Miles, and Justin Arft, "The Epic Cycle and Oral Tradition," in *The Greek Epic Cycle and its Ancient Reception* (ed. Marco Fantuzzi and Christos Tsagalis; Cambridge, UK: Cambridge University Press, 2015), pp. 78-95.

Fowler, Robert, "The Homeric Question," in *The Cambridge Companion to Homer* (ed. Robert Fowler; Cambridge Companions to Literature; Cambridge, UK: Cambridge University Press, 2004), pp. 220-32.

Fowler, Robert L. "Genealogical Thinking, Hesiod's Catalogue and the Creation of the Hellenes," *Proceedings of the Cambridge Philological Society* 44 (1999), pp. 1-19.

Fox, Jennifer, "The Creator Gods: Romantic Nationalism and the En-Genderment of Women in Folklore," *Journal of American Folklore* 100.398 (1987), pp. 563-72.

Frei, Hans W., *The Eclipse of Biblical Narrative* (New Haven, CT: Yale University Press, 1974).

Funke, Peter, "Between Mantinea and Leuctra," in *Politics of Ethnicity and the Crisis of the Peloponnesian League* (ed. Peter Funke and Nino Luraghi; Washington, DC: Center for Hellenic Studies, 2009), pp. 1-14.

Funkenstein, Amos, "History, Counter History and Narrative," *Alpayim* 4 (1991), pp. 206-23.

Gantz, Timothy, *Early Greek Myth*. Vol. 1 (Baltimore, MD: Johns Hopkins University Press, 1993).

—*Early Greek Myth*. Vol. 2 (Baltimore, MD: Johns Hopkins University Press, 1993).

Geary, Patrick J., *The Myth of Nations: The Medieval Origins of Europe* (Princeton, NJ: Princeton University Press, 2002).

Gelb, Ignace J., "Two Assyrian King Lists," *JNES* 13.4 (1954), pp. 209-30.

Gere, Cathy. *Knossos & the Prophets of Modernism* (Chicago: University of Chicago Press, 2009).

Gomme, A.W., "The Legend of Cadmus and the Logographi," *JHS* 33 (1913), pp. 53-72.

—"The Topography of Boeotia and the Theories of M. Bérard," *Annual of the British School at Athens* 18 (1911), pp. 189-210.

Gomme, George Laurence, *Folklore as an Historical Science* (London: Methuen, 1908).

Grabbe, Lester L. "The Case of the Corrupting Consensus," in *Between Evidence and Ideology: Essays on the History of Ancient Israel Read at the Joint Meeting of the Society for Old Testament Study and the Oudtestamentisch Werkgezelschap, Lincoln, July 2009* (ed. Bob Becking and Lester L. Grabbe; OTS, 59; Leiden: E.J. Brill, 2011), pp. 83-92.

Graeber, David, and David Wengrow, *The Dawn of Everything: A New History of Humanity* (New York: Farrar, Straus and Giroux, 2021).

Graf, Fritz, *Greek Mythology: An Introduction* (trans. T. Marier; Baltimore, MD: Johns Hopkins University Press, 1993).

Grafton, Anthony, Glenn W. Most, and James E.G. Zetzel, "Introduction," in Frederick A. Wolf, *Prolegomena to Homer* (Princeton, NJ: Princeton University Press, 1988), pp. 3-36.

Granovetter, Mark, "The Strength of Weak Ties," *American Journal of Sociology* 78 (1973), pp. 1360-80.

Graziosi, Barbara, and Johannes Haubold, *Homer: The Resonance of Epic* (London: A & C Black, 2013).

Gressmann, Hugo, "Die Aufgaben der alttestamentlichen Forschung," *ZAW* 42 (1924), pp. 1-33.

Grethlein, Jonas, "From 'Imperishable Glory' to History: The Iliad and the Trojan War," in *Epic and History* (ed. David Konstan and Kurt A. Raaflaub; The Ancient World: Comparative Histories; Malden, MA: Wiley Blackwell, 2010), pp. 122-44.

Griffith, F.L., "The Decipherment of the Hieroglyphs," *JEA* 37 (1951), pp. 38-46.

Gruen, Erich S., *Ethnicity in the Ancient World—Did It Matter?* Berlin: de Gruyter, 2020).

—*Rethinking the Other in Antiquity* (Princeton, NJ: Princeton University Press, 2011).

Guest, Lady Charlotte, *The Mabinogion: From the Welsh of the Llyfr Coch o Hergest (The Red Book of Hergest) in the Library of Jesus College, Oxford* (London: Quaritch, 2nd edn, 1877).

Guillaume, Philippe, "Exploring the Memory of Aaron in Late Persian/Early Hellenistic Period Yehud," in *Remembering Biblical Figures in the Late Persian and Early Hellenistic Periods* (ed. Diana Vikander Edelman and Ehud Ben Zvi; Oxford: Oxford University Press, 2013), pp. 95-105.

Gunkel, Hermann, *The Legends of Genesis* (trans. W.H. Carruth; HKAT, 1; Chicago: Open Court Publishing, 1901).

Hagedorn, Anselm C., *Between Moses and Plato: Individual and Society in Deuteronomy and Ancient Greek Law* (Göttingen: Vandenhoeck & Ruprecht, 2004).

Hainsworth, J.B., "Oral Poetry and Homer," *Classical Review* 40.1 (1990), pp. 1-3.

Hall, Jonathan M., "Contested Ethnicities: Perceptions of Macedonia within Evolving Definitions of Greek Identity," in *Ancient Perceptions of Greek Ethnicity* (ed. Irad Malkin; Cambridge, MA: Harvard University Press, 2001), pp. 159-86.

—*Ethnic Identity in Greek Antiquity* (Cambridge, UK: Cambridge University Press, 1997).

—*Hellenicity: Between Ethnicity and Culture* (Chicago: University of Chicago Press, 2002).

—"How Argive Was the 'Argive' Heraion? The Political and Cultic Geography of the Argive Plain, 900–400 B.C," *AJA* 99.4 (1995), pp. 577-613.

Hattem, Michael D., *Past and Prologue: Politics and Memory in the American Revolution* (New Haven, CT: Yale University Press, 2020).

Herder, Johann Gottfried, *Another Philosophy of History and Selected Political Writings* (trans. Ioannis D. Evrigenis and Daniel Pellerin; Indianapolis, IN: Hackett Publishing Company, 2004.

—*Outlines of a Philosophy of the History of Man* (trans. T. Churchill; London: Luke Hansard, 1800.

Hertel, Dieter, and Frank Kolb, "Troy in Clearer Perspective," *Anatolian Studies* 53 (2003), p. 71.

Heth, Raleigh, and T.E. Kelley, "Isaac and Iphigenia: Portrayals of Child Sacrifice in Israelite and Greek Literature," *Bib* 102.4 (2021), pp. 481-502.

Hobsbawm, Eric, "Introduction: Inventing Traditions," in *The Invention of Tradition* (ed. Eric Hobsbawm and Terence Ranger; Cambridge, UK: Cambridge University Press, 1983), pp. 1-14.

Hobsbawm, Eric, and Terence Ranger, eds., *The Invention of Tradition* (Cambridge, UK: Cambridge University Press, 1983).

Holmes, J. Teresa, "When Blood Matters: Making Kinship in Colonial Kenya," in *Kinship and Beyond: The Genealogical Model Reconsidered* (ed. Sandra Bamford and James Leach; Oxford: Berghahn Books, 2009).

Hooker, James T., "New Reflexions on the Dorian Invasion," *Klio* 61.1-2 (1979), pp. 353-60.

Ibrahim, Vivian, "Ethnicity," in *The Routledge Companion to Race and Ethnicity* (London: Routledge, 2nd edn, 2020), pp. 18-24.

Iggers, Georg G., "Historicism: The History and Meaning of the Term," *Journal of the History of Ideas* 56.1 (1995), pp. 129-52.

Irwin, Elizabeth, "Gods among Men? The Social and Political Dynamics of the Hesiodic Catalogue of Women," in *The Hesiodic Catalogue of Women* (ed. Richard L. Hunter; Cambridge, UK: Cambridge University Press, 2005), pp. 35-84.

Junod, Henri Alexandre, *The Life of a South African Tribe* (2 vols.; Neuchatel: Attinger, 1913).

Kamenetsky, Christa, "The Brothers Grimm: Folktale Style and Romantic Theories," *Elementary English* 51.3 (1974), pp. 379-83.

Kanigel, Robert, *Hearing Homer's Song: The Brief Life and Big Idea of Milman Parry* (New York: Knopf Doubleday Publishing Group, 2021).

Kasimis, Demetra, "The Tragedy of Blood-Based Membership: Secrecy and the Politics of Immigration in Euripides's Ion," *Political Theory* 41.2 (2013), pp. 231-56.

Kawashima, Robert S., *The Archaeology of Ancient Israelite Knowledge* (Bloomington: Indiana University Press, 2022).

Kennedy, Rebecca Futo, *Race and Ethnicity in the Classical World: An Anthology of Primary Sources in Translation* (Indianapolis, IN: Hackett Publishing, 2013).

Kenyon, Kathleen M., *The Bible and Recent Archaeology* (Atlanta, GA: John Knox, 1978).

Killebrew, Ann E., *Biblical Peoples and Ethnicity: An Archaeological Study of Egyptians, Canaanite, Philistines, and Early Israel, 1300–100 BCE* (Atlanta, GA: Society of Biblical Literature, 2005).

Kim, Uriah Y., *Decolonizing Josiah: Toward a Postcolonial Reading of the Deuteronomistic History* (Sheffield: Sheffield Phoenix, 2005).

Kirkpatrick, Patricia G., *The Old Testament and Folklore Study* (JSOTSup, 62; Sheffield: JSOT Press, 1988).

—*The Old Testament and Folklore Study* (JSOTSup, 62. Sheffield: Sheffield Academic Press, 1988).

Kittel, Rudolf, "Die Zukunft der Alttestamentlichen Wissenschaft," *ZAW* 39 (1921), pp. 84-99.

Kleinberg, Ethan, "Deconstructing Historicist Time, or Time's Scribe," *History and Theory* 62.4 (2023), pp. 105-22.

Knauf, Ernst Axel, "Bethel: The Israelite Impact on Judean Language and Literature," in *Judah and the Judeans in the Persian Period* (ed. Manfred Oeming and Oded Lipschits; Winona Lake, IN: Eisenbrauns, 2006), pp. 291-350.

—, and Philippe Guillaume, *A History of Biblical Israel: The Fate of the Tribes and Kingdoms from Merenptah to Bar Kochba* (Sheffield: Equinox, 2016).

Knoppers, Gary N., "Greek Historiography and the Chronicler's History: A Reexamination," *JBL* 122 (2003), pp. 627-50.

Knox, Bernard, "Introduction," in M.I. Finley, *The World of Odysseus* (New York: New York Review of Books, 2002), pp. vii-xviii.

Koiv, Mait, *Ancient Tradition and Early Greek History: The Origins of States in Early Archaic Sparta, Argos and Corinth* (Tallinn: Avita, 2003).

Konstan, David. "To Hellēnikon Ethnos: Ethnicity and the Construction of Ancient Greek Identity," in *Ancient Perceptions of Greek Ethnicity* (ed. Irad Malkin; Washington, DC: Center for Hellenic Studies, 2001), pp. 29-50.

Kratz, Reinhard G., "Israel in the Book of Isaiah," *JSOT* 31.1 (2006), pp. 103-28.

Kuhrt, Amélie, *The Ancient Near East C. 3000–330 BC*. Vol. 2 of *Routledge History of the Ancient World* (London: Routledge, 2003).

Kundra, Nakul, "Understanding Nation and Nationalism," *Interdisciplinary Literary Studies* 21.2 (2019), pp. 125-49.

Kurtz, Paul Michael, "A Historical, Critical Retrospective on Historical Criticism," in *The New Cambridge Companion to Biblical Interpretation* (Cambridge, UK: Cambridge University Press, 2022), pp.15-36.

—*Kaiser, Christ, and Canaan* (Tübingen: Mohr Siebeck, 2018).

Lahire, Bernard, *The Plural Actor* (trans. David Fernbach; Cambridge, UK: Cambridge University Press, 2011).

Lampart, Fabian, "The Turn to History and the Volk: Brentano, Arnim, and the Grimm Brothers," in *The Literature of German Romanticism* (ed. Dennis F. Mahoney; Martlesham, Suffolk: Boydell & Brewer, 2004), pp. 171-90.

Latacz, Joachim, *Kampfparänese, Kampfdarstellung und Kampfwirklichkeit in der Ilias, bei Kallinos und Tyrtaios* (Munich: Beck, 1977).

—*Troy and Homer: Towards a Solution of an Old Mystery* (trans. Kevin Windle and Rosh Ireland; Oxford: Oxford University Press, 2004).

Lemaire, André, "The Mesha Stele and the Omri Dynasty," in *Ahab Agonistes: The Rise and Fall of the Omri Dynasty* (ed. Lester L. Grabbe; LHB/OTS; London: T. & T. Clark, 2007), pp. 135-44.

Lemche, Niels Peter, "The Greek 'Amphictyony'—Could It Be a Prototype for the Israelite Society in the Period of the Judges?" *JSOT* 2.4 (1977), pp. 48-59.

Leuchter, Mark, "Jeroboam the Ephratite," *JBL* 125 (2006), pp. 51-72.

Levinson, Bernard M., "Goethe's Analysis of Exodus 34 and its Influence on Wellhausen: The Pfropfung of the Documentary Hypothesis," *ZAW* 114.2 (2002), pp. 212-23.

Lévi-Strauss, Claude, "The Structural Study of Myth," *Journal of American Folklore* 68.270 (1955), pp. 428-44.

Levy, Thomas E., and Mohammad Najjar, "Some Thoughts on Khirbet En-Naḥas, Edom, Biblical History and Anthropology—A Response to Israel Finkelstein," *Tel Aviv* 33.1 (2006), pp. 3-17.

Levy, Thomas E., Mohammad Najjar, Johannes Van der Plicht, Neil Smith, Hendrik J. Bruins and Thomas Higham, "Lowland Edom and the High and Low Chronologies," in *The Bible and Radiocarbon Dating: Archaeology, Text and Science* (ed. Thomas E. Levy and Thomas Higham; Oxfordshire: Routledge, 2005), pp. 129-63.

Lincoln, Bruce, *Discourse and the Construction of Society: Comparative Studies of Myth, Ritual and Classification* (New York: Oxford University Press, 1989).

—*Theorizing Myth: Narrative, Ideology and Scholarship* (Chicago: University of Chicago Press, 1999).

Lipschits, Oded, and Joseph Blenkinsopp, "After the 'Myth of the Empty Land': Major Challenges in the Study of Neo-Babylonian Judah," in *Judah and the Judeans in the Neo-Babylonian Period* (Winona Lake, IN: Eisenbrauns, 2003), pp. 3-20.

Littlejohns, Richard, "Early Romanticism," in *The Literature of German Romanticism* (ed. Dennis F. Mahoney; Martlesham, Suffolk: Boydell & Brewer, 2004), pp. 61-78.

Litwa, M. David, "Genealogy," in *How the Gospels Became History: Jesus and Mediterranean Myths* (ed. Dale B. Martin and L.L. Welborn; New Haven, CT: Yale University Press, 2019), pp. 77-85.

Liverani, Mario, *Israel's History and the History of Israel* (London: Routledge, 2005).

Lord, Albert B., *The Singer of Tales* (Cambridge, MA: Harvard University Press, 1960).

Lowie, R.H., "Oral Tradition and History," *Journal of American Folklore* 30 (1917), pp. 161-67.

Malamat, Abraham, *History of Biblical Israel* (Leiden: E.J. Brill, 2001).

—"King Lists of the Old Babylonian Period and Biblical Genealogies," *JAOS* 88.1 (1968), pp. 163-73.

—"Tribal Societies: Biblical Genealogies and African Lineage Systems," *European Journal of Sociology* 14.1 (1973), pp. 126-36.

Malkin, Irad, *A Small Greek World* (Oxford: Oxford University Press, 2011).

—*Myth and Territory in the Spartan Mediterranean* (Cambridge, UK: Cambridge University Press, 1994).

—*The Returns of Odysseus* (Berkeley: University of California Press, 1998).

Martin, Thomas R., *Ancient Greece from Prehistoric to Hellenistic Times* (New Haven, CT: Yale University Press, 1996).

Mason, Rhiannon, "Cultural Theory and Museum Studies," in *A Companion to Museum Studies* (ed. Sharon Macdonald; Chichester: Wiley-Blackwell, 2011), pp. 17-32.

Mazar, Amihai, "The Patriarchs, Exodus, and Conquest Narratives in Light of Archaeology," in *The Quest for the Historical Israel: Debating Archaeology and the History of Israel* (ed. Brian B. Schmidt. Atlanta, GA: Society of Biblical Literature, 2007), pp. 57-66.

Mazar, Amihai, and Israel Finkelstein, *The Quest for the Historical Israel: Debating Archaeology and the History of Israel* (ed. Brian B. Schmidt; Atlanta, GA: Society of Biblical Literature, 2007).

McCauley, Barbara, "The Transfer of Hippodameia's Bones: A Historical Context," *Classical Journal* 93.3 (1998), pp. 225-39.

McDonald, William A., *Progress Into the Past* (New York: Macmillan, 1967).

McEntire, Mark, and Wongi Park, "Ethnic Fission and Fusion in Biblical Genealogies," *JBL* 140 (2021), pp. 31-47.

McInerney, Jeremy, "Ethnos and Ethnicity in Early Greece," in *Ancient Perceptions of Greek Ethnicity* (ed. Irad Malkin; Washington, DC: Center for Hellenic Studies, 2001), pp. 51-74.

McKenzie, Steven L., "The Source for Jeroboam's Role at Shechem (1 Kgs 11:43–12:3, 12:20)," *JBL* 106 (1987), pp. 297-300.

Middlemas, Jill A., "Going beyond the Myth of the Empty Land: A Reassessment of the Early Persian Period," in *Exile and Restoration Revisited: Essays on the Babylonian and Persian Periods in Memory of Peter R. Ackroyd* (ed. Gary N. Knoppers, Lester L. Grabbe, and Dierdre N. Fulton; London: T. & T. Clark, 2009), pp. 174-94.

Miller, James C., "Ethnicity and the Hebrew Bible: Problems and Prospects," *CBR* 6.2 (2008), pp. 170-213.

Miller, Robert D., *Oral Tradition in Ancient Israel* (Eugene, OR: Cascade Books, 2011).

Mink, Louis O., "Narrative Form as a Cognitive Instrument," in *Historical Understanding* (ed. Brian Fay, Eugene O. Golob, and Richard T. Vann; Ithaca, NY: Cornell University Press, 1987), pp. 182-203.

Momigliano, Arnaldo, "Biblical Studies and Classical Studies: Simple Reflections about Historical Method," *BA* 45.4 (1982), pp. 224-28.

Monroe, Lauren A.S., and Daniel Fleming, "Earliest Israel in Highland Company," *Near Eastern Archaeology* 82.1 (2019), pp. 16-23.

Moore, Megan Bishop, *Philosophy and Practice in Writing a History of Ancient Israel* (New York: T. & T. Clark, 2006).

—, and Brad E. Kelle, *Biblical History and Israel's Past* (Grand Rapids, MI: Eerdmans, 2011).

Mroczek, Eva, "The Hegemony of the Biblical in the Study of Second Temple Literature," *Journal of Ancient Judaism* 6.1 (2015), pp. 2-35.

—*The Literary Imagination in Jewish Antiquity* (Oxford: Oxford University Press, 2016).

Na'aman, Nadav, "The Jacob Story and the Formation of Biblical Israel," *Tel Aviv* 41.1 (2014), pp. 95-125.

Nagy, Gregory, *Homeric Questions* (Austin: University of Texas Press, 1996).

—*The Best of the Achaeans: Concepts of the Hero in Archaic Greek Poetry* (Baltimore, MD: Johns Hopkins University Press, 1979).

Nagy, Helen, Larissa Bonfante, and Jane K. Whitehead, "Searching for Etruscan Identity," *AJA* 112.3 (2008), pp. 413-17.

Nilsson, Martin P., *Homer and Mycenae* (New York: Cooper Square Publishers, 1968).

—*The Mycenaean Origin of Greek Mythology* (Berkeley: University of California Press, 1972).

Nissinen, Martti, *Ancient Prophecy: Near Eastern, Biblical, and Greek Perspectives* (Oxford: Oxford University Press, 2017).

Noll, Kurt L., "Was There Doctrinal Dissemination in Early Yahweh Religion," *BibInt* 16.5 (2008), pp. 395-427.

Norman, Judith, and Alistair Welchman, "The Question of Romanticism," in *The Edinburgh Critical History of Nineteenth-Century Philosophy* (ed. Alison Stone; Edinburgh: Edinburgh University Press, 2011), pp. 47-68.

Noth, Martin. *A History of Pentateuchal Traditions* (trans. Bernhard W. Anderson; Englewood Cliffs, NJ: Prentice Hall, 1972).

—*A History of the Pentateuchal Traditions* (trans. Bernhard W. Anderson; Chico, CA: Scholars Press, 1981).

—*Das System der zwölf Stämme Israels* (Stuttgart: Kohlhammer, 1930).

—*The History of Israel* (New York: Harper & Row, 2nd edn, 1960).

Olick, Jeffrey K., and Joyce Robbins, "Social Memory Studies: From 'Collective Memory' to the Historical Sociology of Mnemonic Practices," *Annual Review of Sociology* 24 (1998), pp. 105-40.

Oring, Elliott, "On the Concepts of Folklore," in *Folk Groups and Folklore Genres: An Introduction* (ed. Elliott Oring; Logan, UT: Utah State University Press, 1986), pp. 1-22.

Orlinsky, Harry M., "The Tribal System of Israel and Related Groups in the Period of the Judges," in *Studies and Essays in Honor of Abraham A. Newman* (ed. Meir Ben-Horin, Bernard D. Weinryb, and Sol Zeitlin; Leiden: E.J. Brill, 1962), pp. 375-88.

Parker, Robert, *Greek Gods Abroad: Names, Natures, and Transformations* (Berkeley: University of California Press, 2017).

Parry, Milman, *Studies in the Epic Technique of Oral Verse-Making: II. The Homeric Language as the Language of an Oral Poetry* (Harvard Studies in Classical Philology, 43; Cambridge, MA: Harvard University Press, 1932).

—"Whole Formulaic Verses in Greek and Southslavic Heroic Song," *TAPA* 64 (1933), pp. 179-97.

Patterson, Lee E., *Kinship Myth in Ancient Greece* (Austin: University of Texas Press, 2010).

Pioske, Daniel, "An Archaeology of Ancient Thought: On the Hebrew Bible and the History of Ancient Israel," *HTR* 115.2 (2022), pp. 171-96.

—*David's Jerusalem: Between Memory and History* (New York: Routledge, 2015).

—*Memory in a Time of Prose: Studies in Epistemology, Hebrew Scribalism, and the Biblical Past* (Oxford: Oxford University Press, 2018).

—"Retracing a Remembered Past: Methodological Remarks on Memory, History, and the Hebrew Bible," *BibInt* 23.3 (2015), pp. 291-315.

Provan, Iain, V. Philips Long, and Tremper Longman III, *A Biblical History of Israel* (Louisville, KY: Westminster John Knox, 2003).

Quick, Laura, *Dress, Adornment, and the Body in the Hebrew Bible* (Oxford: Oxford University Press, 2021).

Raaflaub, Kurt A., "Epic and History," in *A Companion to Ancient Epic* (ed. John Miles Foley; Malden, MA: Blackwell Publishing, 2005), pp. 55-70.

—"The Newest Sappho and Archaic Greek-Near East Interaction," in *The Newest Sappho (P. Sapph. Obbink and P. GC Inv. 105, Frs. 1-4)* (ed. Anton Bierl and A. P. M. H. Lardinois; Studies in Archaic and Classical Greek Song, 2; Leiden: E.J. Brill, 2016). pp. 127-47.

Rad, Gerhard von, *The Problem of the Hexateuch and Other Essays* (trans. E.W. Trueman Dicken; London: SCM Press, 1984).

Rahtjen, Bruce Donald, "Philistine and Hebrew Amphictyonies," *JNES* 24.1/2 (1965), pp. 100-104.

Rebillard, Eric, "Material Culture and Religious Identity in Late Antiquity," in *A Companion to the Archaeology of Religion in the Ancient World* (ed. Rubina Raja and Jörg Rüpke; Chichester, UK: Wiley Blackwell, 2015), pp. 427-36.

Reece, Steve, "The Myth of Milman Parry: Ajax or Elpenor," *Oral Traditions* 331.1 (2019), pp. 115-42.

Reid, Donald Malcolm, "Egyptology under Ismail: Mariette, al-Tahtawi, and Brugsch, 1850–1882," in *Whose Pharaohs?* (Archaeology, Museums, and Egyptian National Identity from Napoleon to World War I; Oakland: University of California Press, 2002), pp. 93-136.

—"Rediscovering Ancient Egypt: Champollion and al-Tahtawi," in *Whose Pharaohs?* (Archaeology, Museums, and Egyptian National Identity from Napoleon to World War I; Oakland: University of California Press, 2002), pp. 21-63.

Ridgway, David, *The First Western Greeks* (Cambridge, UK: Cambridge University Press, 1992).

Rogerson, John, *Old Testament Criticism in the Nineteenth Century: England and Germany* (London: Fortress Press, 1985).

Römer, Thomas, "'Higher Criticism': The Historical and Literary-Critical Approach—with Special Reference to the Pentateuch," in *From Modernism to Post-Modernism (The Nineteenth and Twentieth Centuries)* (ed. Magne Saebo, Peter Machinist, and Jean Louis Ska; Hebrew Bible/Old Testament: The History of its Interpretation; Göttingen: Vandenhoeck & Ruprecht, 2013), pp. 393-420.

Ross, Shawn A., "Barbarophonos: Language and Panhellenism in the Iliad," *Classical Philology* 100.4 (2005), pp. 299-316.

Sanders, Seth, "What If There Aren't Any Empirical Models for Pentateuchal Criticism?" in *Contextualizing Israel's Sacred Writing: Ancient Literacy, Orality, and Literary Production* (ed. Brian Schmidt; Atlanta, GA: Society of Biblical Literature, 2014), pp. 281-304.

Schmid, Konrad, *The Old Testament: A Literary History* (trans. Linda M. Maloney; Minneapolis, MN: Fortress Press, 2012).

Scodel, Ruth, "Aetiology, Autochthony, and Athenian Identity in Ajax and Oedipus

Coloneus," *Bulletin of the Institute of Classical Studies. Supplement* 87 (2006), pp. 65-78.

—*Listening to Homer: Tradition, Narrative and Audience* (Ann Arbor: University of Michigan Press, 2002).

Shenhav-Keller, Shelly, "Invented Exhibits: Visual Politics of the Past at the Museum," in *Memory and Ethnicity: Ethnic Museums in Israel and the Diaspora* (ed. Emanuela Trevisan Semi, Dario Miccoli, and Tudor Parfitt; Newcastle upon Tyne: Cambridge Scholars Publishing, 2013), pp. 21-44.

Simon, Erika, "Greek Myth in Etruscan Culture," in *The Etruscan World* (London: Routledge, 2013).

Ska, Jean Louis, "The 'History of Israel': Its Emergence as an Independent Discipline," in *From Modernism to Post-Modernism (The Nineteenth and Twentieth Centuries)* (ed. Magne Saebo, Peter Machinist, and Jean Louis Ska; Hebrew Bible/Old Testament: The History of its Interpretation; Göttingen: Vandenhoeck & Ruprecht, 2013), pp. 307-41.

Smith, Jonathan Z., "A Matter of Class: Taxonomies of Religion," *HTR* 89.4 (1996), pp. 387-403.

—"In Comparison a Magic Still Dwells," in *Imagining Religion: From Babylon to Jonestown* (Chicago: University of Chicago Press, 1982), pp. 19-35.

Smith, Mark S., *God in Translation: Deities in Cross-Cultural Discourse* (Grand Rapids, MI: Eerdmans, 2010).

—*The Memoirs of God: History, Memory, and the Experience of the Divine in Ancient Israel* (Minneapolis, MN: Fortress Press, 2004).

Smith, Neil G., and Thomas E. Levy. "The Iron Age Pottery from Khirbat En-Nahas, Jordan: A Preliminary Study," *Bulletin of the American Schools of Oriental Research* 352 (2008), pp. 41-91.

Sollors, Werner. *The Invention of Ethnicity* (Oxford: Oxford University Press, 1989).

Stager, Lawrence E., "The Patrimonial Kingdom of Solomon," in *Symbiosis, Symbolism, and the Power of the Past: Canaan, Ancient Israel, and their Neighbors from the Late Bronze Age through Roman Palaestina* (ed. William G. Dever and Seymour Gitin; Winona Lake, IN: Eisenbrauns, 2003), pp. 63-74.

Steinmeyer, Nathan, "An Early Israelite Curse Inscription from Mt. Ebal?" *Biblical Archaeology Society*, 25 April 2022, https://www.biblicalarchaeology.org/daily/ biblical-artifacts/inscriptions/mt_ebal_inscription/.

Stone, Lawson G., "Early Israel and its Appearance in Canaan," in *Ancient Israel's History: An Introduction to Issues and Sources* (ed. Bill T. Arnold and Richard S. Hess; Grand Rapids, MI: Baker Academic, 2014), pp. 127-64.

Strine, Casey, "Your Name Shall No Longer Be Jacob, but Refugee: Involuntary Migration and the Development of the Jacob Narrative," in *Scripture as Social Discourse* (ed. J.M. Keady, T.E. Klutz, and C.A. Strine; London: T. & T. Clark, 2018), pp. 51-69.

Thomas, Rosalind, *Literacy and Orality in Ancient Greece* (Cambridge: Cambridge University Press, 1995).

Thompson, Thomas L., *The Historicity of the Patriarchal Narratives: The Quest for the Historical Abraham* (Berlin: de Gruyter, 1974).

Tobolowsky, Andrew, "Benjamin and the Anonymous Ten Tribes of Israel: A Holistic Approach to Tribal Confusions," *VT* 73.3 (2023), pp. 426-44.

—"History, Myth, and the Shrinking of Genre Borders," *Eidolon*, 16 May 2016, https:// eidolon.pub/history-myth-and-the-shrinking-of-genre-borders-e7ad46ca745.

—"Israelite and Judahite History in Contemporary Theoretical Approaches," *CBR* 17.1 (2018), pp. 33-58.

—"On Comparison with Ancient Greek Traditions: Lessons from the Mid-Century," *Journal of Hebrew Scriptures* 23 (2023), pp. 1-30.

—"Othniel, David, Solomon: Additional Evidence of the Late Development of Normative Tribal Concepts in the South," *ZAW* 13.1 (2019), pp. 207-19.

—"Reading Genesis through Chronicles: The Creation of the Sons of Jacob," *Journal of Ancient Judaism* 7.2 (2016), pp. 138-68.

—"Redescribing, But Really, Finally Moving on from Israelite Origins," *Method and Theory in the Study of Religion* 5.35 (2023), pp. 434-44.

—"The Hebrew Bible as Mythic 'Vocabulary': Towards a New Comparative Mythology," *Religions* 11.9 (2020), pp. 459.

—*The Myth of the Twelve Tribes of Israel: New Identities across Time and Space* (Cambridge, UK: Cambridge University Press, 2022).

—"The Primary History as Museum Exhibit: Rethinking the Recovery of the Hebrew Bible's Artifacts," *Method and Theory in the Study of Religion* 32.3 (2020), pp. 233-58.

—"The Problem of Reubenite Primacy," *JBL* 139 (2020), pp. 27-45.

—*The Sons of Jacob and the Sons of Herakles: The History of the Tribal System and the Organization of Biblical Identity* (FAT, 2; Tübingen: Mohr Siebeck, 2017).

—"The Thor Movies and the 'Available Myth': Mythic Reinvention in Marvel Movies," in *Theology and the Marvel Universe* (Lanham, MD: Lexington Books, 2020), pp. 173-86.

Tracy, Stephen V., "The Acceptance of the Greek Solution for Linear B," *Hesperia: The Journal of the American School of Classical Studies at Athens* 87.1 (2018), pp. 1-16.

Turner, Frank, "The Homeric Question," in *A New Companion to Homer* (ed. Ian Morris and Barry B. Powell; Leiden: E.J. Brill, 1997), pp. 123-45.

Ulf, Christoph, "The Development of Greek Ethnê," *Politics of Ethnicity and the Crisis of the Peloponnesian League* (ed. Nino Luraghi and Peter Funke; Hellenic Studies, 32; Cambridge, MA: Center for Hellenic Studies, 2009).

Van Seters, John. *Abraham in History and Tradition* (New Haven, CT: Yale University Press, 1975).

—*In Search of History: Historiography in the Ancient World and the Origins of Biblical History* (New Haven, CT: Yale University Press, 1983).

—*Prologue to History: The Yahwist as Historian in Genesis* (Louisville, KY: Westminster John Knox, 1992).

Vayntrub, Jacqueline, *Beyond Orality: Biblical Poetry on its Own Terms* (The Ancient Word; London: Routledge, 2019).

Vlassopoulos, Kostas, "Ethnicity and Greek History: Re-Examining our Assumptions," *Bulletin of the Institute of Classical Studies* 58.2 (2015), pp. 1-13.

Voutsaki, Sofia, "The Dorian Invasion," *Classical Review* 50.1 (2000), pp. 232-33.

Walsh, Robyn Faith, *The Origins of Early Christian Literature: Contextualizing the New Testament within Greco-Roman Literary Culture* (Cambridge, UK: Cambridge University Press, 2021).

Watts, D.J., and Steven H. Strogatz, "Collective Dynamics of Small-World Networks," *Nature* 393 (1998), pp. 440-42.

Webber, Andrew, "The Afterlife of Romanticism," in *German Literature of the Nineteenth Century, 1832–1899* (ed. Clayton Koelb and Eric Downing; Woodbridge, Suffolk: Boydell & Brewer, 2005), pp. 23-44.

Weingart, Kristin, "Jeroboam and Benjamin: Pragmatics and Date of 1 Kings 11:26-40; 12:1-20," in *Saul, Benjamin, and the Emergence of Monarchy in Israel: Biblical and Archaeological Perspectives* (ed. Joachim J. Krause, Omer Sergi, and Kristin Weingart; Atlanta, GA: Society of Biblical Literature, 2020), pp. 133-60.

Wellhausen, Julius, *Prolegomena to the History of Ancient Israel. With a Reprint of the Article "Israel" from the Encyclopedia Britannica* (Gloucester, MA: Peter Smith, 1973).

—*Prolegomena to the History of Israel. With a Reprint of the Article "Israel" from the Encyclopedia Britannica* (trans. J. Sutherland Black and Alan Menzies; Edinburgh: A. & C. Black, 1885).

Wertsch, James V., "Collective Memory," in *Memory in Mind and Culture* (ed. Pascal Boyer and James V. Wertsch; Cambridge, UK: Cambridge University Press, 2009), pp. 117-37.

West, M.L., *The Hesiodic Catalogue of Women: Its Nature, Structure and Origin* (Oxford: Oxford University Press, 1985).

Whitman, Cedric H., *Homer and the Heroic Tradition* (Cambridge, MA: Harvard University Press, 1963).

Wiedemann, Felix, "Migration and Narration: How European Historians in the Nineteenth and Early Twentieth Centuries Told the History of Human Mass Migrations or Völkerwanderungen," *History and Theory* 59.1 (2020), pp. 42-60.

Wilamowitz-Moellendorff, Ulrich Von. *History of Classical Scholarship* (ed. Hugh Lloyd-Jones; trans. Alan Harris; Baltimore, MD: Johns Hopkins University Press, 1982).

Williamson, George S., *The Longing for Myth in Germany* (Chicago: University of Chicago Press, 2004).

Wilson, Ian Douglas, "History and the Hebrew Bible: Culture, Narrative, and Memory," *Brill Research Perspectives in Biblical Interpretation* 3.2 (2018), pp. 1-69.

—*Kingship and Memory in Ancient Judah* (New York: Oxford University Press, 2017).

Wilson, Robert R., "Between 'Azel' and 'Azel': Interpreting the Biblical Genealogies," *BA* 42.1 (1979), pp. 11-22.

—*Genealogy and History in the Biblical World* (New Haven, CT: Yale University Press, 1977).

—"The Old Testament Genealogies in Recent Research," *JBL* 94 (1975), pp. 169-89.

Wilson, William A., "Herder, Folklore, and Romantic Nationalism," in *The Marrow of Human Experience* (ed. Jill Terry Rudy and Diane Call; Logan, UT: Utah State University Press, 2006).

Wimmer, Andreas, "The Making and Unmaking of Ethnic Boundaries: A Multilevel Process Theory," *American Journal of Sociology* 113 (2008), pp. 970-1022.

Wolf, Frederick A., *Prolegomena to Homer* (trans. Anthony Grafton, Glenn W. Most, and James E.G. Zetzel; Princeton, NJ: Princeton University Press, 1988).

Zerubavel, Eviatar, *Time Maps* (Chicago: University of Chicago Press, 2003).

Zipes, Jack, *The Original Folk and Fairy Tales of the Brothers Grimm: The Complete First Edition* (Princeton, NJ: Princeton University Press, 2014).

Zuckerberg, Donna, *Not All Dead White Men: Classics and Misogyny in the Digital Age* (Cambridge, MA: Harvard University Press, 2018).

Index of References

Index of Authors

www.ingramcontent.com/pod-product-compliance
Lightning Source LLC
LaVergne TN
LVHW022022090625
813403LV00003B/466